Also available at all good book stores

9781785315510

9781785314902

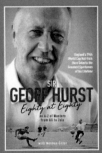

9781801501286

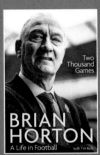

9781785316685

9781785316807

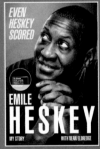

9781785315008

9781785316333

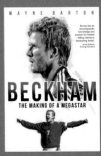

9781785316760

9781785314995

The one and only

Jimmy Greaves

The one and only

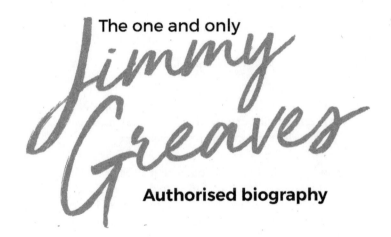

Jimmy Greaves

Authorised biography

By the man who knew him best

NORMAN GILLER

A Norman Giller Books Publication
In association with Pitch Publishing

First published by Pitch Publishing, 2022

Pitch Publishing
9 Donnington Park,
85 Birdham Road,
Chichester,
West Sussex,
PO20 7AJ
www.pitchpublishing.co.uk
info@pitchpublishing.co.uk

ISBN 978 1 80150 365 5

Typesetting and origination by Pitch Publishing
Printed and bound in Great Britain by TJ Books, Padstow

Contents

In loving memory of the
one and only Jimmy Greaves

Acknowledgements

MY HEARTFELT thanks to Irene Greaves for encouraging me to write this authorised biography of her late husband, national treasure and best friend Jimmy, on the understanding that 'it's not treacle and tells the truth about a wonderful but complex man.'

Irene has generously lent her name to a book for the first time because she wants to help paint an accurate picture of a legend of a man, warts 'n' all. As I knew Jim as long as Irene, over 64 years, I feel justified in claiming the book as the definitive biography of The Great Entertainer.

We have chosen for our publication date the 60th anniversary of Jimmy's memorable, magical goal in the 1962 FA Cup final for Tottenham against Burnley at Wembley on 5 May 1962, and hope it's a worthy Diamond Jubilee tribute to The Master.

As with any book of mine with a Spurs theme, I give a share of any profits to the Tottenham Tribute Trust, who quietly do a great job in helping our old heroes as they pay the price for the efforts they made entertaining us in the summertime of their lives and now suffering in the winter of their discontent.

'The Trust and Tottenham Hotspur were among many that did their best to help Jim in his difficult final years,' says Irene, 'and I would like to thank them and all the hundreds of people who contacted me and our family with sympathetic messages. In particular I would like you to mention family friends 'Doc'

Doherty and Jimmy's faithful van driver, Big Andy Keen and our relay of carers and hospital staff who did their best to make Jim's last years as comfortable and pain-free as possible. Jim was always surrounded with love.'

Running through the book are exclusive head-to-head interviews I organised for Jimmy with his good friends Johnny Haynes, Dave Mackay, Gordon Banks, George Best, Brian Clough and Bobby Moore, and I remember each of them with reverence, respect and affection. I acknowledge *The Sun*, *Sunday Express*, Robson Books, Arthur Barker and Weidenfeld & Nicolson, who originally published the words.

There are repeat articles from previous publications of mine, because I cannot rewrite history and in each case Jimmy and I jointly held the copyright. Tottenham Hotspur claim that all historical facts are their intellectual property, and I (begrudgingly) accept that assertion.

I nod gratefully in the direction of the queue of writers who followed in my ghostly footsteps as Jimmy's Boswell, including skilled wordsmiths Martin Samuel, Neil Custis, Dave Kidd, Mark Irwin, Joe Steeples, Bob Patience, Les Scott, and his 2018 biographer David Tossell. I also called on the wisdom of brilliant young film-maker Thomas Boswell – yes, a modern-day Boswell – who kindly included my recollections in his stunning *Greavsie* documentary for BTSport. Highly recommended.

Terry Baker, his agent, manager and friend at the back end of his career, was also a mine of information and worked tirelessly to raise funds to help ease the pressure on Jim and the Greaves family.

Thanks to omniscient Tottenham disciple David Guthrie for his fact-checking, to No 1 son, Michael, for his in-depth knowledge, and gratitude – for their support and encouragement – to Spurs Odyssey webmaster Paul H. Smith and Michael Berry, founder of the leading football retro magazine *BackPass*.

For club information I have over the years dipped into the archives of statisticians Albert Sewell (Chelsea), Les Yates, Andy Porter, John Fennelly (Tottenham), Jack and John Helliar (West Ham), all of them far more knowledgeable than me, and I'm glad to say the two Johns are still with us.

Thanks to the Ford Motor Company for permission to reprint passages from the article from their 1970s World Cup Rally magazine and to Central TV, TVam and LWT for allowing me to use photos of Jim while involved in their programmes.

Bowing the knee, relatively speaking, to brother and sister Paul and Jane Camillin of Pitch Publishing for their positive and productive work in surreal times, Duncan Olner for making me suitably jacketed, Alex Daley for the promotion push; also diligent editor Richard Fletcher and skilled lay-out artist Graham Hales.

Across the years Irene and I have been furnished with photographs by late, great Fleet Street cameramen Monty Fresco, his nephew Monte Fresco, Norman 'Speedy' Quicke and Bob Stiggins, and it is mainly their work that features in the picture sections. Best efforts have been made to clear all copyrights and Irene and I claim rights to those photographs given to us as gifts.

Thanks to all Jimmy's former team-mates and television colleagues, who willingly shared their memories. I just hope I have done the great man justice.

Thanks most of all to YOU for buying the book and keeping alive the memory of the one and only Jimmy Greaves.

'It's a funny old game ...'

Irene and her Jim during good times, 1990

Mr and Mrs Greaves the second time around, two years after Jim's violent stroke in 2015

Introduction

Irene Greaves: 'Jim would want
this to be warts 'n' all'

THIS IS the one and only time I have put my name to a book on my Jim, and I have only agreed to it because I want this to be the story everybody reads about my best mate knowing they are reading the truth. I have trusted Jimmy's close friend Norman Giller to describe his great adventure, warts 'n' all. There has rarely been a life to match it.

So many things written about Jim came from people who did not really know him. He was a wonderful yet complex man, and he would have hated anybody giving him the treacle treatment. We were together for 63 years, the love of each other's lives, and it was a rollercoaster like no other.

For every mountain climbed and bridge crossed, there was a fall waiting at the other side. Jim knew the highs, but there were plenty of lows to balance and often wreck the good times. Only Jim and I know what he went through in those last torturous six years after his violent stroke. It was agonising to see him reduced to an almost mute invalid, confined to a wheelchair and unable to show off what was an incredible, matchless wit. This was the man who during our 63 years of on-off-on marriage often had me crying with either laughter or exasperation and, finally, heartbreak. One thing's for sure: life with Jim was never, ever dull.

Older readers will remember there used to be a popular series 'on the wireless' called *Mrs Dale's Diary*, in which she was constantly saying, 'I'm worried about Jim' [her husband]. It became a catchphrase in the Greaves household, sometimes for a laugh but too often for real.

In those dark days following the stroke, he often asked me to help him end it all and, to be honest, it was a relief and a release when he finally passed in 2021, thankfully in his own bed and not in a hospital surrounded by strangers. He was a loving dad, grandad, great grandad, brother, uncle and my best pal, but after that savage stroke he gradually lost the will to live.

There were – years earlier – other horrible days when he lost himself in the bottle. He became a stranger to everybody, nothing resembling the Jim I had loved since we were teenage sweethearts, both with an East London background and devoted to each other. I divorced him to try to bring him to his senses, and within a few months of fearing he was losing the family he loved so much, he started a remarkable recovery and won his way back into our lives.

Somehow, he picked himself up when all who knew him had written him off as a washed-up former football player, and the way he reinvented himself as a major television and stage performer was beyond belief. Norman Giller was very close to him during that amazing transition period, and when describing it in this book kindly gives me most of the credit for pulling Jim through his crisis.

I was certainly there to encourage and praise him and, when necessary, be his honest critic, but Jim did it all on his own, teaching himself the art of broadcasting and how to turn the camera into a friend. I know from the hundreds of letters I have received that he touched many hearts with his fightback from alcoholism and he was loved way beyond the football world in which he had been – okay, I'm biased – a superstar.

I know enough about football to say there was no greater British goalscorer. You will find plenty of experts on the following pages seconding my admittedly partisan opinion, and as you have kindly bought this book no doubt you share this assessment.

Yet – and this will surprise many people – Jimmy did not have an all-consuming love of the game. In his later years, he much preferred to watch rugby or cricket and rarely went out of his way to switch on a football match. It was a game at which he was a natural genius, but he got much greater satisfaction from what he achieved in the world of television.

I am now going to hand you over to Norman Giller to tell Jim's story. He has, appropriately, called it *The One and Only*.

There will never be another like my Jim.

Irene Greaves

Our last picture together on Jimmy's 75th birthday

Harry Redknapp and Ossie Ardiles among the mourners at the full-house funeral

KICK OFF:

Starting at the end

LET ME first of all present my credentials for being the right person to write this official, authorised biography of the one and only Jimmy Greaves. It means starting at the end of Jimmy's remarkable life, and the final fond farewell that he was given at his funeral at Chelmsford Crematorium on 22 October 2021.

I was privileged to deliver the eulogy on behalf of Jimmy's former team-mates, television colleagues and the army of fans he had accumulated across the nation. There were just 200 mourners shoe-horned into the chapel when we could have filled Wembley Stadium with the thousands who would have liked to have paid their last respects to the Goliath of goalscorers. Among the congregation I spotted Steve Perryman, Harry Redknapp, Cliff Jones, Pat Jennings, Phil Beal, John Pratt, Brian Dear and Martin Chivers, all former club mates who knew exactly how exceptional Jimmy had been as a player. You could also feel the presence of his late old pals Bobby Moore, Johnny Haynes, Gordon Banks, Alan Gilzean, Bobby Smith, George Best and Danny Blanchflower. Now Jimmy was joining them.

These were my parting words, which I repeat here to underline that Jimmy and I had a special bond that transcended football.

They give a summary of what he achieved during his extraordinary time on this mortal coil:

❛ I'm privileged to be the spokesman for Jimmy's many friends, former team-mates, television colleagues and his army of fans around the country as we say a final fond farewell to my old mate of 64 years.

I've been restricted to 700 words but 7,000 would not do the great man justice.

We'll be letting Jimmy down if we don't share a laugh or two at his memory in this celebration of his astonishing life. So with that in mind, let's remember for a moment just how great he was in the box and, Jim, never deadlier than today.

He'd laugh loudest at that and wouldn't want any of us to be morbid and miserable.

Jim was the Great Entertainer, whether with a ball at his feet or a microphone at his lips, and he brought pleasure and sunshine into the lives of millions. A national treasure. Arise, Sir Jim.

That should have been the cue for Jimmy to leap up and shock us all with two fingers to the Establishment. It's a funny old game.

We all know and admire what Jimmy achieved on the football field with Chelsea, AC Milan, nine incredible years with Tottenham Hotspur, West Ham and, of course, England, and later non-League clubs such as Brentwood, Chelmsford and Barnet.

There are plenty of his old team-mates here today who I know will agree with my assessment that Jimmy was simply the greatest British goalscorer of all time.

You have to be way over 50 to have seen him at his peak. He was like Messi with bells on, and I'm not sure the modern master could do it on the mud-heap pitches that Jimmy's generation played on, and with the likes of "Bites Yer Legs" Hunter and Ron "Chopper" Harris trying to kick him up in the air.

After getting off the football express at the ridiculously young age of 31, Jimmy had the character and discipline – with Irene's motivation – to overcome a slight hiccup in his life. He then reinvented himself as a brilliant broadcaster, loved and admired for his irreverent wit and wisdom alongside Ian St John on the ground-breaking *Saint and Greavsie* show.

He was also hugely popular on TV-am and happiest up in the Midlands with his Central TV pals.

Jim was prouder of this period of his life than what he did in football, at which he was a natural genius. He had to learn the TV business from scratch and became a master communicator, mixing humour with biting, no-holds-barred opinions.

He suffered from chronic dyslexia and could not rely on the auto-cue, so what we got every time he was on our screens was the raw, real Jimmy. And everybody from kids to grannies loved him.

Jim was never, ever fazed, whether it was sharing a ring with Mike Tyson, a fairway with Sevvy Ballesteros, taking the pee out of Donald Trump, or causing mischief with his best mate Bobby Moore, two loveable rascals together. What a team they've got up there now!

It says everything for Jimmy's stature that he was never overshadowed by all the megastars he mixed with, yet he remained modest and unassuming. I bet none of you ever heard him boast, yet he had so much to boast about.

Then, when television chiefs prematurely decided his face no longer fitted (the idiots), he converted to stand-up comedy and impressed with his professional delivery in a series of road shows with his long-time friend and agent Terry Baker.

Anybody who ever saw him on stage will confirm that he was as funny as any of the top comedians. Whether on stage, screen or football pitch, Jimmy always scored.

No question that his greatest triumph was his fantastic family and they will testify that he was a loving brother, uncle, dad, grandad and great grandad, and the best pal his girl Irene ever had.

Irene, you were his rock and pulled him through life's traumas, and he loved you heart and soul.

Jimmy had a lousy last few years following his stroke, and only the support of Irene and their wonderful kids – Lynn, Mitzi, Danny and Andy – kept him sane.

But you don't judge a 90-minute match by the injury time. Judge Jim over the full 90 minutes and he had a fabulously full life and we were so lucky he shared much of it with us.

We were all privileged that he passed our way, a 24-carat gold legend. We'll never see his like again and I'll leave you with this memory of something heard a record 357 times in First Division matches [shouted, commentary-style]: "Goal! It's Jimmy Greaves."

Rest easy, mate. You played a blinder.'

Yes, Jimmy played a blinder, and over the following pages I hope to share his great adventure with you. I suggest you fasten your safety belts.

Chapter 1:

A rare diamond of a goal

WE DELIBERATELY chose 5 May 2022 to publish this tribute book as a lasting memory of the greatest British goalscorer ever to set foot on the playing fields of England, James Peter Greaves. It was 60 years to the day that Jimmy scored one of the great Wembley goals against Burnley in the 1962 FA Cup Final, among the most satisfying moments of a career – and life – that can only be described as extraordinary. Fittingly, it was a rare diamond of a goal.

There have been many books written about Jim, 20 of them ghostwritten by me and several biographies conscientiously carved by people who admired but did not really know him. Now we come to the book Jimmy and I had discussed writing just before he was savagely struck down by the stroke that robbed him of his speech and much of his movement. It was going to be called *The Truth*.

Let's wind the clock back to that day Jimmy helped Spurs retain the FA Cup they had won 12 months earlier when becoming the first team of the 20th century to complete the elusive Double of League championship and FA Cup. This is how Jimmy remembered it:

‘I never used to make predictions about scoring. It was the easiest way to make yourself look foolish. But for some reason I felt confident enough about this match to say to my team-mates in the dressing-room beforehand, "Get the ball to me early, lads. I'm going to score a goal inside the first five minutes." It was so unlike me, and when the words came out I wondered if it was somebody else talking. Sure enough, with the game barely three minutes old, goalkeeper Bill Brown found Bobby Smith with a long clearance, and he played it on to me on the edge of the penalty area. I over-ran the ball but quickly regained control and from 15 yards rolled a shot with my left foot through a forest of legs and into the net. One of the newspaper reporters described it as being "as accurate as an Arnold Palmer putt". Just wish I could have putted like that on the greens.

The goal meant so much to me. I had been as nervous as a kitten in Battersea Dogs' Home when joining Spurs from Milan six months earlier because they had won the Double without me and I was terrified of upsetting the balance of their great team. I had been robbed of a goal in the European Cup semi-final against Benfica in the previous month, but this goal against Burnley – the one I had predicted – wiped out all the bad memories.

We went on to beat that smashing Burnley side 3-1, Danny Blanchflower clinching victory from the penalty spot. Danny, who was godfather to my son Danny a few months later, told us that as he was placing the ball on the spot his Northern Ireland team-mate Jimmy McIlroy, Burnley's stylish schemer, sidled up to him and said, "Bet you miss it." Danny said nothing. "As I ran past Jimmy after putting the penalty into the net," Danny told us, "I said, 'Bet I don't...'"

They were some of the happiest times of my football life, and playing for that Tottenham team was a privilege.

I am here as your guide through Jimmy's life and times, the good, the bad and the ugly. In the hope that you feel his presence on the page I will be quoting him at every opportunity, mostly from conversations we had over the years I covered his career as a reporter and then from our close collaborations on our many book projects after his ridiculously premature retirement at the age of 31. Health warning, I will be focusing on his drinking in the first part of the book before opening the floodgates on his considerable footballing feats. Some of it is quite harrowing, but Jim would have wanted me to tell the naked truth.

One of the questions he was continually asked was, 'What was your best goal?' People thought he was jesting when he continually selected one he scored right at the back end of his career while in an alcoholic state with Southern League Barnet.

' It was when I could still be described as a drunk. Barnet were marvellous to me and used to cover up when I went on benders, but I gave my best for them in my sober moments. This particular day I was playing in midfield in a fourth qualifying round FA Cup tie against Edgware when the ball came to me about 30 yards out. I cracked it with my left foot on the half-volley and the ball zoomed towards the right-hand post, but I put so much bend on it that it finished flashing into the top left [corner] of the net. I never used to get that excited about scoring but this was the farthest out that I had ever hit the target, and I ran in celebration towards the touchline with my arms raised. I acknowledged the rapturous applause from two spectators and a dog. It's a funny old game. '

Describing the Barnet goal as his best was Jimmy's way of dodging a question he was always being asked. As he had nearly 500 to choose from, he found it impossible to pick and I tried to find a way to help him choose just one by writing a book with him called *GOALS!* We sent a questionnaire to every major British forward from Jimmy's generation and they described their most memorable goal and also a personal favourite they had had seen live or on screen. A huge majority selected the one Jimmy scored against Manchester United in 1965 and which featured every week in the *Match of the Day* opening titles until colour television came in.

I put it under the microscope in a closing chapter in the book called 'Anatomy of a Goal':

> ‘Jimmy Greaves scored what was by any standards quite a goal for Tottenham against Manchester United at White Hart Lane on 16 October 1965. Typically, Jimmy was embarrassed when so many of the top marksmen we approached selected it as the greatest goal they had ever seen. He wanted them to choose an alternative goal but as, co-editor of this book, I insisted that their first choice should stand.’

Among the players who selected Jimmy's goal were George Best, Johnny Haynes, Geoff Hurst, Denis Law, Tommy Lawton, Francis Lee, Martin Peters, Bruce Rioch, Terry Venables and Frank Worthington. Best and Law played in the game for United, and the rest saw the goal on television.

So what was so special about the goal? This is how Geoffrey Green, doyen of football writers, described it in *The Times*:

> ‘Magic may be an overworked word, but what came next was just that. It was Greaves who set the high point to the banquet. Receiving from Mackay with his back to the United goal some 35 yards out, he sold two

dummies, changed direction and in the bat of an eyelid had shimmied through and past the converging tackles of three of the great defenders, Foulkes, Stiles and Dunne. Next, Greaves drew out the goalkeeper and bypassed him too, before stroking the ball into the gaping net. The stadium erupted; the terraces waved like a forest in a gale and Manchester could only stand and wonder at it. This was the act of a Pelé under the Brazilian skies, Puskas in the sunshine of Madrid. Greaves, the Fagin of the penalty area, the arch pick-pocket of goals, has stolen many spectacular goals but none quite so richly embroidered as this one. '

The after-match comments from the United players who had been on the receiving end were a chorus of acclaim for the goal. 'No defence in the world could have stopped him,' said Nobby Stiles. 'We all knew we shouldn't commit ourselves to tackles against him, but he draws you towards the ball like a bee to honey. You make your challenge and find yourself tackling thin air. Jimmy's some player.'

'It was a goal of pure genius,' said Pat Crerand. 'We all just shrugged our shoulders and got on with the game. When that little so-and-so makes up his mind to score, there's little you can do about it but just feel privileged to see a master at work.'

'Even though it was a goal against us, it brought a smile to our faces,' said George Best. 'We almost enjoyed watching it! In my time in football, I've not seen a better executed goal. Jimmy was in total command of the situation from the moment the ball arrived at his feet. He knew exactly what he was doing, and left a queue of defenders chasing his shadow.'

Sir Matt Busby was celebrating the 20th anniversary of taking charge at United. 'It was nice of Jimmy to give me that goal as an anniversary present,' he joked. 'I don't think I've seen a better goal scored against us. Jimmy is a master of fashioning a goal out of nothing. Only Denis Law can match him for turning a half-chance into a goal. They are the two kings of the penalty area.'

'I had gone off injured and John Fitzpatrick was substituting for me,' said the other great goal-master, Denis Law. 'Watching the goal from the touchline bench was like seeing poetry in motion. I have always considered Jimmy the greatest goalscorer of all time and this is the goal that surely proves it.'

Denis added with a chuckle, 'I hate the wee man.'

When did Jimmy make up his mind that he was going to score? Jim:

‘ It was not premeditated. I never planned to score a goal in my life. Goals just used to happen. They were just an instinctive thing with me. With this particular goal, I remember receiving the ball from Dave Mackay. John Fitzpatrick was breathing down my neck and I turned him, pretending to go off right but then setting off in a straight line. From then on, everything's a bit of a blur in my memory, but I've seen the goal enough times on television to know that I changed direction two or three times to throw Nobby, big Foulksie and Tony Dunne off balance.

If I had any skill, that was it – the ability to wrong-foot opponents. A goalscorer is like a card sharp. While you've got the ball at your feet, you're holding all the cards. You know where you're going, and the objective is to kid the man or the men in front of you that you're going somewhere else. So you set out to deceive them with little feints, sudden

26

changes of direction and acceleration. If you look at pictures of any of the great ball-playing marksmen scoring their goals, you will usually see one or two defenders on the ground behind them. That's because they had a gift for making defenders commit themselves to tackles. It's like a boxer counter-punching. You wait for them to make the lead and then, whoosh, you're off and past them before they can get their balance back. *

What about the final shot?

* I was rarely a whacker of a ball. I couldn't burst the skin of a rice pudding from 15 yards. Power shooting is a different game altogether. You have to distribute your bodyweight in a different way. I was usually on my toes for my goals and used to steer rather than shoot the ball into the net. For that goal against United, I drew goalkeeper Pat Dunne off the line and let him think he was dictating the angle to me while I knew that I was really in charge. He was inviting me to shoot into the left-hand side of the goal and I dropped my shoulder and cocked my right foot to pretend I had accepted the invitation. I waited until he had all his weight on his left-hand side and then moved wide of him and was left with the simple task of a tap-in goal. People are always reminding me of that goal, but I honestly think I scored a better one against Leicester a couple of years later at White Hart Lane. It was similar to the United goal, but what made it even more satisfying was that I collected the ball from a clearance by goalkeeper Pat Jennings. So it was literally an end-to-end move with only the two of us touching the ball and it was that other master, Peter Shilton, that I hoodwinked at the other end. Very satisfying. *

I had to twist Jimmy's arm to get him to talk in any depth about goalscoring. Throughout his career, he would always say that the most important goal was his next one. As the uncrowned king of goalscorers, he deserves the last word on the subject of goals, and I know it will be echoed by all proven marksmen: 'A goal is a goal is a goal!'

From goals to gongs and a subject that irritated me but did not bother Jim in the slightest. Okay, I am biased but in my view he should have been knighted long before his passing. I think the Establishment got their own back on him for continually knocking the honours system. He strongly felt that the UK should have adopted the old-style Russian process of rewarding outstanding sports performances with Masters of Sport medals, and he used to regularly mock the fact that the likes of Bobby Moore, George Best and Denis Law never got the knighthoods their service to football deserved.

For more than 20 years I campaigned for Jimmy to get a gong, and the *Daily Mail* took up the crusade in 2020 but rather overcooked it, with dozens of pages devoted to getting him the knighthood he had earned. How did the Whitehall mandarins react? They gave him a measly MBE, which Jim – if he had been able to express himself – would have told them to stick where the sun don't shine.

Enough to drive a man to drink …

Chapter 2:

Getting sober out of our minds

COME WITH me to my home in Thorpe Bay, Essex, a 1930s-built detached house overlooking the Thames Estuary. It is 20 February 1979 and Jimmy Greaves and I were celebrating his 39th birthday. We had just finished our first book together, *This One's On Me*, which was a ground-breaking, tell-all story about how alcoholism had wrecked his life.

My lovely wife Eileen was making us copious cups of black coffee – Jimmy's latest addiction – and I proposed a toast. Lifting my coffee cup, I said, 'Jim, let's go and get sober out of our minds.'

'What a great idea, Norm,' he said, taking a gulp of the piping hot espresso coffee. 'I've been pissed out of my mind for too many years.'

From then on, neither Jimmy nor I touched another alcoholic drink. It was the turning point in Jimmy's life, which included moments of turbulence, brilliance, madness, magnificence, misery and sadness. Back then, I was a Fleet Street drinker, which in those pre-breathalyser days meant I could put it away with the best of them. Fleet Street was not only the street of ink but also of drink. I stopped drinking to encourage Jimmy to beat his demons, and over the next 35-plus years was an astonished witness to what he achieved with his life. It was sobering to watch.

Anybody who knew Jim intimately in those five lost years after his premature retirement from West Ham in 1971 at the age of just 31 would not have given him a hope of beating the bottle. Boozing on a monumental scale had not only cost him his marriage but a flourishing packaging and travel business that he ran with his brother-in-law, Tom Barden. It had a turnover of more than £1 million and employed 30 people. Jimmy's drinking helped send it to the wall, and the shame of it just made him dive deeper into a sea of alcohol.

To appreciate and understand just how low he had got, let me quote Jim from *This One's On Me*:

‘ Every alcoholic has his own rock bottom. For many, it's the Thames Embankment and a diet of methylated spirits and the ravaged remains of other people's left-overs. The only thing that saved me from the Embankment was that I was always in a position to afford, for the want of a better word, good booze, and I also had the physical fitness to be able to quickly recover from even the severest bouts of drinking. I had more benders than Uri Geller.

My personal rock bottom came in the early hours of a frosty winter's morning when I was ransacking the dustbin in my back garden for empty vodka bottles that had been thrown away by my wife Irene. It was in the winter of 1977. Don't ask me to put times and dates on events of the last five years because the one thing that has been permanently damaged by drink is my memory. I have almost total recall of everything that happened in my football career, but there is some sort of mental blockage on the most horrendous moments of my drinking bouts.

But I do have a nightmare memory of the moment I realised that I was a hopeless alcoholic. I had been sleeping a boozing session off in an armchair in the lounge when Irene – now my ex-wife, I'm sad to say – found my hidden hoard of vodka and in a rage poured all the drink down the sink and threw the bottles into the dustbin. I woke up with a raging thirst, turned cupboards and drawers upside down in a maniacal search for my drinks and finished up kneeling by the side of the dustbin draining the last drops out of the bottles. This was the gutter point of my life.

It looked then like the point of no return. I was having to drink a half-bottle of vodka before I could even get out of bed to face the day. My hands would shake uncontrollably and all I could think about was the next drink. When the pubs opened, I would be standing on the doorstep. My first order would be a pint of Guinness because at least that was nourishing and my only food of the day

By the end of the day I would have got through 12 or 14 pints. No bother. And I could hold my drink so well that only people really close to me would know that I'd been on the booze. Then it would be home to a bottle, sometimes two bottles, of vodka.

I am not putting these statistics down to be dramatic or sensational. I just want you to know and understand how bad my problem had become. The wonder is that I am alive to talk about it. '

Jim had critics – including Arsenal's reformed alcoholic, the crusading Tony Adams – who claimed he did not give enough credit to Alcoholics Anonymous (AA) for his recovery. But I know for a fact that he always quoted their doctrine when approached time and again by people seeking help and advice on how to beat the bottle. I can divulge that he secretly helped many unknown members of the public to follow the AA disciplines, and also gave confidential motivational support to former football colleagues like Billy Wright, Brian Clough and Cliff Jones, all of whom at one time struggled under the devastating influence of alcohol.

Back in the days when I was a Fleet Street reporter, drinking was the culture of the time, both in the worlds of journalism and football. Every club had its hard drinking schools, and I just about remember getting legless with the Chelsea crew led by Peter Osgood, Alan Hudson and Charlie Cooke, the Arsenal gang featuring Frank McLintock, Geordie Armstrong and George Graham (who later become a disciplinarian of a manager), and West Ham with 'Hollow Legs' Bobby Moore, Frank Lampard senior, Brian Dear and young Harry Redknapp first to the Black Lion bar.

Best of all, I enjoyed being in the company at the Bell and Hare club crowded with Tottenham players such as the maestro Dave Mackay, Cliffie Jones and Alan Gilzean, who once – when I asked him to name his favourite partners – told me, 'Bacardi and Coke.' All of them considered drinking harmless and their reward for a game well played or a defeat that needed drowning.

Prominent in the Tottenham and then West Ham drinking pools was one Jimmy Greaves. But what none of us knew then is that he was also drinking heavily alone and in secret.

'Getting sober out of our minds' was not going to be easy.

Jim and I had known (and liked) each other since we were both 17. It was the summer of 1957 and he had started pumping in goals for Chelsea while I had just become assistant sports editor on the West Ham local paper, the *Stratford Express* (a sports staff of two, I might add). As Jimmy had been born in our circulation area at Manor Park, I arranged an interview with him at Stamford Bridge. When I got there, he said with some embarrassment, 'Sorry, mate, can't talk to you. The boss [Ted Drake] has told me not to give any more interviews.' Ted was worried that Jimmy was getting too much attention and that it was affecting his game (a matter of record: Drake 'rested' Jimmy for six weeks because he thought the pressure was getting to him. He recalled him on Boxing Day 1957 and Jimmy scored four goals against Portsmouth. Ted never rested Jim again!).

As compensation for my wasted journey, Jimmy – then of the spiky, crew-cut hair and crepe-sole shoes – bought me a cuppa at the popular Bridge Cafe and we later travelled back to East London together on the District Line. It was the start of a 64-year friendship that climaxed with me delivering his eulogy. It's a sad old game.

While he sharpened his soccer skills, I broadened my vocabulary and found my way to Fleet Street. I went on to write for the *Daily Herald* and then the *Daily Express* as chief football reporter, chronicling many of Jimmy's games and goals for club and country.

Fast forward to the winter of 1978 and we were standing side by side at the grave of our mutual mate Vic Railton, a renowned London *Evening News* football reporter, who had died suddenly of a heart attack at 59. Just that previous weekend, the *Sunday People* had splashed a front-page story by their top investigative reporter Frank Thorne revealing that Jimmy was in a mental home at Warley recovering from a bender. The headline screamed, 'Jimmy Greaves: Drink is killing me.'

It took enormous courage for Jimmy to go to Vic's funeral at the vast, 200-acre City of London Cemetery in Newham, knowing that all eyes would be on him. As we tossed earth on to Vic's coffin after he had been lowered into the grave, I overheard Jim say, 'Rest easy, Vic. See you soon. I'll be next.'

I invited Jim for a coffee at a Wanstead café two miles from the cemetery and we sat sharing memories of Vic, one of the great characters of Fleet Street. It was difficult to believe that this was the same Jimmy Greaves who had just a few years earlier been lauded as the greatest British goalscorer of not just our time but any time. His hands were trembling and his confidence and self-esteem were shot to pieces. He told me he was living in a rented bedsit in a nearby terraced redbrick house while he fought his demons. 'I've fucked up my life,' he said with brutal honesty. 'If I had the guts, I'd top myself. Tried it with a razor blade to my wrists the other day, but swallowed it.'

There was a flash of the old Greavsie humour. 'Ever tried swallowing a razor blade? Don't half hurt.'

I laughed at his punchline but knew what he meant. He really had contemplated slashing his wrists.

As we sat chatting, I was trying to get my head round the fact that here was one of the most accomplished footballers ever to play the game and he was drowning in a sea of sorrow and self-pity. It made no sense and I decided I was going to do my best to help him start believing in himself. Arise Saint Norman.

'There's only one Jimmy Greaves,' I told him, stating the obvious. 'You've got to feed off that. You're still an idol to thousands out there.'

'Yes, idle bastard,' Jimmy shot back, making a play on the word 'idol'. This convinced me we had a lot to work with, and I persuaded him we should get together and write a book in which we could showcase his natural humour and tell the blistering truth about his life and times.

And that's how *This One's On Me* came about ('much better than this book,' I hear you say).

Film producer/director Bernie Stringle, famous for his hilarious chimps in the PG Tips TV adverts, read the book and rang me. 'Fantastic story,' he said. 'What chance Jimmy telling it to camera?'

I said I'd put it to him, and Jimmy's first reaction was, 'He wants me to star in the chimps' tea party. You trying to make a monkey out of me?'

First of all he declined, but after sleeping on it, he told me, 'Sod it, I'll give it a go.'

At the time, he was earning a crust selling ladies' sweaters (provided by a caring fashion-trade pal, Geoff Green) from the boot of his mustard-coloured Jaguar sports car, the one luxury he had managed to hang on to. 'Must have a nice motor,' he said. 'If I'm going to hell, I want to travel in comfort.'

So it was that within two months of the publication of our book, Jimmy was facing a camera and saying the blunt opening line, 'My name is Jimmy G, and I am an alcoholic.' Bernie, himself a recovering alcoholic, used one of our chapter titles – *Just for Today* – as the name for his absorbing, hour-long programme. It was shot in my Thorpe Bay home and along the Estuary beach. Jim spent hours talking to camera and telling his harrowing story before the editing process. 'I shot enough film to make *Gone with the Wind* meets *The Longest Day*,' he said with the sort of punchline humour that would make him loved nationwide.

Jimmy got more valuable experience in front of the camera when he anchored a video I scripted to mark Tottenham's 1982 centenary year. Released on the Betamax system before it was knocked out by the VHS tapes, it has become a real collector's item because few people have the facility to play it. A highlight was Jimmy interviewing emotional former manager Bill Nicholson, who had returned to the club as a consultant after a lost, fish-out-of-water year at West Ham. He surprisingly said off camera to Jimmy, 'I would have selected you for the 1966 World Cup Final. I thought Alf was crazy to leave out his greatest striker, even though the final 4-2 victory over the Germans proved me wrong. But I still say it was a mad gamble by Alf. My way as manager was always to play my best players and my best team. You were comfortably England's best forward.'

Jim and I looked at each other with raised eyebrows. It was the first time we had ever heard Bill refer to the team selection by Ramsey, who had been one of his biggest rivals throughout his club management career and had desperately wanted the Spurs coaching job before moving on to Third Division Ipswich. That job, of course, went to Bill.

We spent a week at White Hart Lane shooting what was then a rare video, and for Jimmy it meant hours of treasured time talking to camera.

Little did we know that he was serving an apprenticeship for the new world that was about to open up to him. Jimmy Greaves, footballer extraordinaire turned television personality.

He had come a long way from East London and Hitler's bombs.

Chapter 3:

Bombs, footballs, schools and scouts

JIMMY HAD his first kick of life on Tuesday, 20 February 1940 in Manor Park, just a few hundred yards from where Vic Railton was later buried in the City of London Cemetery, the scene of our graveside reunion in 1978. Back in the 1940s, it was in the borough of East Ham before East and West were merged into Newham. As was to become his habit, he arrived at the right time and place in the East Ham Hospital maternity ward, the first child of Jim and Mary Greaves. Within weeks, he had been whisked nine miles along the North Circular Road to the relative safety of a terraced house in Ivyhouse Road, Dagenham, just about out of range of the Luftwaffe's falling bombs.

Jim senior, son of Irish immigrants, served with the British Army in India, where he was renowned for being sports mad, shining at football, hockey and tennis. On his demob, he became a guard and then a driver on the London District Line tube trains, while Mary was a housewife looking after Jimmy junior, then his sister Marion and, after the war, brother Paul. It says everything about the brain cells in the Greaves family that both Marion and Paul went on to become headteachers. 'Me,' said Jim, 'I had my brains in my feet.' Completely untrue, of course, because he was one of the most intelligent, streetwise people to cross my path, but was handicapped academically by suffering from what was much later diagnosed as dyslexia. 'Back then,' Jim recalled, 'if you couldn't read you were considered thick. I could read but kept seeing the words out of order, a bit like that classic Morecambe and Wise piano sketch with Andre Previn: "I'm reading all the right words, not necessarily in the right order."'

It was Jim's dad who had the biggest influence on him as a fledgling footballer. Jim Junior:

‘ Dad played football into his 40s with at least three local amateur clubs, and like so many of his generation lost his best years to the war, so there was no chance of him playing professionally. He taught me the importance of being two-footed and used to Dubbin my boots for me, so that I always had good, supple daisy roots, eventually size 8s. For several years, he was treasurer of Fanshaw Old Boys, a team that got its name from a Dagenham school where the likes of the Allen brothers, Les and Dennis, Ken Brown, Terry Venables and Martin Peters attended. It was a football-potty neighbourhood and Dad passed his love of the game on to me.

One of my happiest childhood memories is of him giving me an old leather-panelled football that the Fanshaw players had knocked the hell out of, and it became my constant companion and all the boys living near me came pleading to have a kick. We used to organise street games with me as the king of the castle because I owned the ball. Before that, we'd had to make do with tennis balls that we kicked around until they were bare with no cover. Those were the days when you could safely play in the streets with coats for goalposts because few people could afford cars, although our neighbours working at the nearby Ford factory used to do overtime to be able to buy the Prefects, Anglias and then Escorts that they helped build. I was a cocky little sod and used to challenge the big lads of the Fanshaw men's team to try to get the ball off me during their training sessions. You could say I had a bit of a swagger, and my Dad used to encourage me to show off my dribbling skills in kick-abouts with the grown men. '

Jimmy senior was promoted to driver on the recently extended Central Line, and the family moved to a newly built house on the Huntsman Road estate in Hainault, five miles from the heart of Dagenham and a short walk from Hainault station. It was like moving to a foreign land but Jimmy managed to hang on to his friendship with Dave Emerick, a classmate at Southwood Lane Primary School and a pal for life. Dave (later a long-distance runner who completed more than 80 marathons):

'Jim and I were inseparable in our school days, giving each other confidence and sticking up for each other if there were ever any problems. From the first time I saw him kick a ball, I knew he was something special. Even from the age of about eight, he used to have it instantly under control and he could go past other boys as if they weren't there. It was like watching a ghost going through walls. Now you see him, now you don't. Jim was in demand for playing football every weekend, so didn't form a special affinity with any club, but when he was free we would go together to watch Spurs play at White Hart Lane. That was in their push and run days and I recall Jimmy once running on the pitch at the end of a First Division match to get the autograph of Wolves and England skipper Billy Wright. A few years later, they were England team-mates. '

The move to Hainault gave Jim a major problem. Suddenly, he realised that if he passed his 11-plus exam he would be going to a rugby-playing grammar school. His dyslexia came to his rescue. Jim:

‘ Because it was taking me so long to read the questions, I did not have time to complete the exam and so I failed the 11-plus and got a place in the nearby Kingswood Secondary Modern School, where I became something of a local hero on the football pitch and eventually, would you believe, head boy. Scored goals galore and started attracting the professional scouts. I suppose you could say I cheated in the exam by deliberately not trying, but that was how mad I was on playing football. The last thing I wanted was going to a rugby school, yet many years later I would have chosen rugby ahead of football. I became hooked – a deliberate joke – on the game in middle-age and would have loved to have had a go at being a scrum-half. Collecting the ball at the base of the scrum and then squirming past tackles with lots of dummy passes and side steps really appealed to me. But when I was a kid with a boys' team called Lakeside Manor, I saw nothing but a football future ahead for me. It was almost taken for granted that I would make a living out of the game, although Dad wanted me to have a safety-net career and had got me an interview for a job in the print as an apprentice compositor at *The Times* when Chelsea came calling. ’

Sir Geoff Hurst, who was learning the football arts 30 miles away in Chelmsford, told me:

‘ Everybody in Essex schools football knew about Jimmy. He was the talk of the game and his scoring feats even then were extraordinary. You needed to be around where and when I was growing up to realise why he has always been gigantic in my personal rating of footballers. If there's been a greater British goalscorer then I've not seen him and, for Jimmy, it was cruel fate that he was not in England's 1966 World Cup-winning team. I was a year younger than Jim and was in awe of him because of the way he monopolised matches in our local Essex school games. He once scored 11 goals in a 13-0 victory against the school where Martin Peters was a pupil. "I watched from the sidelines," the two-years-younger Martin later told me. "I've never seen an individual performance to touch it." We were all expecting an announcement that he was going to join Spurs, and it came as a shock when he chose Chelsea on the "wrong" side of London. When I signed as an apprentice for West Ham in 1956, he was already a star in the making and getting headlines. That season, 1956/57, he scored the little matter of 114 goals for Chelsea. Astonishing.

I remember my first meeting with Jimmy away from football. Our daughter Claire was just a couple of months old and I was pushing her in a pram through our local supermarket in Essex when I came face to face with Jimmy. He was a huge star with Spurs then and I was just making a name for myself at West Ham, where manager Ron Greenwood had converted me from a plodding midfielder to a striker, not in Jim's class but I was managing to make an impact. We both did a double-take as we met in the supermarket, laughed at the coincidence and then got involved in a conversation. I was so in awe of him that when I wandered back into the High Street, I realised I had left Claire in the supermarket and rushed back and retrieved her. A year later, Greavsie and I were together in the England squad. What was that Jim always said about it being a funny old game? *'*

It was a widespread belief that Jimmy would kick off his professional career with Tottenham Hotspur. Manager Arthur Rowe made a hush-hush visit to his Hainault home in 1954 when Jimmy was 14, and Jim senior assured him his son would be very happy to sign for Spurs when he left school the following summer. But Rowe became unwell and while he was recuperating at home a bowler-hatted 'Mr Pope' popped up on Jimmy's doorstep. This was the pseudonym for a rascal of a Chelsea scout called Jimmy Thompson. The reason he used another name was to keep the Football Association off his back, because he had been continually reprimanded for 'tapping up' players in a bid to get them to play for Chelsea. He persuaded Jimmy Greaves senior that Jimmy Greaves junior would be much better off plying his trade at Stamford Bridge rather than White Hart Lane, and he handed over £50 in Irish fivers to convince Jim's dad that he was a man to trust!

Thompson, who had played for 19 clubs as a have-boots-will-travel centre-forward in the 20s and 30s, made such a fuss of Jim that he convinced him he was something very special. So he was bemused rather than amused to find that 'Mr Pope' had used the same selling line to the most talented of his schoolboy team-mates. When he reported as instructed under the big clock at Liverpool Street Station on the day he was signing for Chelsea, he found he was joined by seven other young footballers, including Ken Shellito, Mel Scott and David Cliss, with whom he had recently played in a London Schools representative match. The irrepressible Thompson arrived, gave the boys a train ticket and a Polo mint each and then led them on to the Tube train for the journey to Fulham Broadway and Chelsea Football Club. He was the Fagin of football.

John Sillett, who had signed for Chelsea a year earlier to join his older brother Peter, watched the arrival of the latest batch of Drake's Ducklings, as Thompson called them in deference to Chelsea manager and former England centre-forward Ted Drake. Forgive me if you can pick up on me being emotional as I type this paragraph. I have just heard that John has joined Jimmy in the great football stadium in the sky. They were the best of mates for nearly 66 years, and I interviewed him very recently for this book. He was one of football's great characters was John Sillett and a born raconteur:

‘ My brother Peter and I chuckled when we saw Jimmy Thompson marching his latest ducklings into Ted Drake's office. He was like a pied piper. What we later discovered was that he got £100 a head for each boy Chelsea signed and then another ton if they made it into the first team, and that was on top of his £20-a-week wages. He was laughing all the way to the bank. Don't forget that was when we were on £15 a week, maximum, in the season and eight quid a week in the summer.

I always remember that Thompson had a strawberry-red Sunbeam saloon in the days when few footballers could afford a car. Only one thing wrong: he couldn't drive. His daughter used to act as his chauffeur. He was dancing around after signing David Cliss and Greavsie, waving his bowler in the air as if he'd just won the pools. They were the two hottest prospects in the game. Clissy was unlucky to break a leg early in his Chelsea career and was never the same afterwards. He started a window cleaning business with my brother Peter, but both found out they were afraid of heights and couldn't climb ladders, so he emigrated to Australia and had a fair playing career down there.

Peter and I took Jimmy under our wing and introduced him to the joys of downing a pint after a game, so I suppose we started him on the slippery slope. But we had some great laughs, and he was the one who started calling me Schnoz after the American comedian with the huge conk, Schnozzle Durante. It was a name that stuck with me for life and few people knew I was named John.

Jim was a fantastic footballer, from another planet. I reckon he was at his best at Chelsea, scoring goals willy nilly. Bang, he'd put the ball into the net. Bang, we'd concede a goal. Bang, he'd get another. As fast as he scored them, you could bet on us letting them in at the back. Peter and I were full-backs and so you can imagine the stick Jimmy gave us. But we had great fun drowning our sorrows. If you want me to be serious for a minute, let me say from my heart that Jimmy Greaves was by a country mile the greatest goalscorer this country has ever produced and what he would call "a proper geezer". I was proud to have him as a pal. '

In his final season in youth football – 1956/57 – Jimmy netted an incredible 114 goals for the Chelsea youth team, including seven in one game, which caught the attention of manager Drake. Jim:

'After my seven goals, I was summoned to Ted Drake's office. It was the first time I'd had a face-to-face with him. "I'm told you scored seven goals on Saturday," he said in his Hampshire burr. "Did you know I once scored seven goals in a match?" I nodded shyly (there was not a schoolboy who didn't know the legend of how he scored seven goals from eight shots for Arsenal against Aston Villa at Villa Park in 1935). "Then take it from me," he continued, "that you must store the memory of each of those goals away in your mind as if it's a film. I can remember every one of my goals and it warms me on wintry nights. Seven goals! It only happens once in a career." That was it, and he signalled me to leave his office. In the next match, I scored eight goals. Then, against West Ham, I failed to find the net. That's football, famine or feast. At the end of the season, Chelsea chairman Joe Mears presented me with an illuminated address, a framed certificate congratulating me on my 114 goals in a season. My next match at the start of the following season was for the first team at, of all places, White Hart Lane. '

Chapter 4:

Chelsea, the 'All the Best' club

SO IT was that on Saturday, 24 August 1957, a 17-year-old Jimmy Greaves ran out on to Tottenham's White Hart Lane pitch for his Football League debut in the royal-blue shirt and white shorts of Chelsea. By the final whistle at 4.45pm, he was the talk of football and being hailed as a boy wonder. He had scored an astonishing goal, one that some surviving witnesses continue to talk about 65 years later.

This is how Jimmy remembered that *first* match and that *first* goal as we sat in my Thorpe Bay home sipping coffee and collaborating on our *first* book in 1978. It was all about firsts and thirsts ('Another coffee please, Eileen'):

‘ People wouldn't believe that I travelled to White Hart Lane by bus all by myself for my league debut after I'd been instructed to meet the rest of the team at the ground an hour before kick-off. In those days it took two buses, one to get from Hainault to Ilford and then another double-decker to the Regal Edmonton. So there I was walking down Tottenham High Road with thousands of other people aiming for the Lane, where I had sometimes been as a schoolboy spectator on the rare weekends when I didn't have a schools or junior club match. Nobody knew who I was and it was surreal to think I was about to play in front of them all. I reckon I could have taken off with the butterflies whirling in my tummy. Not anxiety as much as excitement.

I was carrying my boots in a small holdall, along with my shin-pads and a bar of Fry's milk chocolate that my mum had given me. There was also a stick of Wrigley's chewing gum. As I boldly presented myself at the players' entrance, the steward looked at me as if I was an intruder. "Move along, son," he said. "Can't collect autographs here." He tried to keep a straight face when I told him that I was playing. I fished out a club identification card that I'd been given and he reluctantly let me through after studying it with incredulity.

Most of my team-mates were already in the visitors' dressing-room and trainer Albert Tennant pointed me towards my peg, where my number 10 shirt hung, no name on the back, of course, in those days. Physio Harry Medhurst threw me a pair of shorts that, when I put them on, came down to my knees and had enough room in them for Billy Bunter and his sister Bessie. But I had long been an admirer of Alex James, the Scottish ball player at Arsenal, and if baggy shorts were good enough for him, so they were for me.

I looked nervously around the dressing room and smiled and nodded to my team-mates, who I knew fairly well following a recent trip to Holland with them for a warm-up match. Our line-up was a familiar one for Chelsea fans except for my name in the forward line. It read:

Reg Matthews, Peter Sillett, Dickie Whittaker, our captain Derek Saunders, John Mortimore, Alan Dicks, Peter

Brabrook, Ron Tindall, Les Allen, Baggy Shorts Me, Jim
Lewis

Goalkeeper Reg Matthews was puffing away at a fag
and looked much more nervous than me, and I could not
imagine how he was going to catch a ball. Both Les Allen
and Peter Brabrook were from my neck of the woods and I
was on nodding terms with them. Jim Lewis was a famous
amateur from Walthamstow Avenue and Peter Sillett
was already one of my best mates along with his brother,
Schnoz. I sat waiting to get my instructions from manager
Ted Drake, but there was no sign of him.

Five minutes before we were due to go out, he came
striding into the dressing room and took centre stage.
"Right, lads, you know what you've got to do,' he said. "Go
out there and give it everything you've got. All the best."

With that, he turned on his heel and walked out of the
dressing room, leaving me gaping and wondering whether
he had forgotten I was making my First Division debut.
It was the shortest pre-match talk I'd ever known from a
manager, and I quickly learned why the more experienced
Chelsea players dubbed us the "All the Best" club.

There was huge rivalry between the two clubs, and
nobody knew what to expect in what was the first game of
a new season. As we ran out on to the pitch first, there were
deafening boos from the home fans mixed with cheers from
the ten thousand Chelsea supporters among the 52,000
crowd, most of them wondering who was that little guy in
the baggy shorts. Only the real Bridge fanatics knew what
I'd been achieving with the youth team.

Spurs followed us on to the pitch, led by skipper Danny
Blanchflower, who was going to mark me in the then

tradition of the right-half marking the inside-left. Numbers on the shirts still meant something. This was a shadow of the Spurs team that I would ultimately join, managed by Jimmy Anderson and including only four of what would be the Double side. Bill Nicholson was on the touchline as a track-suited Tottenham coach, just a couple of years after a recurring knee injury had forced his retirement as a key midfield player in the push and run days. One of the main players in that great Spurs Double team was alongside me for Chelsea, Les Allen. And former Chelsea centre-forward Bobby Smith was leading the Tottenham attack. Confusing enough for you?

Danny, as you would expect of a master craftsman, did a thoroughly professional job marking me. He was expert at shepherding opponents into a cul de sac, and leaving the likes of big Maurice Norman and John Ryden to do the heavy tackling. Danny was all silken skill and elegance. Thank goodness Dave Mackay had not yet joined the Tottenham ranks. He would have been sure to have let me know he was on the pitch!

Alfie Stokes gave Spurs the lead in the 75th minute and we seemed to be drifting towards an opening-day defeat, with little impact from James Greaves. Then, with four minutes to go, I got lucky and managed to outwit the close-marking Danny at last, and as goalkeeper Ron Reynolds came charging towards me I side-stepped [him] and slid the ball into the empty net. It was the start of me always scoring in a major debut match, and I just hoped the players' entrance steward was watching. '

This is exactly how Jimmy described his goal, modestly forgetting to mention that he left not only Danny on his backside but also

John Ryden and Maurice Norman before drawing Ron Reynolds off his line and wrong-footing him with a shrug of the shoulder and finishing nonchalantly with a clinical right-foot shot. It was a magnificent goal that sent the crowd into ecstasy, including the Tottenham fans (well, some) who recognised genius when they saw it.

Reporters in the press box stood applauding, and competed with each other for who could give the most fitting description of the gem of a goal. 'The goal of the century from a wonder kid who will dominate our football for years to come,' gushed 'Man in the Brown Bowler' Desmond Hackett in the *Daily Express*; 'Astonishing,' wrote Geoffrey Green in *The Times*; 'Remarkable,' commented Bernard Joy in the *Evening Standard*; 'A goal in a million,' screamed the *People*.

The eloquent Danny Blanchflower stoked the furnace of praise. 'The lad has a great future,' he said. 'He scored one of the greatest goals I've ever seen. Unfortunately, I had the best view of it, sitting on my backside and admiring the finish. He completely hoodwinked me and most of my colleagues in defence. I've not seen a debut to match it.'

Jimmy Greaves senior read all the headlines with a mixture of pride and concern. 'Don't let it go to your head son,' he said. 'The press can break you as well as make you.'

This was as near as Jim's dad got to quoting Rudyard Kipling's 'If' classic:

> 'If you can meet with triumph and disaster
> And treat those two imposters just the same
> You'll be a man, my son.'

Jimmy junior was determined to remain balanced, accepting praise and criticism with controlled equanimity. And anyway, he had other things on his mind. He had fallen in love.

Like me a 1940 baby, Jim and I were among the first to be spared the discipline and demands of two years' National Service. One of his best mates, born in 1939, went off to join the army, asking him to 'look after' his girlfriend Irene Barden while he was off serving his country. Jimmy took it rather literally. He and the beautiful girl from Harold Hill via Bethnal Green fell madly in love, and in 1958 the teenagers got married at Romford Register office, a few months ahead of the arrival of their gorgeous daughter Lynn. It was unquestionably the best match of both their lives.

The new Mr and Mrs Greaves moved into a one-bedroom rented flat inside the then Isthmian League Wimbledon's ground overlooking the pitch at Plough Lane, helping to pay the rent by weeding the terraces. Many years later, Jim told me:

‘ They were wonderful days at Plough Lane. Everybody was telling us we were too young to get married and that we would regret it. The old pros said it would affect my career. I worked my socks off to prove them wrong. Nobody ever associated me with hard work, and they always talked about me being a natural as if all I had to do was to go out on to the pitch and everything would just click into place. But I promise you, I beavered away to keep myself fit and worked at improving my skills. I will own up to not liking long-distance running without the ball, but those stories of me taking lifts on milk floats were greatly exaggerated. I might have done it a couple of times and also once on a tractor as a joke and it shot round the village world of football that I was always taking short cuts. I would have backed myself over 20 yards against almost anybody apart from whippets like Cliffie Jones and Frank Blunstone. But unless I had a ball at my feet, I found it pointless running long distances.

Chelsea trainer Albert Tennant – we didn't call them coaches back then – was a stern, unsmiling but sincere man who taught me how to improve my acceleration by running on the balls of my feet, and youth team manager Dickie Foss was always the man I turned to for advice on positioning and tactics. He did more than anybody in my early days to help me lay the foundation to my career and to see and understand what was going on right across the pitch rather than just in my patch.

Ted Drake? A lovely man but no way should he have been in charge of that club. He fluked the league championship in 1954/55, making him the first to win it as both player (Arsenal) and manager. But it was thanks to his ageing but very capable players, led by Roy Bentley, that they took the title in a scrambling season rather than anything to do with his tactics. Ted, idolised in his playing days, was from the outdated "up and at 'em" school of football and his tactical theories did not stretch much beyond "all the best". He was an eternal optimist who I can never remember thinking we were going to be beaten. "This is one of the worst sides I've ever seen," he would say, regardless of the status of the opposition. "Just get out there and do what you know you've got to do. All the best."

A true story about Ted always makes me laugh. He was once driving Terry Venables and me to the training ground, Terry sitting in front in the passenger seat. Ted droned on and on about the secret of winning football matches was getting the ball into the box, and was rabbiting on as we pulled up at a red light. He kept chuntering on and the lights changed without us moving. The bloke in the car behind quite rightly honked us, and Terry said, "The lights have changed, boss." Ted looked across at him and did a double-take and then came out with the classic, "Bloody hell, I thought you were driving."'

Ted got bitten by the youth bug, inspired by the Busby Babes and the Cullis Cubs. Thanks largely to Jimmy Thompson's unconventional but successful recruiting drives, we had some magnificent young footballers but Ted did not have a clue how to mould us into a team. If an organiser like Walter Winterbottom or Bill Nicholson had been in charge, I think we would have swept up all the trophies. But we were just a bunch of kids playing it off the cuff and often coming off second best.

We used to have the most ridiculous results. I recall us once losing 6-5 to Manchester United and can still see our left-winger Frank Blunstone flinging his boots across the dressing room afterwards and complaining bitterly to the defenders, "If we scored eight, you could bet on you lot letting in nine." Nobody disputed it.

It was like being at Butlin's, a real holiday-camp atmosphere. Our lack of success did nothing to harm the dressing room spirit and even in defeat you would find us falling about laughing at things that went on at the club. We were still kids waiting to grow up.

One of the best laughs I had while at Chelsea was during a league match with Everton after they had scored against us. Actually, we scored it for them and I still rate it one of the all-time unforgettable goals. If there had been action replay machines around in those days, I am sure they would still be showing it as a comedy classic. A long shot from an Everton player slipped under the body of our chain-smoking England international goalkeeper Reg Matthews. Reg scrambled up and chased after the ball, hotly challenged by our big, bold captain Peter Sillett, who thought he had a better chance of clearing it. They pounded neck and neck towards our goal. Reg won the race and then, instead of diving on the ball, elected to kick it away. He pivoted beautifully and cracked the ball dead centre – straight into the pit of Peter Sillett's stomach. The ball rebounded into the back of the net and Peter collapsed holding his stomach. The rest of us players collapsed in laughter.

Big Peter and his brother Schnoz were two of the great characters of the team. And what drinkers! They could sink pints until the cows came home and show no ill effects at all. I never used to be able to keep pace with them during our after-match drinking sessions, but it was me who went on to have the big drink problem. I was later told that I had a chemical imbalance that made me less capable of holding my liquor, but in those early days I thoroughly enjoyed my boozing.

They were very happy times and Irene and I grew together, maturing from teenagers into worldly people. She was the one person I trusted to always give me the best advice and guidance. It was me who eventually cocked it up in my piss artist days. I made her life hell and she quite rightly kicked me out. Who wants a permanent drunk for company? But before the booze took over we had a smashing life, and those early days at Plough Lane remain in the memory as golden times.

I was a modest drinker back then and vaguely recall being drunk on my wedding day simply because I could not handle the shorts that were being poured down me. I was strictly a beer man and the whiskies and brandies that went down my throat before and after the ceremony went straight to my head.

In those days, footballers just couldn't afford to go on the piss. From what I have seen, the young players of today drink a lot more than [I did] during my teenage-to-early-20s period. We used to be pint sinkers but now the orders are more likely to be Bacardi and cokes or gin and tonics. I have seen them pay out in a single round what I used to earn in a week at Chelsea. Worse, I hear many of our young stars take recreational drugs, which were never on the scene "in my day".

Thinking back, I now realise it was not a lack of thirst but a scarcity of money that prevented me from indulging myself more in the procession of pubs that run off the King's Road. My wages when I married Irene at the age of 18 were £17 a week in the season and £8 during the summer.

It was while at Chelsea that I developed a drinking habit, but it was certainly never a problem. I had a recent reunion at Hereford with my old mate Peter Sillett and his brother John. We had some good laughs about the mad, good old days at Chelsea. John reminded me of a match we played against Preston when I scored a hat-trick to put us 3-0 in the lead. I was a bit of a Jack the lad then and arrogantly informed my team-mates, "I've done my bit, now you lot have a go. I'm finished for the day." By the time we were halfway into the second-half, Preston had pulled back to 3-3 and Peter Sillett said, "Come on, Jim, you'll have to make a comeback." I scored a fourth goal and then went into my shell again. Preston made it 4-4 and Peter pleaded, "Just one more, Jim. That's sure to finish them off." I duly scored a fifth to give us a 5-4 victory at Deepdale. My five goals knocked Preston off the top of the table.

To give you an indication of how the status of professional footballers has changed, I was one of the few players in the Chelsea side with a motor car. I bought my first car, a 1937 Opel convertible, for £30 from my brother-in-law Tom. In those days, as long as you had a provisional licence and L-plates up, you could drive unaccompanied. I had never driven in my life but somehow steered it right across London to home after collecting it for the first time.

After that, I progressed to a 1938 Standard "8" and that became like a team bus with all the players trying to crowd in it after training and matches while we headed for the nearest pub for a pint. [It was] years before the breathalyser, of course. I drank no more, no less than most other players then. To me, a pint was the reward for a job well done. ʼ

Despite the six-week rest that Ted Drake gave him, Jimmy finished his first season as Chelsea's top scorer with 22 goals, including a hat-trick against Sheffield Wednesday. It was only a matter of time before England came calling.

Chapter 5:

England and the Haynes partnership

GEOFFREY GREEN of *The Times*, Jimmy's favourite football writer, described it as 'a partnership made in heaven', the pairing for England of Greavsie and Fulham pass master Johnny Haynes. They were brought together for the first time in Jimmy's England Under-23 debut against Bulgaria at Stamford Bridge on 25 September 1957, just a month after his sensational start for Chelsea at White Hart Lane.

It always rankled with Tottenham that Haynes had slipped through their net. He was born and brought up in Edmonton and played his early football within sight and sound of the Spurs ground. They literally took their eye off the ball and allowed Johnny's schoolboy pal Tosh Chamberlain to persuade the gifted midfield schemer to follow him to Fulham's Craven Cottage.

Jimmy and Johnny hit it off straight away, and Bulgaria were dispatched 6-2. Greavsie, the talk of football, scored two goals and missed a penalty, robbing himself of a hat-trick. This was Jimmy talking about Johnny Haynes and the England of Walter Winterbottom, pre-Alf Ramsey:

'Johnny Haynes was far and away my favourite partner when I made my breakthrough into the England squad, under the scholarly eye of Walter Winterbottom. The national press used to knock lumps off Winterbottom – who we players behind his back sniggeringly called Cold Arse – yet to be fair he was a warm-hearted man and far more approachable than his successor, Alf Ramsey. The Fleet Street assassins came down on him with a ton of dung when he (quite rightly in my view) ignored me for the 1958 World Cup finals, took Bobby Charlton but did not play him. England came home after the quarter-finals with tails between legs and with bruised egos.

A former schoolteacher from Lancashire who had played a few games pre-war for Manchester United, Walter was the first man appointed England team manager in the immediate post-war year of 1946. He was shackled and stifled by a team selection system that put all the responsibility on his shoulders but most of the power in the hands of a bunch of amateurs who (and I'm being polite here) could not have organised a booze-up in a brewery.

It was Walter who awarded me my first England cap, and so I will always have a soft spot for him. He also has my sympathy for having had to do the job with his hands tied while answerable to football club chairmen blinded by vested interest and who had never kicked a ball in their lives. The farcical situation throughout most of his 16 years in charge was that he *managed* the team but did not *select* it. We were literally being run by the butchers, bakers and candlestick makers.

In the first half of his reign, Winterbottom was given access to arguably the greatest English footballers of all time. The names of the prominent players of that era echo like a roll-call of footballing gods: Stanley Matthews, Tom Finney, Tommy Lawton, Raich Carter, Len Shackleton,

Wilf Mannion, Nat Lofthouse, Stan Mortensen, Jackie Milburn, Frank Swift, Billy Wright and a poised and purposeful right-back called Alf Ramsey. They were all superheroes of the game when I was growing up dreaming of one day playing for England.

With players of that quality to call on, England should have cemented their traditionally held reputation as the masters of world football. It is an indictment of the overall system rather than Winterbottom's management that even with all this talent on tap, English football went into a decline. Our game was in the throttling grip of the barons of the Football League, the club chairmen who put club before country at every turn. Winterbottom was lucky if he got his players together a day before an international match, and often they would arrive just a few hours before the kick-off. It was nothing unusual for England team-mates to meet each other for the first time in the dressing room shortly before going out to play.

Despite the stature of his job, Winterbottom managed to keep a low public profile. The only time he used to make it into the headlines was after an England defeat, when the football writers would line up like a firing squad. It was a standing joke in Fleet Street that the sports desks of the national newspapers had "Winterbottom Must Go" headlines set up for every match.

I eventually made my England debut against Peru in Lima in 1959 during a disastrous South American tour. I managed to score our goal in a 4-1 defeat, and on the trip I got a taste of the appalling organisation that had bugged our footballers for years.

Our travel schedule would have worn out Captain Cook. It's no secret that I was the worst flier imaginable, and was out of the school that believed if God had meant us to fly he would have given us wings. It was quite likely something psychological to do with the Manchester United air crash of 1958, when eight Busby Babes were among those killed in a snow-hit nightmare in Munich after their plane failed to get off the ground. That tragedy cut deep with everybody in the game.

England's faithful trainer and physio Harold Shepherdson knew I was a nervous – even paranoid – flier and sat with me on the flight from Rio de Janeiro to Lima. He did his best to take my mind off the fact that we were in the air. Anybody who ever saw my attempts at heading a ball will know I am happiest with my feet firmly on the floor. As Shep was talking, I just happened to look out of the plane window and nearly died of shock. We were flying below the peaks of the Andes and were so low you could actually see the pack horses on the high passes bringing the copper ore out of the mountains.

Just then John Camkin, an awfully posh journalist with the *News Chronicle,* came walking casually down the aisle from the direction of the pilot's cabin. John had been a bomber crew navigator during the war and flying to him was just like taking a bus ride down the High Street. He stopped by Shep and said very casually, "I've just been talking to the captain of this old ship. He tells me he normally takes the short route over the top of the Andes but because of the BBC's heavy camera equipment he has decided to fly through the Southern Pass, which will make the trip a bit longer and just a little dicey."

It took several seconds for this travelogue to sink in and then I leaned across Shep and said, "Excuse me, Wing Commander Camkin. Can you please go to the flight deck and tell Captain Biggles that the VIP passengers on board have had a vote and they have decided that the best thing he can do is chuck the fucking cameras overboard and fly a little higher!"

Old Shep fell about laughing. But I was too scared to raise a smile. Camkin went on to help revolutionise the commercial side of football with his good mate Jimmy Hill at Coventry City. He made them a high-flying club.

England played Brazil, Peru, Mexico and the United States during a span of just 15 days. We were beaten 2-0 by world champions Brazil, 4-1 by a Peruvian side packed with highly skilled individualists, and then 2-1 by Mexico in the high altitude of Mexico City. We took all our frustration out on the United States and hammered them 8-1 (after being held to a 1-1 draw at half time), and the result was some sort of revenge for Winterbottom's humiliation against them in the 1950 World Cup when they somehow beat England 1-0. The result also provided sweet satisfaction for skipper Billy Wright, playing his 105th and final match for England. Just a few months earlier, I had managed to score five goals for Chelsea against Billy and the Wolves defence, and Billy later told me that was the day he decided he should hang up his boots.

Three of the players in our 18-man squad – Roy Gratrix, Graham Shaw and Ron Baynham – travelled halfway round the world without getting a kick at a ball, and Wilf McGuinness got on for only 45 minutes. It was my first close-up look at international football from the inside. I was not impressed. In Brazil, for instance, we trained under the full blast of a midday sun for a match that was kicking off at 4pm – mad dogs and English footballers! We were cajoled into working really hard in the training sessions, which I felt was pretty pointless because we were all knackered after a full league season. I have to confess that I was never the most enthusiastic of trainers, but even the fanatics in our squad had to admit we were being over-cooked.

The press were going for Walter's jugular but called off their witch hunt when England hit a winning streak during which we scored 32 goals and conceded eight in winning five matches in the 1960/61 season.

The highlight was a 9-3 victory against Scotland at Wembley. I managed to bang in three goals, but the real star of an extraordinary performance against a Scottish side including Dave Mackay, Billy McNeill, Denis Law and Ian St John was our skipper Johnny Haynes, who paralysed the Scots with his pin-point passes. He got two goals himself, with Bobby Smith, Bobby Robson and Bryan Douglas also getting in on the scoring act. Their goalkeeper Frank Haffey emigrated to New Zealand, where he became a nightclub comedian. Nothing was funnier than the ball continually whipping past him and if ever a Scot asked the time, you would say, "Nine past Haffey".

Johnny was magical that day and we carried him off shoulder high. I promise it is not sour grapes when I say that was an even better England team than the one that lifted the World Cup in 1966. If you could have grafted this Haynes-inspired attack on to a team containing the 1966 England defence, you would have had the greatest England international side of all time.

Unfortunately, this 1961 team came to the boil too early. We were past our peak by the time the 1962 World Cup came round, and we were eliminated by Brazil after struggling through to the quarter-finals. It was during that match against Brazil that I caught a stray dog that had invaded the pitch. As I carried him to the touchline, he urinated all the way down my England shirt. The great Brazilian winger Garrincha later adopted the dog and called it Yimmy Greaves. I think he was taking the pee.

Anyway, the 3-1 defeat by Brazil signalled the end for Walter. All of the Fleet Street critics came back out of the woodwork, and this time they showed no mercy. I was one of several players accused of wearing the England shirt like a white flag of surrender. Johnny Haynes was described as a selfish captain who thought only of himself. This was tame compared with the burning oil poured on Winterbottom. I remember what my dad had said after I was being lauded following my league debut performance for Chelsea at Tottenham, "The press can make you and they can break you."

Walter, a thoroughly decent man who could talk the ears off an elephant, gave an insight into the pressures he was facing when he revealed that his wife, Ann, was being greeted with stony silence in supermarkets and local shops and that his son, Alan, came home crying from school after being teased and taunted.

I believe that Winterbottom knew that his time was up even before the 1962 World Cup finals, and when Denis Follows was preferred to him for the FA secretary's job, which should have been his by right, he resigned.

He had received the sort of mean, miserly treatment that stopped him becoming a more successful manager on the world stage. He was expected to run our football in the days when the £20-a-week players were treated like slaves – and the most shackled one of them all was Walter himself. He was never given the freedom he needed (and deserved) to do the job properly. *

Jimmy was capped 25 times by Winterbottom, scoring 22 goals. Walter became a high-powered general secretary of the Central Council of Physical Recreation and then the first director of the Sports Council, and was knighted for his services to sport in 1978, 12 years after the man who (pun intended) had been waiting in the wings, Alf Ramsey.

The departure of Winterbottom also signalled the end of the reign of England's 'Mr Football', Johnny Haynes. In August 1962, the sports car in which he was returning late to his Blackpool hotel was blown by a gust of wind into the path of another vehicle. Haynes suffered broken bones in both feet and a badly injured knee. He told Jimmy that that the police officer who attended the accident reassured him by saying, 'Don't worry, son, you've only broken your legs.' He missed almost a season and when he returned to the Fulham side he was not quite the same player. Prior to the accident, he had captained England 22 times and – at 27 – was expected to lead them into the 1966 World Cup finals. He never played for England again.

John held his passing-out parade with Fulham, even briefly managing them after a tearful Bobby Robson had been sacked in 1968. But he hated managerial responsibility and disappeared off to Durban City, helping them win the Springbok championship. He returned from South Africa with his second wife, Avril, and stunned us all by choosing to live among the 'auld enemy' in Scotland. He had done very nicely out of his betting shops, and he helped Avril run a dry-cleaning business.

Not long before his tragic death following another car smash in 2005, I brought Johnny and Jimmy together to talk about old times:

JG: What the hell are you doing living among the Jocks, Haynsie? I thought you hated them.

JH: Not at all, James. I thought players like Dave Mackay, Denis Law, Jim Baxter and even your old sparring partner Ian St John were among the best footballers in the business. Scots are good people at heart, and have made Avril and me feel very at home in Edinburgh.

JG: Do you resent the sort of wages the top players are getting today? Blimey, some of them earn more in a week than you and I picked up throughout our careers.

JH: You're talking to the man who got lots of stick when it became public knowledge that I was on £100 a week. I'm delighted to see players getting paid well for what, let's face it, is a very short career at the top. I was more resentful, Jim, when we used to get a maximum 20 quid a week, and clubs were packing the crowds in. Where on earth did all that money go that they took at the gates?

JG: Straight into the bins of the chairmen and directors, I bet. Nowadays, you can hardly find a player in the Premier League who has English as his first language.

JH: Football is an international language that everybody understands. The overseas players are only doing what you did, Jim, when you buggered off to Milan. It's all about earning as much as you can while you can. It's a worry that not enough home-grown talent is coming through, but the standards are so high that I think we'll find a new generation of youngsters eventually forcing their way into the first-team squads because of the way they have been inspired by what they see.

JG: Is there any one British player you would fork out loadsamoney to buy if you were a club chairman with limitless funds?

JH: My personal favourite is Paul Scholes at Manchester United. He reads the game well, goes where he is needed on the pitch, never ducks responsibility, passes well, and has a little bit of devil about him. What a pity he's called it a day with England. They need his drive in midfield.

JG: What about David Beckham?

JH: A very good player with a dream of a right boot. But you know what I'm going to say, James. He's too one-footed and so therefore a bit predictable. It's easy for any team to work out what to do to nullify him when he's playing for England. Just stop the ball getting to him, and suddenly the team is half as effective. And he hasn't got a Jimmy Greaves to pass to.

JG: And there's nobody around of your class who can put the ball on a handkerchief from 40 yards with either foot. But that's enough of that, Haynsie. People will start talking about us. Of all the games we played together, which one stands out above all the others?

JH: It has to be the 9-3 against Scotland. But if we're honest, Jim, we were lucky that day to find them with a very dodgy goalkeeper.

JG: Poor old Frank Haffey. The Scots took the piss out of him so much over that game that he emigrated to New Zealand. They used to say, 'What's the time? Nine past Haffey.'

JH: Tell you what, Jim, I remember us having a bloody good night after that win. There was you, Bobby Smith and me, and I have hazy memories of a nightclub. Sorry, perhaps I shouldn't talk about a boozing night.

JG: Leave off, John. I never regret memories of those celebration nights after matches, or even when we were beaten and drowned our sorrows. Smithy and I got legless after that Scottish win. Blimey, it's not every day you put nine past the Jocks!

JH: Missing out on the '66 World Cup Final must have been a real killer blow for you.

JG: It hurt like hell, if you want to know. But I'd have done the same thing in Alf's shoes. The rest of the boys were magnificent against Argentina and Portugal, and there's that old saying, 'Never change a winning team.' It must have been bad for you, too. I thought you'd be a cert to lead us.

JH: No, that car crash did for me, Jim. I damaged my cruciate ligament, and I was never quite the same after that. Alf Ramsey was always asking George Cohen how I was doing, and being the honest bloke he is, George told him that I was not quite ready to play for England again. And that was the truth. Obviously, I would have given anything to lead England out in the final, but Bobby Moore made quite a good job of it! What a player! One of the few truly world-class defenders we've ever produced.

JG: If you had to pick one England international from our era who would have made it as a big star in today's game, which one would you select?

JH: Not just because you're facing me, James, but it would be you. Goodness knows how many goals you would score now that they can't tackle from behind.

JG: Behave yourself, John. I mean a player not here in this room!

JH: It's a tough one. Just one player. It's got to be Tom Finney. I partnered him on the left wing in my early days with England. He was something special, and was comfortable in any position in the forward line. Stanley Matthews was a magician, but not my personal taste. For me, it would have to be Finney. Can you imagine what he would be worth in today's transfer market? He would cost as much as the crown jewels. After Tom, I would choose Bobby Charlton. I suppose he played the role in the '66 World Cup finals that would've been mine if I'd been able to extend my England run. He was a beautifully balanced player, and his shots from outside the box were spectacular. Oh yes, and we mustn't forget Duncan Edwards. He would have been a great player in any era. I cried my eyes out when he died following the Munich air disaster. He was going to become a world star, no doubt about it.

JG: Finally, Johnny old friend, a very personal question. Did you look after all that dough you made as a £100-a-week player?

JH: You know me, James. I never exactly threw my money around. The best thing I did was invest my earnings in the betting shops. We sold our chain to the Tote in 1976 and made a tidy profit. The only luxury I allowed myself when Fulham suddenly turned me into a relatively well-off footballer was a brand new Jaguar sports car. Cost just over three grand, and that was the car I smashed up in 1962, wrecking my career. Like you say, Jim, it's a funny old game.

Just a few months later, Johnny died in hospital in Edinburgh following a car crash the day after his 71st birthday. Jimmy had lost a great friend. Football had lost a great servant.

Chapter 6

Tragedy and then the Italian Job

ANY PSYCHIATRIST trying to get to the bottom of why Jimmy turned to the bottle could not dismiss the tragedy that struck him and Irene in the autumn of 1960. Their son Jimmy Junior, who was four months old, died following a bout of pneumonia, devastating them both at a time when they were in turmoil over whether to move to Italy and a promised life of luxury.

Lifelong friend and near neighbour Dave Emerick recalled:

‘ It was the night England hammered Spain 4-2 at Wembley. Jim scored and had a cracking game, and the next morning I called round to congratulate him. When he opened the door to me, he was sobbing. "What's wrong, mate?" I asked, having expected him to be all smiles. "It's baby Jim," he replied. "We've lost him. Died in his cot." He and Irene should have been on top of the world, but instead they were heartbroken. Jim had always wanted a son, [but] now he was gone. I had no words for him and just hugged Jim and Irene and left them alone with their grief. What could anybody say? ’

This all happened at the same time Jim was wrestling with a secret offer made to him by Italian scout Gigi Peronace, who told him

AC Milan wanted to sign him with a promise to treble the £20 a week he was earning with Chelsea, plus a huge signing-on fee of £10,000. This was when the average price of a semi-detached house was around £2,500.

It was the hardest thing for Jim to talk about when we were working on our first book, *This One's On Me*. Eighteen years after the loss, he was still struggling to discuss it. Eventually, I got him talking:

‘ We continue to think of baby Jim as if he's still with us. His loss was a nightmare experience that nearly drove Irene and me out of our minds. We were just out of our teens and having to deal with a tragedy that nobody could handle. I had been brought up a Roman Catholic, but I said lots of unrepeatable things in the direction of God.

In the middle of all this, I get an approach on the old hush-hush from AC Milan, via first of all a freelance journalist and then an international scout called Gigi Peronace, who could have walked right off the set of *The Godfather*. I slept on it, talked it over with Irene and then told Gigi he would have to make a formal approach to Chelsea chairman Joe Mears, a smashing bloke who was also chairman of the Football Association. He would have wanted everything to have been done above board.

I had reached a point with Chelsea when they knew I was unsettled. I was banging in goals right, left and centre and we were leaking them in even quicker. There was, I thought, a lack of ambition at the club and a move to Italy sounded just the change of scenery and surroundings we needed. Just to make everything even more interesting, Irene told me she was pregnant again, this time with Mitzi, who would soon join our lovely eldest daughter Lynn. Life was kicking me in the balls and then lifting me to the skies. No wonder I was turning to drink.

Joe Mears telephoned me to tell me what I already knew, that AC Milan were interested in buying me, and he swore me to secrecy. My impression was that he did not want to sell me but if I was determined to go, then at least in Italy I could not cause any embarrassment by banging in goals for a rival club.

Chelsea and Milan had top-secret talks and the next thing I knew I had to report to an Italian hospital in the heart of London for a medical check-up. This, of course, was all on the quiet. If any of my friends had seen me in hospital, they would have thought I was undergoing an autopsy. The things they did to me! They inspected my blood, my urine, my sight, my reactions and every bone in my body, including bones in places where I didn't know I had places!

They took about 50 X-rays during my two days in the hospital and at the end of it all the Milan representatives shook their heads and looked doubtful and mournful, as if there was no hope for the patient. Apparently, a couple of small bones in the small of my back had broken when I was a kid and had interlocked while mending. The Italians reckoned this made me a very dodgy investment. Their fear was that my back would give me trouble later in my career. As it happened, they should have been more concerned about my elbow.

This hospital revelation frightened the life out of me. I had visions of being in a wheelchair before I was 30. Then a Harley Street specialist studied the X-ray plates and delivered the considered verdict that hundreds of people were walking around with the same bone abnormality. He said Milan need have no fears. I was passed 100 per cent fit and everything was set for me to sign. Giuseppe Viani, Milan's manager, came to London to clinch the deal. I was offered what was then an eye-watering £10,000 as a signing-on fee. This would be paid over my three-year contract at £3,000 a year, with a £1,000 down payment in my hand the moment I signed the contract. It may not seem a vast amount in these inflationary times, but you must remember that with the maximum wage set-up it would have taken me ten years to earn that much in English football.

Chelsea's consolation for selling me was £80,000. Not a bad profit on a player who had cost them just a £10 signing-on fee. And an under-the-counter 50 quid in Irish fivers. It was then a record for an English club, although Turin were soon to top that figure when buying Denis Law from Manchester City for £100,000.

Senor Viani talked numbers like a bingo caller. He told me I could earn at least £5,000 a year with Milan on top of the signing-on bonus payments. Their basic wage was only about £20 a week, but they had huge bonus incentives. The only thing he conveniently forgot to mention was their fining system, which cost me hundreds of pounds once I got to Italy. Anyway, I signed the contract that was to bind me to Milan, although for the remaining few months of the season I was to continue to play for Chelsea until the Italian embargo on foreign players was lifted. I got my £1,000. Chelsea got a £10,000 down-payment. For Milan, it was like putting a deposit on an item of furniture. I had the Chippendale legs.

The signing of the contract heralded one of the worst years of my life. And little did I know it then, but it also put me on the long and winding road to alcoholism.

There was a smell of revolution in the air in English football at about the time I was making my decision to go to Milan. League footballers, led by the then players' union chairman Jimmy Hill, were pressing for a new pay deal. The Football League had tossed out a demand for an increase in the £20 maximum wage and the players were in the mood for strike action.

I was a passionate advocate of the players' union case for a new deal and even after signing for Milan attended meetings in London, where there were strike threats that would have stopped the League ball rolling. But my old mate Jimmy "The Beard" Hill, showing the eloquence that was to make him a nationwide television personality, put the players' case so well that the League bosses capitulated and conceded that in future there would be only a minimum wage. The soccer slaves had at last escaped their shackles.

I felt delighted for everyone in the game but was – as the football cliché goes – as sick as a parrot for myself. The fact that Denis Law, Joe Baker, Gerry Hitchens and I had taken the lira bait helped the players clinch the new deal. The league bosses were frightened of a mass exodus and so gave in. Johnny Haynes, then the England captain, was on the Italian wanted list, but Fulham chairman Tommy Trinder boldly announced, "Johnny Haynes is a top entertainer and will be paid as one. I will pay him £100 a week to play for Fulham."

In my opinion, this was the funniest line Tommy Trinder ever delivered and my good pal Johnny Haynes was laughing all the way to the bank.

Let's face it, I had got involved with Milan for purely mercenary reasons. Money was the only motive. I wanted to play football in Italy like I wanted a hole in the head. I had allowed myself to be seduced by the promise of sudden wealth but in passing judgement on me, remember that I was a mere 20-year-old when Milan first hooked me.

My immaturity showed in the way I reacted to receiving the £1,000 signing-on fee from Milan. I immediately went out and blew it on a year-old Jaguar. What a flash git I must have appeared to onlookers. I felt very grand!

I tried everything possible to wriggle out of the Milan deal, particularly when Joe Mears told me Chelsea would be willing to pay me £100 a week to stay at Stamford Bridge. Jimmy Hill, my then adviser Bagenal Harvey, Joe Mears, England manager Walter Winterbottom and that great administrator Sir Stanley Rous all put their heads together in an effort to find a way around my problem. In the company of R. I. Lewis, a top solicitor, I even went to Italy to plead with Milan for a cancellation of my contract, but they made no secret of the fact that they would get me banned from ever kicking a ball again if I backed out of our agreement.

They finally hooked me with the bait they use so well. Money. They offered me a new contract. This time, I was to receive a £15,000 signing-on fee immediately I put my name to paper. I would still have preferred to have remained in England but they had me over a legal barrel. So I signed my second contract at Alassio in June. They paid me £4,000 and said I would get the other £11,000 when I returned from London in July.

I still wasn't keen on the idea of pulling up my roots and moving to Italy but I knew I just had to resign myself to it. To add to my misery, I ended my career with Chelsea in dispute. My final match was at Stamford Bridge against Nottingham Forest. I scored four goals and the Chelsea fans carried me around the pitch as if I were the FA Cup. There was hardly a dry eye in the house. Then the club decided they wanted me "one more time" in a meaningless, end-of-season friendly fixture in Israel. I refused to make the trip and Chelsea slapped a 14-day ban on me that deprived me of an England cap in an international match against Mexico at Wembley.

Even now, I burn with anger when I think back to that ridiculous suspension by Chelsea. I served them well for four years, scored 132 goals in 169 league matches and then they cashed in on my talent by making a profit of £79,990 on my transfer to Milan. Yet just because I did not want to go on an unimportant tour with them, they childishly forced me to finish my career at Chelsea under suspension.

Yes, enough to drive a man to drink.

Those were the days when I started visiting pubs as a regular habit, a hobby even, rather than as an afterthought. When I was standing at a bar with a pint of beer in my hand, it was as if the problems of the Milan affair would shrink to manageable proportions.

Two particular drinking sprees stand out in my memory from that period. The first was when I was on my way out to Milan to make my debut for them in a prestige friendly against Botafogo in June 1961. They wanted to show me off to their supporters but agreed that I could then return to London to await the birth of our third child (our marvellous Mitzi), who was due to arrive the following month. It would help mend our broken hearts after the loss of Baby Jim.

I was accompanied on the flight to Milan by *Daily Express* sports columnist Desmond Hackett and photographer Norman Quicke, a close pal who lived around the corner from us in Upminster. When they made Des

Hackett, the man with the brown bowler, they threw away the mould. He was an astonishing character who brought colour and life to every story he wrote even if – as he often used to say with his tongue in his cheek – "I never let facts spoil a good story!" Des loved the good life and when we got to Heathrow Airport with two hours to spare before our flight, he decided he (or the *Daily Express*) was going to treat me to a lobster and champagne lunch.

We were just finishing off our second bottle of champers and considering starting on a third when Speedy Quicke thought of looking at his watch. "Our plane," he informed us, "left ten minutes ago." It was very unprofessional, but I was never in a hurry to climb aboard a plane.

We caught the next flight out and arrived six hours later than scheduled, and at the wrong airport. Thirty miles away on the other side of town at Linate Airport, a welcoming committee from AC Milan waited for me with growing impatience and concern. It was just as well they didn't see me stepping off the plane after we had touched down at Malpensa. I have already admitted to being the world's worst flier bar none. To give myself Dutch courage, I had piled into the champagne cocktails during the flight and was flying pretty high without need of a plane by the time we got to Italy.

I played the next day and scored a goal in a 2-2 draw with the very capable Botafogo team. The fans seemed happy with my performance and the Milan officials said they looked forward to my return in July after our new baby had arrived. You could say that was the birth of my problems with the club. Mitzi was scheduled to arrive on 15 July and I made provisional plans to join Milan on 17 July. Mitzi, showing a woman's prerogative, was late and I cabled

Milan to tell them I would be staying with Irene until the baby was born. They showed a great sense of understanding by threatening to fine me £50 for every day I failed to make an appearance. From that moment on, there was no way Jimmy Greaves and AC Milan were going to get along. I cabled a reply that regardless of any action that they might take I was not going to join them until the baby had been born. This time they accepted the situation, but there was already a bad taste in my mouth.

Mitzi finally deigned to make her appearance on 6 August. Just by coincidence, I bumped into my old Chelsea buddy John Sillett at the maternity hospital a few hours after Mitzi was born and we decided to go to the local Old Bell at Upminster for a drink or two to wet the baby's head. Seven hours later and in the early hours of the morning, we were happy but legless in the cellar of the Old Bell. The baby's head was being drowned. We were hiding down in the cellar from John's mother-in-law, who was on the warpath because he was supposed to have returned home hours earlier.

With a good drink inside me, the problems of Milan seemed a million miles away. But four days later, I at last reported to my new club. It was the start of a four-month nightmare. I know it sounds dramatic but I literally became a prisoner in Milan. The Italian football set-up, as I discovered to my misery, is totally different to ours. They treated their footballers like mindless morons, not giving them an inch of trust and hitting them in the pocket with hefty fines at the slightest hint of disobedience. I was depressed by the whole scene. Perhaps if I had been older I might have been able to cope with the situation. I had applied an adolescent mind to adult problems and kept coming up with the wrong conclusions.

We Greaves watchers fed hungrily on every line coming from Italy. Each day for more than three months, there were stories being relayed back from Milan on Jimmy's rollercoaster life and times in the land of the lira, and a posse of reporters were regulars on visits to the San Siro stadium. It got to the point where I became a member of what was known as the Jimmy Greaves Club. Each of the reporters who visited Jimmy in Milan purchased a special commemorative tie that had a map of Italy overprinted with his initials and a football. The ties were manufactured by the north London factory owned by Jimmy Burton and his business partner Dave Mackay, who would soon be Jimmy's team-mate.

More appropriately, the tie should have shown a wine bottle with the cork exploding. The people with whom Jimmy did most of his drinking were the same journalists who were filing stories back to England about his 'spoilt brat' antics.

Jimmy agreed with much of what was being reported and was only too happy to feed us stories about his bust-ups with the club. He knew Milan would finally get so sick of it all that they would be glad to see the back of him.

Among the members of the exclusive club were top football scribes Clive Toye, Des Hackett and Speedy Quicke (*Daily Express*), Bill Holden and Ken Jones (*Daily Mirror*), Peter Lorenzo (*Daily Herald*), Maurice Smith (*The People*), Laurie Pignon and Tony Stratton-Smith (*Daily Sketch*), Ian Wooldridge (*News Chronicle*), Peter Moss, Roy Peskett and Brian James (*Daily Mail*), Donald Saunders (*Daily Telegraph*) and Brian Glanville (*Sunday Times*). Sad to say, as I write only two of that old club are still standing.

Back to Jim:

‘ Between my signing for Milan and then joining them, they had taken on a new coach, Nereo Rocco. He was a big, burly disciplinarian who had about as much humour as a ruptured bull. Poor old Nereo. I made his life hell. And he didn't exactly bring the sunshine of happiness into mine.

Thinking back on it, I feel sorry for Rocco. His job was to get the best out of me for his employers, AC Milan. But I was not interested and went out of my way to make his life difficult. If he had been a different sort of bloke, he might have found a way to melt the ice between us, but it seemed the only answer he had for me was to be as tough and cruel an enforcer as possible.

As soon as I arrived in Milan, I had to join Rocco and the rest of the players for pre-season training in a hideaway camp at Gallarate, which is about 40 miles outside Milan. Training camp? It was more like a prison camp. The idea behind having us locked – and I do mean locked – together was to build a team spirit. All I reckoned it did was make the players sick of the sight of each other before a ball was kicked. We were never allowed out of each other's company. It was like one long, boring game of follow-my-leader, with the bullying Rocco out in front barking orders at everybody like a sergeant major. His English was just a little better than my almost non-existent Italian and we used sign language to each other that just about stopped short of Harvey Smith gestures [V-sign].

We used to have a mass walk-about together after breakfast, followed by a training session in the morning, lunch and then a training session in the afternoon. The rest of the time we spent relaxing together. Always together. We were never allowed outside the hotel unless Rocco was with us and to add to the frustration, everything was rationed. Rocco used to order my food and then sit opposite me making sure I ate it. He allowed us only two cigarettes a day, one after lunch and one after dinner. I was a fairly light smoker when I joined Milan, but this attempt at dictating when and how many cigarettes I should have simply made me seek out every chance to snatch a crafty smoke.

As for drinking beer, that was considered one of the mortal sins. Wine was served with our meals, but anybody looking for more than one glassful was risking the wrath of the eagle-eyed Rocco. None of the players liked the strict discipline, but most of them were so accustomed to it that they just accepted it as their fate. Mind you, they all took every opportunity for secret cigarettes in the loo or an ice-cold lager at the hotel bar if they were convinced Rocco was not about.

Gianni Rivera, the then Golden Boy of Italian football, watched my consistent rebellion against the system with astonishment bordering on disbelief and once asked me in fractured English, "Yimmy, why-a you do these things? Why you-a fight Rocco all the time? It is surely easier to give in and do-a as he wants. The money, it is-a good, no?"

I don't think his English was quite good enough to grasp my explanation that I valued my freedom as an individual above everything else. No amount of money could compensate for the loss of it. All my life, I have been a non-conformist and throughout my four months in Milan I battled to retain my liberty and individual identity. I had hardly been out there five minutes when I realised there was no way it was going to work.

What with not being able to understand what was being said around me, I quickly got brassed off and homesick. I was on the point of packing my bags and returning home when my solicitor arrived at the training camp to check on my progress. I gave him a real ear bashing and told him exactly how I felt and that I was ready to catch the first available flight out of Milan. "Three years of this," I said, "and they will be locking me away in a mental home."

My solicitor, a wonderful English gentleman who unfortunately died a few years later in a plane crash, did a good job for me throughout the Milan episode, but looking back on it I regret ever having taken legal advice. I think that if right from the off I had just flatly refused to join Milan, they would have climbed down. But once I started moving in legal circles, my hands were tied. I just had to do everything by the rulebook and my solicitor again explained that my contract was watertight and that I could not just walk out on Milan. He arranged the next best thing by talking Milan into letting me go home for a couple of days to see my family and friends. Back to good old British beer.

Once home, I didn't want to go back, but Irene knocked that stupid idea out of my head with a good common sense talk. She always has had her head screwed on much tighter than me and she kept me from making silly decisions that I might have regretted later. I returned to Italy for the start of the season and my pal Jimmy Hill, fresh from his triumph in the fight for a new deal for league footballers, came with me for a few days to help iron out the differences I had with Milan.

But the inevitable split had only been delayed. In my short spell with them – it seemed like a lifetime – I was top scorer with nine goals in 14 games, but I hated every second of the football. The game out there was being strangled to death by stifling defensive systems and we never played with more than two forwards in attack. I was never one for looking for trouble on the pitch, but it was so spiteful and vicious that even I was moved to try to kick things other than the ball. The first time I lost my temper was with a player from Genoa who spat in my face after tripping me up. I responded by kicking him in the shins, for which the referee awarded Genoa a free kick. They scored from it and Rocco went berserk over my retaliation. He punished me the only way he seemed to know how – with a fine.

My brother-in-law Tom and his wife, Nancy, brought Irene out to join me and things looked a little brighter until I discovered I was still a prisoner. We had a sightseeing day out at Venice soon after they arrived and for that I was fined £500 for breaking city limits.

Tom knew better than anybody the hell I was going through. On an earlier visit, he and I had sat on the balcony of the team hotel late one night knocking back lagers and enjoying a nice relaxed time. One of Rocco's spies reported back to the Godfather and the next day two workmen came to my room and nailed planks of wood across the door leading to the balcony. I blew my top and ripped them down.

Rocco became obsessed with getting me to knuckle under and become just another sheep in his flock of highly paid but unhappy footballers. He used to deliberately sit at the bottom of the stairs in our hotel to make sure I did not sneak out. Tom and I risked death one night to escape him. We climbed out of a window three storeys up and edged along a narrow ledge looking for an escape route, while Rocco was stationed downstairs watching the main exit.

Tom and I were giggling like little boys at the way we had dodged Rocco when we came up against a brick wall. The ledge had led to a dead end. We finally sneaked out by causing a distraction downstairs, Tom pretending to order enough drinks to keep us occupied in the hotel for the whole night. While Rocco was busy cancelling this enormous order, Tom and I tip-toed out the rear exit. It cost me a fine of about £300, but it was well worth it to get the better of Godfather Rocco.

At this distance, I can accept the criticisms that were being made of me at the time. The English newspapers tagged me as the spoilt young brat of football. A lot of what they said about me was true, although they gave the false impression that I was a wealthy young man. Much of my £4,000 signing-on fee had been eaten up by legal fees and air fares, and Milan, understandably, never did get around to paying me the outstanding £11,000. I was getting fined so often that my wages were sometimes lower even than when I was playing for Chelsea. I was perhaps a young brat, but nobody was spoiling me.

The Italian Press murdered me. They could not have done a better assassination job had they been given a contract by the Mafia. Typical of the filth that was being written by their gutter press was a story that accused me of holding a wild orgy in the flat into which Milan had moved me. This all came about because a reporter had looked into our living-room through binoculars and had seen Irene and Nancy walking about in shorts.

A few days later, Rocco and I had a right up-and-downer, insulting each other through an interpreter after he had carpeted me for going to the airport to meet Irene on the eve of a match. Italian clubs ban their players from going near wives, girlfriends or anything in a skirt on the day before and after a match. They lock their players away in hotels in a bid to keep sex and soccer apart. But I was an "old" married man of three years and saw no harm in meeting my wife after she had flown into a strange country. But I suppose Rocco was worried by the "sex maniac" image the newspapers had given me. He must have had visions of Irene and me running naked along the runway at Milan airport.

Tommy Steele, that likeable Bermondsey-born entertainer and football fanatic, dropped in to see me during a trip to Italy. He had heard and read about all my problems and wanted to see for himself the sort of treatment I was receiving. I took Tommy along to an after-match meal and he just could not believe the childish way we were treated. He was appalled by the do-this-do-that discipline that reduced grown men to the role of robots. We were told what we could and couldn't eat, what drink we should have and when we should go to bed – to sleep, naturally. "I can get you out of this, Jim," said Tommy, his eyes alight with enthusiasm. "I'll hire a private plane, smuggle you aboard as one of my musicians and have you home in next to no time."

Now Tommy is one of the world's great leg-pullers but he was deadly serious and started to work out exactly how he could spirit me out of Italy. He was all ready to put his escape plan into operation when I heard on the grapevine that my deliberate policy of non-cooperation had at last pushed Milan to breaking point.

They were buying a Brazilian as a replacement for me and turfed me out of my flat and put Irene and me into a pokey little backstreet hotel. There was no way I was going to stand for that and so, at my own expense, I booked us into a five star hotel where the brigade of British press boys who had shared many of my experiences were staying.

I was less of a prisoner now and got down to some really serious drinking in the company of the British journalists, who were a great set of blokes and helped make my miserable stay in Milan a little more tolerable.

It seems like a lifetime ago when I look back over 18 years to my days in Milan. At this distance, a lot of it seemed like good fun, but most of the time I was in a badly depressed state. I made myself ill with worry, lost weight and was in a run-down condition.

I was drinking a fair amount but stuck mostly to beer and was young enough to run off hangovers in training. Drinking was certainly not a problem then, but it had become an accepted part of my life.

The first I knew for certain that Milan were ready to let me go was when Chelsea chairman Joe Mears and his wife Betty called to see me during a holiday trip to Italy. They thoughtfully brought us a two-pound bag of tea, although as far as I was concerned a couple of packs of bitter would have been more welcome.

Joe told me that Milan were preparing to offer me for sale and that if I agreed to return to Chelsea, they would pay me a guaranteed wage of £120 a week. I told him that naturally I was interested but did not want to build my hopes up because Milan were being so bloody-minded about everything. I had just had a furious row with them because they refused to let me have my passport after a club trip to Yugoslavia. I went to the British Consulate to complain and Milan were ordered to hand it back to me. When I called into the office to collect the passport, it was thrown across the room at me. Things had got that bad.

Even on the pitch, I was being treated like a leper. I suppose the players blamed me for Rocco's bad moods and refused to pass the ball to me unless it was absolutely necessary. I remember scoring a goal against their bitter rivals Inter Milan and not a single player came to congratulate me, even though I had waltzed past three defenders before sticking the ball into the back of the net. I trundled back to the centre circle and turned in the general direction of poor old Rocco and gave him a double reverse V-sign.

Not long after, Milan at last officially announced that they were ready to receive offers for me and Bill Nicholson, the Spurs manager, got word through to me that he was very interested. This was the best bit of news I'd had for months because Tottenham were the club I rated above all others. They had just become the first club this century to win the league and FA Cup Double and the prospect of playing for them was immediately appealing.

Chelsea and Spurs were the two front runners for me and Milan tried to get them locked in an auction. But they were outsmarted by Bill Nicholson and Chelsea secretary John Battersby. They knew what Milan were up to and came to a secret agreement to put in identical bids. Both of them offered £90,000 and then the three of us put our heads together at a private meeting. After a long talk with Bill Nick and John Battersby, I told them that Tottenham were the club I preferred to join.

Battersby agreed to drop out of the bidding so that Spurs could have a clear field. Nick would have done the same for him if I had chosen to return to Chelsea. My old club had been prepared to make me the highest-paid player in Britain at £120 a week, but I settled for the £65-a-week plus bonuses offer from Tottenham.

There were two main reasons. One – I felt that returning to Chelsea would have been a backward step, perhaps to the problems I had wanted to escape just a few months earlier. Two – I really fancied playing for that Tottenham team. The thought of it excited me. I reckoned I would be playing with the greatest club team in the history of British football. Nothing has happened since to make me either regret my decision or change my rating of that team.

Anyway, Bill Nick continued the negotiations on his own. He did not want me saddled with the label of the Football League's first £100,000 player and so did a deal at the odd price of £99,999.

Nick took three days hammering out the details of the deal. Two days later, I was on my way home.

After getting into my drinking stride in Milan, I can look back at the move to Tottenham as the period in my life when knocking back booze became more than just a habit.

It started to become a necessity, like water to a plant. And I loved every drop of it.

Bell and Hare, here I come.'

Chapter 7:

The Glory Glory Years

JIMMY ARRIVED back in England in late October 1961 as autumn was giving way to winter. As he drove his white Jaguar saloon away from Milan in a pea-souper of a fog, he felt like a suddenly released prisoner. 'I didn't get time off for good behaviour,' he joked. 'It was more a reprieve on the grounds of mercy. I was honestly going mad in Milan. It was a disaster from start to finish and I was more to blame than anybody. Put it down to youth and inexperience. Another time, another coach other than the anti-British Rocco and I would probably have made a go of it, but even before I set foot in Italy I knew I had made a blunder. Now as I drove home, I had just one target in mind, to be successful with the club I should have gone with in the first place, Tottenham Hotspur.'

On his return to England, cash-strapped Jimmy and his growing family – Danny was on his way to join Lynn and Mitzi – temporarily moved in with Irene's parents. Whoever thought he had come back from Milan a millionaire was about a million pounds out in their assumption.

Before he could make his debut for Spurs, he had to face a Football League inquiry into possible irregularities in his transfer. Welcome home, Jim! After being totally exonerated of any wrongdoing, he was free to resume his career. He celebrated by getting drunk.

What nobody realised is that the traps for Jimmy becoming an alcoholic had been laid. The loss of baby Jim, the nightmare in Milan and now joining the Bell and Hare drinking school. There was no escape.

When he first drove into White Hart Lane in the autumn of 1961, he was shown where to park by 16-year-old apprentice Philip Beal:

' It was like royalty arriving, and I accidentally found myself as the welcoming committee of one. I pointed out where there was a space for his gleaming white Jaguar and almost bowed as I welcomed him to the club. I honestly felt honoured to be the first to greet him. A few years later, somebody reported that I was always the first name that Bill Nicholson wrote down when selecting his team. Quick as a flash, Jim said, "That's because he writes it in alphabetical order." Talk about puncturing your ego. Like everybody else, I loved Jim not only for his fantastic ability but because he was such a likeable bloke. No airs and graces. He was on another planet to most of us as a footballer but was always unassuming and one of the lads. '

Were the Tottenham fans happy at the signing of Jimmy? He played his first match in the lilywhite shirt at Plymouth Argyle's Home Park in a reserve game in front of a 13,000 crowd, many making the midweek journey down to Devon from north London. It was a record attendance for what was then known as a Combination match. Over to Jim:

' I considered myself the luckiest footballer on earth the day Bill Nick arrived in Milan to sign me for Tottenham.

Not only was he rescuing me from what I reckoned was the prison of Italian football, but he was also giving me the chance to join what I believed was the finest club side in Europe. It was in the previous season that Spurs had pulled off that historic Double. I had played against them with Chelsea, and I can vouch for the fact that they were, to use a Cockney understatement, "a bit tasty".

They purred along like a Rolls-Royce, with Danny Blanchflower, John White and Dave Mackay at the wheel. When they wanted to touch the accelerator, there was Cliff Jones to break the speed limit down either wing; and if they needed a full show of horsepower, Bobby Smith was put in the driving seat. These were the nucleus of five world-class players around which Bill Nick had built his team. He had got the perfect blend and I remember thinking when I played against them, "Blimey, there's not a weakness in this team. They can win the lot."

"The lot" in those days meant the league championship and FA Cup, two trophies that were harder to win then because – and of this I am convinced – the game was a lot tougher and more demanding. In comparison, today's football has become a virtual non-contact sport. And remember, we were all on a 20-quid-a-week maximum wage at the time, which is why I nipped off to Italy.

Just to give you an idea of the overall standard of the First Division in 1960/61, I was playing in a Chelsea side that included such international-class players as Peter Bonetti, Frank Blunstone, Peter Brabrook, the Sillett brothers, Bobby Evans, Bobby Tambling and young Terry Venables. I managed to bang in 41 goals that season. We finished in 12th place in the table.

Wolves, dripping with international players, scored 103 First Division goals and could do no better than third. Defending champions Burnley, blessed with the talents of Jimmy McIlroy, Jimmy Adamson, Alex Elder, Jimmy Robson, Ray Pointer, John Connelly, Brian Miller and Gordon Harris, netted 102 First Division goals, and were back in fourth place. We were all puffing and panting trying to keep up with Spurs.

Runners-up Sheffield Wednesday had England internationals Tony Kay, Peter Swan, Ron Springett and John Fantham at their peak. Blackpool missed relegation by a point, despite being able to call on such skilled players as Tony Waiters, Jimmy Armfield, Ray Parry, Ray Charnley and the legendary Stanley Matthews. I couldn't believe it when Kay and Swan, who I found smashing lads, got themselves caught up in a match-fixing scandal and finished up in jail. You never know where this life is going to take you.

Each team back then also had at least two hatchet men, with instructions to stop the clever players playing. The likes of "Bites Yer Legs" Norman Hunter, Tommy Smith and "Chopper" Harris were coming through the ranks and about to make themselves felt. Just talking about them brings me out in bruises. In today's game, they would have been red-carded every time they stepped on a pitch if they tried to tackle as they did in the 1960s and '70s, when football was not for the faint-hearted.

There was class running right the way through the First Division – and not a foreign player in sight. This was the quality of the opposition that the "Super Spurs" side had to overcome to pull off the league and cup Double that had eluded every great team throughout the 20th century.

They did it with a style and flair that made them one of the most attractive teams of all time. There were defensive deficiencies, but you never heard a murmur of complaint from the spectators, who were always given tremendous value for money.

For me to join the team in late 1961 was like being given a passport to paradise. I considered it like coming home. I was a casual Spurs fan when I was a kid, and it was odds-ón my joining them from school until that lovely rascal of a Chelsea scout called Jimmy Thompson sweet-talked my dad into encouraging me to go to Stamford Bridge.

I wondered how the Tottenham fans would react to me moving to their manor at White Hart Lane, and realised they were quite keen on the idea when I played my first game in a Spurs shirt in a reserve match at Plymouth. There was a record crowd for a reserve game of 13,000 and I know many of them were Spurs supporters, because over the years I have met loads that say they were there!

My other concern was how the Spurs players would take to me. They had been reading the day-to-day accounts of my exploits in Italy, where I had been waging a verbal war in a bid to get back into British football. Those who knew me only by reputation must have been thinking I was a real troublemaker, and – having just won the "impossible" Double without me – understandably looked on me as an intruder who could possibly rock their happy and successful boat.

Thank goodness it didn't take me long to kick their doubts into touch. I got lucky and kicked off with a hat-trick against Blackpool on my first-team debut, and I settled into the side – both on and off the pitch – as if I had been at Tottenham all my life.

I am never comfortable talking about goals that I scored, but I have to admit that one of the goals in my first match was a little bit special. Dave Mackay took one of his long throw-ins, Terry Medwin flicked the ball on and I scored with what the newspapers described as "a spectacular scissors kick". From that moment on, I was accepted by the Tottenham fans and players as "one of them".

All these years later, I can say that the Tottenham team of that period was the best side I ever played with, and that takes into account England matches. I get goosebumps just thinking about some of the football we used to play; it was out of this world, and I consider myself as fortunate as a lottery winner to have had the chance to be part of the dream machine. '

Tottenham made a monumental bid for the major prize – the European Cup – in Jimmy's first season, during which the 'Glory Glory hallelujah' choruses raised the White Hart Lane roof. There are conflicting opinions as to when the 'Battle Hymn of the Republic' was adopted as the club's theme song. Some insist it was being sung by Spurs supporters at Molineux in April 1960 as Tottenham powered to a 3-1 victory that stopped Wolves being first to the league and cup Double.

Older supporters vaguely remember it being sung back in the early 1950s after a cartoon had appeared in the Tottenham match programme showing Arthur Rowe daydreaming of the Double. The caption read, 'While the Spurs go marching on'.

There was an explosion of noise every time Spurs played European Cup ties at White Hart Lane in 1961/62 as they saw off Gornik, Feyenoord and Dukla Prague. There was also good humour to go with the fanatical support. A small group of Spurs supporters always dressed as angels, carrying witty placards and waving them – without malice – at opposition fans. There was never a hint of hooliganism. That scar on the face of soccer was a decade away.

Tottenham were desperately unlucky to lose a two-legged European Cup semi-final against eventual champions Benfica, propelled by the rising master Eusebio. To his dying day, Jimmy insisted that a 'goal' he scored, which would have put Spurs into the final, was wrongly flagged offside by the linesman.

They quickly picked themselves up after their exit from Europe and the following month retained the FA Cup, with Jimmy scoring that exquisite goal in the third minute to put them on the way to a 3-1 victory over Burnley.

The Tottenham team was: Brown; Baker, Henry; Blanchflower, Norman, Mackay; Medwin, White, Smith, Greaves, Jones. No substitutes then, of course. Jim:

'The FA Cup win over Burnley took us into the European Cup Winners' Cup, and I had some fun and games on the way into the final. We played OFK of Belgrade in a bad-tempered semi-final and I managed to get myself sent off for the only time in my league club career. In the first leg in Yugoslavia, I instinctively retaliated early in the second half after their centre-half had kicked me in the shin when we were miles away from the ball.

The referee only saw my part in the scuffle and pointed me towards the dressing room. I did not go immediately and there was a lot of pushing and shoving before Cliff Jones, not playing because of injury, came on from the touchline and escorted me back to the dressing room past flying bottles and coins. "Don't worry, Jim boyo," he said as he put a protective arm around me. "I won't let the bastards hurt you." The Welsh dragon was on fire inside Jonesie and he was prepared to fight the world to keep me safe.

Our trainer Cecil Poynton quietly came up to me at the end of the game and said, "Hope you're proud of yourself. You're the first Spurs player [to be] sent off for nearly 40 years. You should be ashamed of yourself." "Who was the last player?" I asked. "Me," he said in his thick West Midlands accent. "And now at last I can pass the shame on to you." **'**

Jimmy automatically missed the second leg at White Hart Lane, but Tottenham went through 5-2 on aggregate. No British team had won a major trophy in Europe when Spurs travelled to Rotterdam for the final against holders Atletico Madrid, and hopes that they could break the duck were suddenly diminished when their main motivator, Dave Mackay, failed a fitness test on the day of the match.

The absence of Mackay was a devastating blow because he had been a major force in Tottenham's magnificent success over the previous two seasons. As it sank in that they would have to perform without his battering-ram backing, a blanket of gloom descended on the Spurs camp.

Mackay's absence plunged manager Bill Nicholson into a morose mood, and he added to the air of pessimism when he ran through the strengths of the opposition during a tactical team talk. Jim:

' I had never known Bill so downbeat and pessimistic. He made Atletico sound like the greatest team ever to run on to a football pitch, and he bruised rather than boosted our confidence.

Our skipper Danny [Blanchflower] was so concerned about the sudden gloom and doom environment that he stood up and made one of the most inspiring speeches of his career. Using a mixture of fact and blarney, word-master Blanchflower pumped confidence back into us and made us believe in our ability to win. He countered every point that Bill had made about the Madrid players by underlining Tottenham's strengths, and he convinced us that we were superior to the Spaniards in every department. It was a speech of Churchillian class and content and we went into the final with renewed determination to take the trophy back to White Hart Lane.

What Danny, who was also assistant manager, kept from all of us was that he himself was only half-fit and had a pain-killing injection in his dodgy right knee that enabled him to play. Typically, all he had was positive thoughts. What a captain. '

This was how Tottenham lined up for the game of their lives, with Tony Marchi stepping into Dave Mackay's place: Brown, Baker, Henry, Blanchflower, Norman, Marchi, Jones, White, Smith, Greaves, Dyson

Bill Nicholson, one of the finest tacticians in the game, deserved credit for the fact that Greavsie was in position to give Spurs the lead in the 16th minute. He had spotted, during a spying mission to Madrid, that the Atletico defence was slow to cover down the left side, and he instructed that full use should be made of the blistering speed of Cliff Jones. Moving with pace and penetration, Cliff sprinted to meet a neatly placed pass from Bobby Smith and Greavsie drifted into the middle to steer his accurate centre into the net with his deadly left foot.

The goal was a real pick-pocket job, and Tottenham's fans roared their 'Glory Glory' anthem as the Spaniards suddenly wilted.

Jimmy, a seven-year-old football urchin in a photo taken by his Dad with a Kodak Box Brownie camera in their back garden in Dagenham in 1947 before the family moved 'down the road' to Hainault. Have a close look and you will find it's with two of his mates.

The start of the adventure. Jimmy at Chelsea, aged 17 the week after his goal-scoring debut at Spurs. This photo was taken by the late Daily Express cameraman Norman 'Speedy' Quicke, who for several years was Jim's neighbour and baby sitter. He presented Jim and Irene with free copies of all his photos.

Jimmy on his way to the first of his record 357 First Division goals when making his debut for Chelsea at Tottenham on Saturday, 24 August 1957. 'One of the greatest goals I've ever seen,' said Spurs skipper Danny Blanchflower. 'And I had a better view of it than anybody!'

Scanned from Jimmy's scrapbook, he is 17 and with the man who poached him for Chelsea using the pseudonym 'Mr Pope'. His true identity was Chelsea scout Jimmy Thompson, who snapped him up under the noses of Spurs and West Ham.

It is 1958 and 18-year-olds Jimmy and Irene become Mr and Mrs Greaves the first time around. They spent the first year of their married life in a one-bedroom flat at Wimbledon's Plough Lane.

A second goal for Chelsea against Spurs, this time at Stamford Bridge in 1961, the year that Tottenham completed their historic Double of League title and FA Cup. He scored this one with his right boot. Defenders could never work out whether he was right- or left-footed. 'I tended to favour my left,' revealed Jimmy, 'but my Dad taught me from a nipper to be two footed.'

Jimmy on his way to a hat-trick in the 9-3 slaughter of Scotland at Wembley on 15 April 1961. Frank Haffey was in goal for the Scots and for months when anybody asked the time, the answer would invariably be, 'Nine past Haffey.'

Skipper Johnny Haynes, one of Jimmy's favourite England playing partners, is shouldered off in triumph by team-mates Peter Swan and Jimmy Armfield after the 9-3 defeat of Scotland. Within three years, Swan was on his way to prison for match fixing. Johnny is hugging the Home Championship trophy. Jimmy, on the left, is looking pleased with himself after his three goals. He was still a Chelsea player at this point.

To mark his last match for Chelsea on 29 April 1961, Jimmy was made captain. He's here with Nottingham Forest skipper Bob McKinlay before the kick-off at Stamford Bridge. He then signed off with four goals in a 4-3 victory.

Carried off by Chelsea supporters sad to see him go but delighted with his four goals.

Jimmy officially signed for AC Milan in June 1961, and it was the start of a four-month nightmare. From the moment of his arrival he wanted to be playing at home in England.

One of the nine goals Jimmy scored for AC Milan in his 14 appearances. Spurs manager Bill Nicholson soon rescued him in return for a transfer fee of £99,999.

Jimmy, master of all he surveys at Tottenham. He scored a club record 266 goals for Spurs, although some statisticians claim it was 268.

Scanned from Jimmy's scrapbook, the goal that made him an instant hit with the Spurs fans in his 1961 debut against Blackpool. It's the famous scissors-kick wonder strike that was the best of his three-goal banquet.

This is a ball! The two most prolific goalscorers in League football are brought together by England in 1959 but Greavsie and Cloughie could not get a goal between them.

The third minute FA Cup Final goal that Jimmy had promised before the 1962 FA Cup Final against Burnley. His shot was as precise and accurate as an Arnold Palmer putt.

A goal in elite company as Jimmy scores the winner for England against the Rest of the World in a 1963 showpiece match at Wembley to mark the centenary of the Football Association. But for superb saves by legendary Russian goalkeeper Lev Yashin, he would have had a hat-trick.

Marked by Henry Newton, Jimmy powers the ball into the Nottingham Forest net in 1965, one of a record 24 goals he scored against the Midlands club.

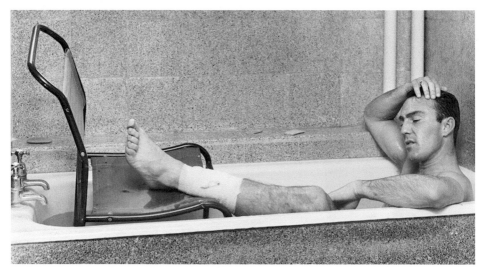

Jimmy nurses his gashed left shin in the bath at the Hendon headquarters of the England 1966 World Cup squad. He already senses his World Cup is over.

As the final whistle blew to signal England's 1966 World Cup victory, spectator Jimmy said he felt like the loneliest man at Wembley.

It was on the wings that Tottenham were monopolising the match, with Jones and tiny Terry Dyson running the Spanish full-backs into dizzy disorder. Atletico, strangely enough, also had a winger called Jones, but he was not in the same class as Tottenham's Welsh wizard.

Dyson and Jones combined to set up goal number two in the 32nd minute, exchanging passes before releasing the ball to Smith, who laid it back for John White to rifle a low shot into the net.

It was a rare but crucial goal from White, who had made his reputation as a maker rather than taker of goals. His signature was stamped on most of Tottenham's attacks as he prised open the Atletico defence with beautifully weighted passes. Blanchflower, White and the tall, stately Marchi were working like trojans in midfield to make up for the absence of the one and only Mackay.

At most clubs, Marchi would have been an automatic choice for the first team, and he played with such skill and determination that his contribution was in the Mackay class. There can be no higher praise.

Atletico Madrid revived their flickering flame of hope in the first minute of the second half, when Enrique Collar scored from the penalty spot after Ron Henry had fisted the ball off the goal-line. Jim:

> ‘ This was when we had to keep our nerve. We did not have Dave Mackay to lift us with his brandished fist and warrior-like competitive drive that would have frightened the lives out of the Spaniards. Danny's knee was giving him hell and we somehow survived a 20-minute storm from the Atletico attack.
>
> It was "Dynamo" Dyson, having the game of a lifetime, who ended the Atletico comeback when his hanging cross was fumbled into the net by goalkeeper [Edgardo]

Madinabeytia, who had one eye on the menacing presence of burly Bobby Smith.

Terry the Titch became a giant of a man and laid on a second goal for me before putting the seal on a memorable performance with a scorching shot at the end of a weaving 30-yard run. His first goal was something of a fluke, but the second was a masterpiece.

As we paraded the Cup in front of our ecstatic fans, Bobby Smith shouted at fellow Yorkshireman Dyson in his typically blunt way, "If I were you, mate, I'd hang up my boots. There's no way you can top that. You were out of this fucking world."

I made a point of going to Dave Mackay and telling him that we would not have got to the final without him. As I hugged one of the greatest footballers of all time, he could not hold back the tears. He was experiencing exactly what I was to go through on the day England won the World Cup in 1966: pleased for your team-mates but choked for yourself.

We were into the history books as the first-ever British winners of a major European trophy, but Dave had missed the party and worse was to come.

The following season dawned with no hint that it was to see the break-up of the "Super Spurs". The heart was ripped out of the our team in a tragic and painful way, and a black cloud of despondency enveloped the club. The nightmare was slow and drawn out.

It started on the evening of 10 December 1963 at Old Trafford when we were playing Manchester United in the second leg of a European Cup Winners' Cup tie. Dave broke a leg in a collision with Noel Cantwell that surely left the United skipper losing sleep about the validity of his challenge. For ever after, Dave called Noel "Cuntwell" and never forgave him for the tackle that would have finished most careers.

Just a few weeks later, Danny Blanchflower was forced to retire because of that recurring knee injury. Tottenham had lost the brains of the team and the heart of the team, and we were devastated by a tragedy at the end of the season. John White, the eyes of the team, was sitting under a tree sheltering from a storm on a north London golf course when he was killed by lightning. We had lost the three most vital cogs in our machine.

John's tragic death came only a matter of months after the passing of his father-in-law Harry Evans from cancer. He was assistant manager to Bill Nicholson, who with trainer Cecil Poynton had to go to the mortuary to identify John's body. "The worst moment of my life" was how Bill described it to me. White was a master footballer and the Nicholson plan was to build his new Tottenham team around the immense talent of the 27-year-old Scot.

Bill Nick got busy in the transfer market and bought Alan Mullery from Fulham, Laurie Brown from Arsenal, Cyril Knowles from Middlesbrough, Pat Jennings from Watford, Jimmy Robertson from St Mirren and Alan Gilzean from Dundee to take over from the old warhorse Bobby Smith.

He took a breather, and then went shopping again, this time buying centre-half Mike England from Blackburn to replace injured Maurice Norman, and Terry Venables was brought in from Chelsea. He also tried and failed to buy Bobby Moore!

Bill Nick was attempting to build another "Super Spurs". He never quite made it. The new Tottenham team had some memorable moments together in the mid-60s, but to be honest I know we never touched the peak performances of the Blanchflower/White/Mackay era.'

Secretly, Bill Nicholson had also tried to bring Edmonton-born England skipper Johnny Haynes to White Hart Lane to team up with his old England side-kick Jimmy Greaves. But the bold attempt fell through when Fulham chairman Tommy Trinder, the Cockney comedian, said, 'If I sold 'Aynsie, the Fulham fans would hang me from the crossbar by my bollocks.'

The Blanchflower-White roles eventually went to Alan Mullery and Terry Venables; good as they were, they struggled to be accepted by the hard-to-please Spurs fans used to the Blanchflower-White chemistry.

Jimmy had become accustomed to the pace set by Danny and John, and he struggled to adapt to their successors' style of delivery. Both were given a tough time by the Spurs supporters, who had been spoiled over recent years. They unkindly but understandably compared the newcomers with their great idols.

Venables was not always happy playing at White Hart Lane after his success as the midfield boss at Chelsea, and when he eventually moved on to Queen's Park Rangers, who would have taken any bets that one day he would return and buy the club!

One of the new-look Tottenham squad who did win the hearts of the fans was Alan Gilzean, who formed a wonderful partnership with Greavsie. Jimmy found Gilly a joy to play with, and he felt that Alan was never given sufficient credit for his delicate touch play and finishing finesse in the penalty area. He was a master of the flick header, and could bamboozle defences with deceptive changes of pace and clever ball control.

Missing the command of Blanchflower, and the drive of Mackay, the 1963/64 season was relatively barren for Spurs after three years of non-stop success. But they still managed to finish fourth in the league in a season that would be remembered for the start of Liverpool's 'Red Revolution' under the mesmeric management of Bill Shankly, a close friend yet fierce rival of Bill Nick.

Ownership of the Spurs had moved from the Bearmans to the Wales late in 1960, with first Fred Wale and then Sidney as chairman. They considered Tottenham a family club, and allowed Bill Nick to get on with the job of managing without interference. Under the Wale influence, the Tottenham directors ran a tight, well-organised ship. But they were also tight with their wage policy and Bill Nick was never, ever paid what he was worth. Jim:

> ‘ Bill was not the sort of person you could ask, "How much d'you earn?" He was a typically proud, tight-lipped Yorkshireman. But I know for sure he never earned more than £200 a week while making millions for the club. That's why I was quick to volunteer when I heard they were giving him a long overdue testimonial match.
>
> He was the reason I had preferred to join Spurs rather than return to Chelsea when both clubs were willing to rescue me from the misery of Milan. I could have earned a lot more money back at the Bridge, but liked and trusted Bill Nick and loved the team he had built.
>
> We were like a big, happy family. Bill was a sort of a miserable but much-loved Big Daddy. ’

Chapter 8:

Drinking for England

RUNNING PARALLEL with his club career, Jimmy was stitching together one of the finest England records as a goalscorer. He became the top marksman and in ratio of goals per match was far and away the most prolific sharpshooter of his generation. I sat at the great man's feet for hours listening to him recounting tales of playing and drinking for England, and feel I should keep out of the way of his storytelling. Jimmy was one of the most captivating of raconteurs (I reckon it was the Irish blood in him) and here he is in full flow on his international experiences:

'Dear old Alf Ramsey – Sir Alfred the Great – saw through me in five minutes flat. He was a shrewd judge of people who quickly had me weighed up as a carefree, non-conformist character whose thinking on football was completely the opposite of his cautious, methodical, well-organised approach to the game.

He knew me for what I was from the moment of our very first conversation outside the boundaries of football. It took place just before one of Alf's early games in charge of the England team against Czechoslovakia in Bratislava. Alf was giving us the after-match agenda in that false posh voice of his, as Cockney as me but doing his best to hide it. "The coach will be ready to leave 45 minutes after the game and we shall go back to the hotel together," he said with that unblinking stare of his that gave listeners the feeling they were being hypnotised. There was an uneasy shuffling of feet and I could sense that my drinking pals in the England squad were waiting for me to act as their spokesman.

"A few of us were wondering, Alf," I said, "whether we could nip out for a couple of drinks before going back to the hotel?"

Now I'm going to quote Alf's reply verbatim because, as I was to discover over the years, he only swore when he wanted to make himself perfectly understood. "If you want a fucking beer, you come back to the hotel and have it."

He had made himself perfectly understood!

It wasn't said in a nasty way and there was a hint of a twinkle in those cold brown eyes of his as they fastened on to me from beneath rich, thick eyebrows. Alf was just letting us know that he was in charge. From that moment on, Alf had me marked down in his photographic memory as a ringleader of the drinking squad.

I scored two goals in a 4-2 win over Czechoslovakia to give Alf a great start to his first tour as England manager. As I remember, he bought one of the early rounds when we got back to the hotel together. Downstairs in the hotel, we found a nightclub and the entire squad had a good celebration drink. Flying to East Germany the next day, several of the hung-over officials as well as some players were distinctly unwell during a bumpy flight that helped confirm my belief that man is not made to fly.

Contrary to what a lot of people think, Alf and I got on quite well with each other even though we were opposites in our attitudes about football. He could shift a drink or two when he wanted and I have had several long sessions with him after matches when he has let himself go and really given the gin and tonics a good hiding. When he dropped his mask, he was a different person altogether to the sombre, unsmiling man the public knew. He had a nice sense of humour and a lot of warmth and charm. There were times when I stretched his charm to breaking point.

We had a good drinking school in that England squad. My long-time pal Bobby Moore was the man I always roomed with. I would have to put him pretty high in the table of international drinkers, but it didn't stop him being just about the greatest defender English football has ever produced. There has never been anybody in the world to touch Mooro for consistency and constant high-performance output. And there are not many footballers who could match him in a drinking contest. Mooro had hollow legs and after top-pressure matches could go through pints of lager without showing any effect from the booze whatsoever. He was in no way a drunkard but enjoyed winding down with a glass in his hand after the match action was over.

Our liking for a good bevvy got Bobby and me into several scrapes together long before the infamous Blackpool affair at West Ham. It reached the point where it was rumoured that Alf was ready to relieve Mooro of the England captaincy before the 1966 World Cup triumph.

The first time we upset Alf was on the eve of England's departure for a match against Portugal in Lisbon in May 1964. Bobby and I called for volunteers for an evening stroll into London's West End from the Lancaster Gate Hotel where we were staying. With "elbow men" like Mooro, "Budgie" Byrne and thirsty me leading the outing, it was odds on the stroll would become something of a stagger before the night was through. In tow along with Budgie we had Gordon Banks, Bobby Charlton, George Eastham and Ray Wilson. We stopped off at a favourite drinking oasis called The Beachcomber and it was fairly late – close to midnight – when we got back to the hotel. Each of us realised our absence-without-leave had been noticed when we found our passports lying on our beds.

This was Alf's stunning but subtle way of letting us know he was not pleased. He left it until the eve of the match four days later before mentioning our little escapade. After our final training session, he said, "You can all go and get changed now apart from the seven players who I believe would like to stay and see me."

Sheepishly, we stood gathered around Alf while the rest of the squad went back to the dressing room with quizzical looks over their shoulders. Alf was short, sharp and to the point. "You are all lucky to be here. If there had been enough players in the squad, I would have left you behind in London. All I hope is that you have learned your lesson and will not do anything silly again."

Alf named all seven of us in the England team and we repaid him by beating Portugal 4-3 in an epic match. Two of the AWOL men – Budgie Byrne and Bobby Charlton – scored the goals, Budgie helping himself to the sweetest of hat-tricks. Alf allowed himself quite a few G&Ts that night.

Less than two weeks later, Mooro and I were in Alf's bad books again. This time it wasn't booze but music that got us into trouble. We were both Ella Fitzgerald fans and slipped out of our New York hotel on the eve of the match against the United States to catch the "First Lady" in concert. Neither Bobby nor I were playing against the States (who were hammered 10-0) and we saw no harm in taking a night off. Alf didn't say very much, but there was a coldness in his manner at breakfast the next morning that left us in no doubt that he was displeased. He was quietly fuming that we had broken that all-do-things-together bond

Our next stop was Rio de Janeiro for a match against Brazil and, boy, did we have a hectic time there. We stayed nine days for an international tournament and we worked and played hard both on and off the pitch.

Budgie Byrne, the incredible character who I think I would have to put top of the international drinkers league table, was the life and soul of the party. He was full of funny tricks, such as pushing me fully clothed in my new England suit into the deep end of the hotel swimming pool. Budgie then had to dive in to pull me out. It was a frightening experience that convinced me I should learn to swim. Ironically, the next day Budgie, a strong swimmer, nearly drowned off the Copacabana beach when he got trapped in rough water. Somehow, he managed to get ashore but not before going through a nightmare that almost sobered him up!

The football tournament got our full concentration and effort. We were holding Brazil to a 1-1 draw with just 20 minutes to go when Pelé hit one of his purple patches and lifted them to a flattering 5-1 victory. This really choked us. Alf knew how we felt and, with four days before the next match, let us off the leash for the night.

At dawn the next morning, a team of seven dishevelled-looking England footballers were beaten about 6-0 in an impromptu match by a side of a dozen Copacabana beach boys whose skills were out of this world. The result, thank goodness, never got into the record books.

We flew up to Sao Paulo from Rio to watch the second match of the mini-World Cup between Brazil and Argentina and I can honestly say I have never witnessed scenes like it. Because there were no seats left in the stand, the entire England party – including players, journalists and officials – were assigned to touchline benches that were just two yards from the pitch and eight or so yards from the fenced-in capacity crowd. It was far too close for comfort.

As soon as we sat down, the spectators spotted us and set up a deafening chant of "Cinco-Uma!" – Portuguese for five-one – and a derisive reminder of our defeat in Rio. Budgie Byrne couldn't resist the bait and stood up on the bench and started conducting the fans like the man in the white suit before a Wembley cup final. The Brazilians loved it and started chanting in time to Budgie's waving arms.

Budgie's choir switched their attention to cheering the Brazilian team when they came out on to the pitch and lit up the night sky by firing dozens of three-stage firework rockets high above the stadium. Then we had fireworks of a different kind on the pitch.

Right from the first whistle, Argentinian defender [Jose] Mesiano made it clear that his one intention was to stop Pelé from playing. He kicked him, tripped him, spat at him, wrestled him to the floor and pulled his shirt any time he seemed likely to get past him. Finally, after about 30 minutes of this almost criminal assault, Pelé completely lost his temper. He took a running jump at Mesiano and butted him full in the face.

The Argentinian was carried off with a broken nose and, incredibly, the Swiss referee let Pelé play on! He clearly feared for his life if he sent off the idol of Brazil so I couldn't really blame him, although Pelé should have been sent for an early bath.

The calculated, cynical fouling by the Argentinians had knocked all the rhythm and style out of the Brazilians and the stadium became as quiet as a morgue when two minutes from the end the player substituting for the injured Mesiano scored his second goal of the match to make it 3-0 to Argentina.

Budgie Byrne unwisely chose this moment to do an insane thing. He stood on the bench again to face the fans and, holding up three fingers, invited them to join him in a chant of "Three-Zero". It was the worst joke of Budgie's life. Suddenly bricks and fireworks rained down from the terraces as the fans turned their disappointment on us. They would have much preferred to have reached the hated Argentinians but we were nearer targets.

The usually impassive Alf Ramsey took one look at the avalanche of bricks, fireworks and rubbish coming our way and gave the shortest tactical talk of his life. "Run for it, lads," he said. Luckily, the final whistle had just blown and we made a mad dash for the centre circle. We later awarded Brian James, of the *Daily Mail*, an imaginary gold medal for being first to the halfway line despite starting at least five yards behind all us players. Frank McGhee of the *Daily Mirror* was voted an award for bravery for sitting it out at the touchline desk where he was writing his report, but was later big enough to admit that the only reason he stayed in the firing line was because he had his foot trapped in the struts of the desk.

Frank glared through his glasses in the direction of Budgie and said, "I felt like a bleedin' scorpion. I'd made up my mind that before I killed myself, I would have throttled that mad bastard Byrne. He could have got us all killed."

It was Budgie's quick wits that finally got us off the pitch in one piece. As the fans began to scream blue murder despite the intimidating presence of dozens of armed police, Budgie shouted the wise instruction, "Grab yourself a Brazilian player."

He then seized goalkeeper Gilmar lovingly by the arm and walked with him off the pitch, knowing full well that no fans would try to harm one of their idols. We all followed Budgie's lead and went off arm in arm with bewildered Brazilian players.

You may think that we were over-reacting, but uppermost in the minds of everybody in that stadium was the fact that just ten days earlier 301 people had been killed in a riot at the national stadium in Peru, where Argentina had been the opponents.

I think the way Argentina had played against Brazil that night – brutally and coldly vicious – stayed imprinted on Alf Ramsey's mind and was one of the reasons he made his controversial, headline-hitting "animals" outburst against them during the 1966 World Cup.

Seven months before the 1966 tournament in England I went down with hepatitis, an illness that affects the liver but was not brought on by anything to do with my boozing. It drained me dry of energy and strength. I was out of the game for 15 weeks and by the time I returned in the February, Alf was well ahead with his team-building programme.

I have never worked harder in my life to recapture fitness, even cutting right back on my drinking. This was a time in my life when I could control myself. I was desperately keen to play in the finals because I was convinced England were going to win. Everything was right for us. We had a great pool of players, vital home advantage and the right mood running through the game at league level. No disrespect to Alf, but I reckoned England would win no matter who was in charge.

That damned hepatitis attack robbed me of a vital half-yard of pace, but I still believed I was good enough and sharp enough to represent England better than any other striker around. That may sound conceited, but any goalscorer who lacks confidence and belief in his own ability is in trouble. I believed in myself and I know that Alf thought I was the right man for the job.

Both Mooro and I clinched our places in the World Cup team during the tour leading up to the finals. Alf toyed with the idea of putting Norman Hunter in the No. 6 shirt, but Bobby produced a succession of regally impressive performances that convinced Ramsey that he should retain the West Ham skipper. That decision more than any other won the World Cup for England because Bobby emerged as the player of the tournament, never putting a foot wrong.

I was beginning to motor with some of my old enthusiasm and snap, and a goal against Yugoslavia and four against Norway persuaded Alf that I should be in the attack for the opening World Cup match against Uruguay.

We were on a hiding to nothing against Uruguay because everybody expected us to win and anything less than victory meant a lot of stick for England. Uruguay were interested only in stopping us from scoring and packed their penalty area with nine defenders. It was an undistinguished start, but even after the goalless draw I still knew in my heart that England were going to win the World Cup. What I didn't know is that they were going to do it without me.

Alf made two changes for the second match against Mexico, replacing Alan Ball and John Connolly with Terry Paine and Martin Peters. Ballie, another of my drinking partners, was sick with Alf and talked about going home. But over a lager we helped him see the sense of staying on and he played a prominent part in England's victory against West Germany in the final.

We began to find our momentum against Mexico. I did not score but felt satisfied with my contribution towards England's 2-0 win. I missed a couple of chances against France in the third match, but we beat them comfortably 2-0. After the game, I had four stitches inserted in a gash on my shin. It was an injury that provided the excuse for my exit from the quarter-final against Argentina and Geoff Hurst took my place for his World Cup debut. He gladly grabbed the opportunity and headed a fine goal from a perfect Martin Peters pass to give England a 1-0 victory.

Argentina were less violent but just as niggling as they had been against Brazil in Sao Paulo, and their captain Rattin, a gifted but temperamental player, was sent off for trying to referee the match. I agreed with Alf's uncharacteristic outburst afterwards when he described the Argentinians as "animals". I was delighted to see that by the time they came to stage the 1978 World Cup, they had tamed their tempers and flourished through their great talents.

The semi-final against Portugal was the classic the match with Argentina could have been. I was still nursing the injury, which was practically healed, and watched from the touchline as Bobby Charlton majestically conducted England's well-deserved 2-1 victory.

At the end of the semi-final, I felt in my bones that Alf was not going to select me for the final. My dream of helping England win the World Cup was about to be smashed. I was fit for selection and the press boys began churning out "Greaves must play" or "Greaves must not play" stories – according to how they saw it. But only one bloke knew for sure whether I was going to make it. Alf Ramsey. And he wasn't saying a dicky bird.

The Saturday of the final came and still I did not know for sure whether I was in or out. But I sensed that Alf was being a little distant and guessed he had made up his mind to pick an unchanged team. I knew for certain at midday and I had guessed right.

In fact, I had been so sure that on the morning of the match, my room-mate Bobby Moore had woken up to find me packing my bags. "What are you doing, Jim?" he queried, sitting up in bed at the start of what was to be the greatest day in his life. "Just getting ready for a quick getaway once the match is over," I told him. "You can do that tomorrow morning," he said. "We'll all be on the bevvy tonight. Celebrating our World Cup win."

Alf didn't say much to me. Just said he had decided on an unchanged team and thought I would understand. "Sure, Alf," I told him. "They'll win it for you."

"I think so," he said, and then was gone to talk to other players who had been left out.

People have often asked me since what Alf had to say to me when he told me I was out of the side. What could he say? He knew I was choked but he was doing what he believed to be right. There were ten other blokes in the squad as unlucky as me, so there was no reason why Alf had to sort me out for a special word of sympathy. Not that

I was seeking anybody's sympathy. I felt sorry for myself and sick that I was out, but Alf did his job and England won the World Cup.

It says a lot for the wonderful team spirit that Alf had built up that all 11 of the players who had been left out swallowed their self-pity and gave their total support to the 11 players who were representing us against West Germany. We were out there on the pitch with them in spirit and I felt as exhausted as if I'd played after the game had gone into extra time. Geoff Hurst went on to complete his now historic hat-trick to clinch a 4-2 victory and, of course, the World Cup. It could not have happened for a nicer bloke.

I danced around the pitch with everybody else but even in this great moment of triumph, I felt a sickness in my stomach that I had not taken part in the match of a lifetime. Great as it was for the country, it was my saddest day in football.

As the celebrations got into full swing, I quietly slipped off home with my brother-in-law Tom. I was told later by Mooro that Alf thought I had deliberately snubbed him after the game, but that is far from the truth. I was delighted for Alf and didn't want to spoil his moment of glory by letting him see the hurt in my eyes.

Late that night, I went off on a family holiday. The 1966 World Cup was suddenly history.

I played just three more times for England. Then, after about a year out of the international picture, I suddenly started pumping in goals for Spurs in something like my old style. There was quite a campaign in the press for my reinstatement and Alf – by then, Sir Alf – was moved to say, "I am being crucified because I am not selecting Greaves, yet he has told me that he does not want to play for England."

I was astonished by that statement because deep down I still wanted to play for my country and, despite what some people may have thought, was always passionately proud to wear the white shirt of England. Early in my career, I was the victim of a damaging misquote. It was claimed that I had said that I "had no fire in my belly" when playing for England. I never uttered those words but they appeared in print and many people took them as gospel and thought I played with less than total commitment when on international duty. I promise you I always gave my best for England and can point to 44 goals in 57 matches as evidence.

Alf completely misunderstood me if he really did believe that I had asked him not to select me to play for England any more. What I had said to Alf during my last training session with his squad at Roehampton was that I would rather not be called up unless I was going to play.

At the time, Alf had got into the habit of including me in his training squad and then not naming me to play in the match. He told me it was useful to have a player of my experience on the sidelines. All it did was frustrate me and as quite an active businessman in those days I knew there were plenty of things I could be doing rather than continually wasting hours at training get-togethers which, for me, had no end product.

So that was the end of my England career, nine years that I had mostly enjoyed. Believe me, I was always proud to play for my country and I enjoyed the goals – and the pints. '

Excuse me while I interrupt with some of my own 1966 World Cup memories. I was lucky to spend the entire tournament with the England squad, on quotes duty for the *Daily Express*. I watched with interest the brittle relationship between not only Jimmy and Alf but his skipper Bobby Moore. You needed to know their history to understand why there was little love lost between them.

Mooro was the ringleader of many pranks, and he and Jimmy went several bridges too far with their mickey taking of Ramsey and his Dick van Dyke voice. Alf was a sensitive, proud man and he knew what they were up to. The England manager was once overheard saying to trainer Harold Shepherdson, 'Those two will take the piss once too often.'

Once when the England team coach was overtaking a hay-carrying horse and cart driven by two gypsies, Bobby said, 'They're going to make Alf's bed up.' Alf, sensitive and secretive about his Romany background, was sitting at the front of the coach and turned purple with suppressed rage.

It was an open secret that during the European tour in the weeks before the World Cup, Alf toyed with replacing Bobby with Norman Hunter. He left him out for two successive matches, but when Bobby was recalled he set his game up to top gear and it was clear to everybody that he was a class above not only Norman Hunter but every central defender in the world.

Alf knew better than anybody that Bobby was key to England winning the World Cup. They buried their mutual suspicion of each other and concentrated on the one objective of capturing football's biggest prize. But there was never, ever any real warmth between them.

Mooro and Greavsie, drinking pals and hoping to play together with Spurs after the World Cup, laughed at Alf's expense again on the day following the boring opening goalless draw against Uruguay at Wembley on Monday, 11 July. I joined the players on a guided tour of the Pinewood Studios, which had been arranged as a diversion from the pressures of the tournament.

Sean Connery, who was shooting his latest James Bond film *You Only Live Twice*, showed us around, along with Yul Brynner and Norman Wisdom, who were both also making films at the sprawling studios. At the end of the tour, Ramsey stepped forward to make a short 'thank you' speech. 'I would like to thank,' he said in that distinctive, clipped posh-Cockney accent of his, 'everybody at Pinewood Studios and in particular Mr Seen Connery.' I was standing with the mickey-taking masters Mooro and Greavsie. Bobby had us all falling about as he said in a stage whisper, 'That's the funniest thing I've ever shawn or heard.'

Alf sensed he was being laughed at and shot a killer look in our direction. Another strike against Mooro and Greavsie.

I knew that Jimmy was definitely fit for the final. He had played in a secret match behind closed doors against an Arsenal team at their London Colney training headquarters the day after the semi-final victory against Portugal. All the England reserves had played as Alf kept them match fit, just in case of injuries to his first-choice players. The players in the team that had beaten Portugal stood on the touchline cheering on their squad colleagues, much of it in joking tone, but Alf was in no mood for comedy. He kept a close watch on Greavsie's performance.

Jimmy was marked by Arsenal skipper Frank McLintock, who told me, 'There's no doubt that Jimmy is fit. He was his usual sharp self and popped in one of his typical solo goals. I was sure Ramsey would pick him for the World Cup Final. I wouldn't have had the nerve to keep a world-class striker on the sidelines, not a player with Jimmy's unique finishing ability.'

Later that day I heard loud, uncontrollable laughter coming from the team meeting at Hendon Hall. I peeped through the open door and saw Alf and all the players in hysterics as they watched film of their training matches leading up to the final. Projectionist Derek Cattani, official FA cameraman, was playing his film backwards at double speed. It was hilarious. The laughter was just what the doctor ordered.

But then the door was closed and Alf got down to the serious business of showing his players how they could beat West Germany and become champions of the world. Jimmy did not get a mention in the briefing, and guessed he was going to miss the match of a lifetime.

It was after breakfast on the morning of the final, and out of sight of the growing army of newspapermen and broadcasters, that Ramsey called a private team meeting. I later learned that he said, simply, 'Gentlemen, it will be an unchanged team. I want to thank all of you for your efforts so far, and I know you'll all pull together this afternoon. It's our team spirit that makes us stronger than the rest. I don't want to announce the team until we get to Wembley, so please keep it to yourself.'

Alf took his former skipper Jimmy Armfield to one side and told him, 'I'm putting you in charge of the rest of the squad. There are seats reserved for you in the stand. Regardless of the score, bring them down to the pitch side with five minutes to go. I want us all to be together at the end, no matter what the result.'

In fairness to Ramsey, he was not keeping the team from the press so much as from the Germans. He did not want his rival manager Helmut Schoen to know his line-up until as late as possible. Alf was sure that the German boss – along with most good judges – would be convinced that Jimmy Greaves was certain to play.

In the German headquarters at the Homestead Court Hotel in Welwyn Garden City, Schoen was holding a team meeting where it was not Jimmy Greaves on his mind but Bobby Charlton. He had watched Bobby's exceptional display against Portugal and decided to sacrifice his most talented player, Franz Beckenbauer, to man-mark the England schemer. It was a tactical decision that would have a huge impact on the final.

The England players had sat in a darkened room at Hendon Hall watching television film of West Germany's victory over Russia in their semi-final, with Alf continually stopping the action and giving each of his players specific instructions in how to play them. He ordered Bobby Charlton to shadow Beckenbauer. Two of the most creative players in the world were about to cancel each other out.

Alf was a man with a plan, and his fellow Dagenhamite Jimmy Greaves was not part of it. And neither were any wingers.

Jimmy had guessed he was out and without a word to anybody had packed his bags ready for a quick getaway once the match was over. Hendon Hall had become Heartbreak Hotel.

He smuggled the cases to his brother-in-law Tom. They would be leaving with their wives, Irene and Nancy, the next day for a Caribbean holiday. For Jimmy, the World Cup campaign was over.

Greavsie would give his team-mates his full, sincere support at Wembley but inside he felt sick and empty. For months he had been telling people, including me, that England would win the World Cup. He just did not envisage being a non-playing spectator. 'I was,' he said profoundly, 'the loneliest man at Wembley.'

Alf did not see fit to say a word to him. He considered there were ten other excluded players who would then also deserve an explanation.

I felt I had betrayed a good pal by writing that Alf should leave him out of the biggest game that any footballer could play.

And over the next 50+ years, Jimmy never, ever let me forget what I had written in the *Express* on the morning of the match. He had always done it in jest, but deep down I know he must have felt I was putting the boot in on a friend. It was 12 years later, when we were writing the first of our 20 books together, that Jimmy conceded he was playing below par in the 1965/66 season. The hepatitis that put him in hospital in the autumn of 1965 had robbed him of a vital half-yard of pace.

He worked harder than at any time in his career to get his match fitness back, and was still considered England's major striker going into the World Cup finals. But a wild kick from a French defender – picking on Jimmy rather than the fearsome Nobby Stiles – opened a deep gash on his left shin that required several stitches.

'I had no idea how bad it was until I looked down and found that my white sock was blood red,' he told me. 'An alarm bell went off in my head at that moment that maybe my World Cup was over.'

Following the banquet, with an empty Jimmy Greaves seat, Alf – knowing my closeness to Greavsie – asked, 'Is Jimmy okay?'

'You know Jim,' I replied. 'He just doesn't want any fuss, so he's quietly nipped away.'

Alf was a relieved man. His gamble of leaving out England's greatest goalscorer had come off. If the Germans had won, he knew he would have been crucified.

Let's leave the 1966 World Cup behind with a smile that captures Jimmy's no-holds-barred humour. Eleven years after the finals in England, there was a five-a-side Queen's Jubilee tournament at Wembley Arena (the Empire Pool as it was called then) featuring veterans of 66. France were among the competing teams, and the social itinerary included a Thames pleasure boat trip from Westminster.

Looking across the deck, Stiles saw among the French players his old adversary Jacques Simon, a maestro of a playmaker. Nobby, who never took prisoners, had flattened him with a tackle at Wembley during the World Cup that was so fierce some FIFA and Football Association officials demanded Alf Ramsey drop the Manchester United midfielder, famously known by his nickname The Toothless Tiger.

It was always Nobby's contention that what looked to many like a criminal assault had been accidental rather than intentional.

'I'd never had the chance to apologise,' Nobby said. 'Knowing he spoke English, I went over to him and started to explain that it was a badly timed rather than deliberately malicious tackle. I was just softening him up and he was smiling when Greavsie went and poked his nose in. He'd sussed what I was up to and spoiled it all by creeping up to Simon and saying in a loud whisper, "Don't listen to the dirty little bastard! He kicked me up hill and down dale for ten years."'

It was a typical Jimmy prank, and Simon and Stiles fell into each other's arms laughing.

Greavsie had scored again.

Chapter 9

Bobby Moore on tape

WHEN JIMMY first switched to media work as he came out of his alcoholic haze, I set up an interview with his old mate Bobby Moore. With me in charge of the tape recorder, this is Greavsie and Mooro discussing the good and bad times they had together on and off the pitch:

JG: What a jammy git you were, Mooro, to last 90 matches as England captain. I did my best to cost you the job.

BM: There were a couple of times when Alf was on the point of giving me the chop after incidents involving you, James. He went ballistic in New York in 1964 after you'd talked me into breaking a curfew to sneak away from the team hotel to see Ella Fitzgerald singing at Madison Square Garden.

JG: Dear old Alf. When we told him we'd been to see Ella, he thought it was an elephant at the circus. All he knew about was football and westerns.

BM: Yeah, he loved his westerns. Remember when we were in East Germany and Alf found out there was a western showing with subtitles? He rounded us up and we all went off to the cinema. The film was dubbed in German and as the subtitles started crawling along the bottom of the screen they were in Polish!

JG: We pissed ourselves. Alf loved us to do things together, to go round as a team as if tied by a rope.

BM: You were too much of an individualist for him, Jim. Don't forget that we were together on the best day of my life and the worst of yours.

JG: Knew you'd bring that up. We were room sharing in the Hendon Hall hotel during the 1966 World Cup. It was weird when we woke up on the morning of the final because you knew you were going to captain the side and I guessed I wouldn't be playing. Alf had not said a dicky bird to me, but I sensed I'd been given the elbow.

BM: What could Alf do, Jim? You'd been injured for the quarter and semi-final and the team had been magnificent in both games. If there had been substitutes then you would have got on, and Geoff probably wouldn't have got his hat-trick.

JG: That's all blood under the bridge, Mooro. I always knew we would win the World Cup, but, to be honest, I never envisaged that I'd be a spectator. Remember the team outing after the opening match of the finals when we went to Pinewood film studios. Sean Connery was making the Bond movie *You Only Live Twice*, and showed us around the set.

BM: I know what's coming. The famous Alf speech. He said, 'On behalf of the team, I'd like to thank Seen Connery for his guided tour.'

JG: And you said instantly, 'That's the funniest thing I've ever shawn or heard.' I fell about laughing and Alf was not best pleased with us taking the pee. I wonder if people realise how close you came to not playing in the finals?

BM: Oh, you mean the West Ham contract business. I was virtually blackmailed into signing a new contract with the club just before the first match against Uruguay. Ron Greenwood came to the hotel with all the papers, and it was made clear to me that as I was out of contract with West Ham I would not, under FIFA rules, be eligible to play for England. I'd been hanging out for a hoped-for move to join you at Tottenham, but West Ham kept copping a deaf ear to their approaches. So I put my name to the contract and tied myself to the Hammers. I wasn't being greedy. I just knew I was getting paid half of what many of the players at other clubs were earning.

JG: You'd have loved it at Spurs. Bill Nicholson never made a secret of his admiration for your footballing talent, and if you'd joined us in those mid-60s I reckon we could have got the league title to go with the FA Cup we won in '67.

BM: Don't rub it in, Jimbo. I was always a fan of that Tottenham team's style of play under Bill Nick. I got several pulls on the old hush-hush, including from you that Bill wanted me, but West Ham would not budge. No disrespect to West Ham but the overall strength of the Spurs squad was far superior back then to what we had at Upton Park.

JG: You were England captain for Alf Ramsey's greatest triumphs, but also for the bad times. There were, for instance, the cock-ups he made with the substitutions in Mexico in 1970.

BM: Yes, it was the one weakness with Alf apart from his lack of communication skills with the media. He hated the substitute rule because it had never been part of his thinking in all his time in the game. He never experienced it at club level, and just didn't feel comfortable with the rule. His decision to take off Bobby Charlton, who was motoring nicely in the 1970 quarter-final against West Germany, was a shocker. Franz Beckenbauer was standing close to me as Bobby got the hook, and his eyes lit up. He'd suddenly been given hope that Germany could turn the game around.

JG: And you were involved in Kevin Keegan's embarrassing exposure at Wembley.

BM: That was in the 1974 World Cup qualifier against Poland. I'd been dropped after I'd had a bit of a nightmare in the game in Poland. I sat alongside Alf, and had never seen him so lacking in ideas as England struggled to get the ball into the net. I kept on at him in the second half to get a substitute on to mix things up a bit. But the longer the game went on, he just seemed to freeze. Sitting to my right were our subs, including Ray Clemence, Kevin Keegan and Kevin Hector. Suddenly, with just five minutes to go and with me nagging him, Alf finally decided he should send on a sub. 'Kevin, get stripped,' Alf ordered. This was the moment when the drama on the bench turned to farce. Ray Clemence helped Kevin Keegan off with his tracksuit bottoms, but he was so eager that he tugged his shorts down to his knees. While he was suffering this over-exposure, he became even further embarrassed when Alf made it clear he meant Kevin Hector not Keegan. I helped Hector off with his tracksuit bottoms, but by the time he got on there were just 100 seconds left – the shortest England debut on record. He had on e chance and missed a sitter from three yards. England went out of the World Cup, and it eventually cost Alf his job.

JG: The most shocked I'd ever known you, Bob, was when I dropped in from nowhere to see you in Mexico City when you were under lock and key in the British ambassador's villa.

BM: That was when I'd been sent back from Colombia after being arrested on that crazy charge of stealing a bracelet from a jeweller's shop on the eve of the 1970 World Cup. Talk about a stitch-up.

JG: I'd arrived in Mexico at the end of the World Cup rally to find out that you'd been nicked. Our mutual mate Norman did some detective work and found out where you were being held until allowed to rejoin the England squad. I climbed over the wall of the villa to avoid all the press and photographers at the front, and the ambassador's wife caught me wandering around the garden. She gave me a bollocking and then demanded that I go to the front door. When I rang the door, she let me in!

BM: She almost fainted, Jimbo, when your first words to me were, 'Show us the bracelet then, Mooro.' I was so pleased to see you after the nightmare I'd been through. We cleared the ambassador out of all his drink that night.

JG: Once we'd settled down, your larger-than-life neighbour from Chigwell, Lou Wade, was allowed to join us, remember? He stood 6ft 7in and wore a garish check jacket that made him look like a Las Vegas gambler.

BM: The look on her face when Lou walked in was one of total disbelief. He helped give the ambassador's drinks cabinet a hammering.

JG: It was disgraceful the way Alf and the rest of the Football Association freebie chasers left you out to dry in Colombia. You could have got thousands out of the jewellery shop for destroying your reputation with a false charge.

BM: I thought of going down that road, Jim, but it would have cost a fortune in legal fees, and knowing what crafty people they were I ran the risk of them inventing some witness who would have pointed the finger at me. Bobby Charlton was in the jewellery shop with me at the time of me supposedly stealing the bracelet. Can you imagine him having anything to do with anything that dodgy?

JG: Or anything dodgy. You could trust him with your last bottle of water in the desert. Remember our dance, Mooro?

BM: You, you silly sod, suddenly grabbed hold of me in the penalty area in the middle of a First Division match between West Ham and Tottenham. You twirled me around as if it was a Cockney knees-up. It was hilarious. Can't imagine that happening in today's game. It's all so bloody serious. As we danced you said, 'See you later at the Black Lion', one of our watering holes.

JG: Happy days. Of course, we wound up together at West Ham.

BM: Yes, and you got me in trouble again. New Year's Day 1971.

JG: Here we go. I'm going to get blamed for the 'Blackpool affair' now.

BM: Well, it was you, Jim, who called the cab to take us to Brian London's nightclub when you heard one of the hotel porters say there was no chance of the cup tie being played the next day because of all the snow on the pitch.

JG: Let's be honest, Mooro, eskimos couldn't have played football in those conditions. And by the way, I didn't call the cab. Two arrived for a TV crew who only needed one. On the spur of the moment, we took the spare cab.

BM: I felt sorry for Clyde Best, who we dragged along with us at the last minute.

JG: Yes, Clyde came along for the ride and Stag [Brian Dear] for the drink. We were not pissed when we got back to the Imperial, but we had been seen having a few pints in the nightclub by a supporter. He reported us to the club after we had lost to Blackpool on a skating rink pitch that should have been ruled unfit for play.

BM: It all blew up five days later. Everybody had kept quiet about it because, unbeknown to me, Eamonn Andrews was planning to hit me with the *This Is Your Life* book, and they waited until after the show before the newspapers started headlining what had happened at Blackpool.

JG: I thought Ron Greenwood let you down big time. I didn't care about myself because I was planning to get out of the game at the end of the season. But he just threw you to the wolves. We were both suspended and even Alf Ramsey dropped you for a match. If you'd played, it would have meant you beating Billy Wright's record of captaining England 90 times, instead of equalling it. The biggest mistake we made, Mooro, was losing that cup tie at Blackpool. If we'd won or got a replay, nothing would have come of it. Greenwood could have punished us privately, but decided to let the press have a field day. He used us as scapegoats.

BM: D'you think he was getting his own back for what happened on the plane?

JG: Oh, you mean when that rascal Freddie Harrison spiked his drinks.

BM: We were in the upstairs bar of a Jumbo jet on the way to New York for a friendly match against Pelé's Santos. You and I were knocking back pints when Ron joined us and asked for a Coke.

Freddie, my business partner, decided to lace the Coke with Bacardi, a pretty juvenile thing to do, but we giggled behind Ron's back.

JG: During the next hour or so Ron must have had five or six Cokes, all of them doctored by the mischievous Freddie. Ron finally realised what was going on and, to his credit, he laughed it off. The alcohol made his tongue much looser than he would have liked and he confessed he was thinking of resigning.

BM: Yes, that was embarrassing. And when he went back to his seat, he dropped off into a heavy, drink-sedated sleep. Peter Eustace, who was not exactly Ron's greatest fan since being dropped from the team, had the rest of us in fits of laughter as he leant over the snoring Greenwood, miming as if telling him exactly what he thought of him. Ron would have had a fit if he'd woken up.

JG: He never mentioned the resigning business again, but the Blackpool farce certainly gave him the chance to get his own back.

BM: Let's be fair, Jim, for all his faults Ron was a gentleman who gave a lot to the game. He was as good a tactician as I ever met in the game, and he taught me a lot when I was a kid with the England Under-23s and then when he took over from Ted Fenton as manager at Upton Park.

JG: Yeah, Ron was out of the Walter Winterbottom school. A scholar and a gentleman. He couldn't understand how you and I could be less than serious about the game when we were off the pitch. It's history that I hit the bottle, but you could always outdrink me without showing any effect. We used to say you had hollow legs.

BM: I've always enjoyed a good drink, James, as you know. I couldn't believe it when you publicly admitted you were an alcoholic. All of us admire the way you've beaten your problem.

JG: Enough of rabbiting about me. This interview is supposed to be about you. With a gun to your head, who would have been your first choice for a world team from all the players you played with or against?

BM: That's easy, Jim. Pelé by a mile. He had everything – perfect balance, could shoot with either foot, had tremendous vision, was as brave as they come and had the agility of a gymnast. When we appeared together with Sylvester Stallone in the film *Escape to Victory...*

JG: You were more wooden than the goalposts, Mooro.

BM: Thanks, Jimbo. I didn't expect an Oscar. Anyway, Pelé scored with a fantastic bicycle kick. What the public didn't know is that they shot that scene 30 times, and then used the first take! There's no question that Pelé was the greatest goalscorer of them all, with you the best of the Brits.

JG: If I was picking a world team defence, Mooro, I'll say this to your face because it's what I say behind your back. You would be my first choice.

BM: Stop it, Jim. You're making me blush.

JG: Could never understand why you didn't get a shot at a top manager's job. Nobody in the game had a better pedigree than you.

BM: Well, I went for the top one, the England post. Sent a handwritten letter to the FA and didn't even get a reply. Then Elton John gave me the impression I'd got the Watford job and the next I knew he'd given it to Graham Taylor without a dicky bird to me. That disappointed me, Jim. Not so much that I didn't get either job but the way it was handled. Very disrespectful.

I wanted to update the interview for a book Jim and I were writing about the greats of the game, and for me there was no greater defender than Mooro, who I had known as long as I'd been friends with Greavsie. We used to go to many boxing shows together. Jimmy and I had arranged to meet him at the Capital Gold studio in January 1993, but got a call from their switchboard sending his apologies and asking us to postpone our meeting until a later date.

The interview never took place. Within a month, lovely Mooro had succumbed to his cancer.

One of England's greatest ever footballers – 'Sir' Bobby Moore – had gone and suddenly everybody cared.

But where were they all when he needed them? Jimmy shared my view that the football establishment should have been ashamed of the way they treated Bobby after he had hung up his boots.

Bobby and Jimmy were loveable rascals together, and two of the finest footballers ever produced on the playing fields of England. Both should have been knighted. Somebody hold my coat while I punch a few stuck-up noses.

Chapter 10:

The G-Men on the road to Wembley

BACK ON the club circuit after the 1966 World Cup, Bill Nicholson's latest 'Super' side saved their peak performances for the FA Cup in the 1966/67 season, culminating in a well-earned FA Cup Final triumph over London neighbours Chelsea at Wembley. Of the side that won the trophy in 1962, only Dave Mackay and Greavsie had survived, along with Cliff Jones on the substitutes bench.

Jimmy had recovered from the hepatitis that had robbed him of half a yard of pace during the build-up to the 1966 World Cup finals; nobody ever takes that illness into account when discussing his contribution to the World Cup triumph, halted by a shin injury received in that group game against France.

The fact that Mackay was there to lead out the Tottenham team as skipper in the 1967 FA Cup Final was the sort of story that you would expect to come from the pages of *Roy of the Rovers*. 'Miracle Man' Mackay had made an astonishing recovery after breaking his leg a second time following his controversial collision with Noel Cantwell at Old Trafford in 1963. Listen to Jimmy reminiscing on that Cup-winning squad:

' Dave Mackay motivated a team that had Pat Jennings building himself into a legend as the last line of defence.

Big Pat was a bundle of nerves when he first arrived from Watford, and couldn't be trusted to hold a mug of tea without spilling it. Bill had to recall dear old Bill Brown a couple of times until Pat started to believe in himself. Then there was no greater goalkeeper in the game, and with those huge mitts of his he could have strangled King Kong.

Baby-faced Irish international Joe Kinnear had come in as right-back in place of the energetic Phil Beal, who was unlucky to break an arm after playing an important part in getting us to the final. Joe, a neat, controlled player, was partnered at full-back by Cyril Knowles, a former Yorkshire miner who took the eye with his sharp tackling and some polished, if at times eccentric skills. He used to give Bill Nick babies with his dribbling in front of his own goal, but he'd been a winger before dropping into defence and liked to show off his skill. The fact that it was in our box gave us all many heart-in-the-mouth moments. I remember our coach Eddie Baily saying to him once after he had dribbled the ball in the six-yard box, including along the goal-line, "For fuck's sake, get rid of the thing if you're anywhere near our goal. You almost made my old girl a widow."

Joker Cyril said in his deliberately exaggerated Yorkshire tones, "Ay oop, lad, I'd 'ave organised a whip round for her."

He had a brother, Peter, who was a gifted inside-forward with Wolves, but he'd been nobbled by the Jehovah's witnesses and gave up the game to spread the word. I told Cyril that if his brother ever came knocking on my door, I'd tell him where to stick his book. Me religious? Just let's say it makes me cross.

Cyril, often as silly as a box of lights, became a cult hero, with anything he attempted – good or bad – accompanied by chants of "Nice one, Cyril" from the White Hart Lane faithful. I used to tell him he was a slice or two short of a full loaf. Eddie Baily often got close to calling him a cult.

Standing like a Welsh mountain in the middle of the defence was the majestic Mike England, one of the finest centre-halves I ever played with or against. Bill bought Mike from Blackburn Rovers to take over from Maurice Norman after Mo had broken a thigh bone in a meaningless friendly against Hungary when they were warming up for the 1966 World Cup. I don't think Jack Charlton would have got a sniff of the England No. 5 shirt if our Norfolk Swedebasher had been fit.

Mike was a class player from head to toe. Just imagine if Bobby Moore had arrived to play alongside him! Yes, Bill Nick tried hard to sign him, and I had the job of whispering in Bobby's shell-like when we were on England trips. Bobby was desperate to join us, but West Ham dared not let him go after his performance in the '66 World Cup. They had to pay a king's ransom to hold on to him, and he was worth every penny.

My old mucker Dave Mackay was the immoveable link between defence and attack as he adapted his game from buccaneer to anchorman, helping to stoke the fires of the engine room where Alan Mullery and Terry Venables were forging a productive partnership. It's fair to say they never quite touched the peaks that Spurs fans had seen in the "Glory Glory" days of Blanchflower/White/Mackay, but – let's be honest – few midfield combinations have ever reached that sky-scraping standard. Mullers was as solid and reliable as the military tank after which he was nicknamed, and Venners had more swagger than a barrow boy on a beano. I remember the day Tel and I did a number on Liverpool. While I pretended to be tying my bootlace, he was making a fuss about their wall not being back the full ten yards at a free kick. The Saint and Tommy Smith took the bait and started effing and blinding the referee while I, still in a crouching position, rolled the ball past goalkeeper Tommy Lawrence. After the game, Bill Shankly shouted at me in the car park, "Greavsie, you're a thief. Come and join Liverpool and play for a proper team." Yes, happy days.

Jimmy Robertson was a flying Scot on the right wing, where his speed was a vital asset. Bill Nick later swapped Robbo for Arsenal winger David Jenkins. Some said Arsenal got a Ferrari and we got a Robin Reliant. It certainly wasn't one of Bill's better deals.

Because Chelsea were neurotic about keeping Gilly and me under lock and key in that first all-London final, they forgot to tight mark Robbo and Frankie Saul and they got the goals that mattered. Tommy Docherty, Chelsea's larger-than-life manager cut from the same tartan cloth as Shanks, came up to me as I was waiting to go and collect my medal. "Well done, wee man," he said. "Just wish you'd stayed in Italy." **'**

Three months after this triumph, Tottenham drew 3-3 in the Charity Shield against Manchester United at Old Trafford, a match that has gone down in footballing folklore because of a wind-assisted goal scored by Pat Jennings. The Irish international goalkeeper hammered a huge clearance from the Spurs penalty area that went first bounce over the head of Alex Stepney and into the back of the United net.

The bewildered look on the faces of the players of both teams was hilarious to see. I was reporting the match for the *Daily Express*, and afterwards Pat told me:

‘ I decided to clear the ball up to Greavsie and Gilly, and a strong following wind grabbed it and took it all the way first bounce into the United net. Jimmy and Alan had their backs to me and could not believe it when they realised it was me who had scored. Greavsie said he told Alan, “D’you realise this makes Pat our top scorer for the season? He’ll never let us forget it.”

I’ve left out the colourful adjectives. The air was often blue around Jimmy and I always wondered and worried over whether he would drop the “f” bomb while on air. ‘I shared your concern,’ said Jim. ‘I was always on my best behaviour, I swear.” ’

The Greavsie era at Tottenham was drawing to a close, leaving a remarkable legacy of a club-record 220 First Division goals (including a record 37 in 1962/63), 32 FA Cup goals and 266 in all competitions; or 268, according to which record book you believe. Those bare statistics hide the fact that many of the goals were of the spectacular variety, fashioned like a skilled sculptor with clever feints, dizzying dribbles, astonishing acceleration and then finished with a pass rather than a shot into the net.

Those old enough to have witnessed a Greaves goal will confirm that I am not exaggerating when I say we actually felt privileged to have been there to see it. We were keeping company with a genius, a Goya of goals. How many would a peak-powered Greaves score in today’s game, with no Norman Hunter-style bites-yer-legs tackling from behind, billiard-table surfaces and the relaxed, often-confusing offside law?

And what would he be worth in the transfer market? Let the bidding begin at £99.999m!

There were calls for Greavsie to be reinstated in the England team when he hit a purple patch with 27 First Division goals in

1968/69, but Jimmy seemed to be almost visibly losing his appetite for the game the following season.

He had built up a flourishing packaging, sports shop and travel business with his brother-in-law Tom Barden, and football was no longer the be-all-and-end-all for him. Yet he was still by some distance the most dynamic finisher in the 'old' First Division. To try to bring the best out of Greavsie, Nicholson went shopping and bought Martin Chivers as a new playmate from Southampton.

Sadly, he arrived at Jimmy's side just as the goal master was losing his motivation. The crunch came when Spurs wore their white shirts like flags of surrender against Crystal Palace in a fourth-round FA Cup replay at Selhurst Park. Palace striker Gerry Queen dismantled the Spurs defence for the winning goal, and I recall the headline on my report for the *Daily Express*, which announced, "Queen Is King at the Palace."

Greavsie, trying to settle into his new partnership with Chivers, was dropped for the first time in his nine years at Spurs. It was his final curtain at Tottenham. With many Spurs fans in tears, genius Jimmy was allowed to move on to West Ham for an unhappy last season in league football, while Martin Peters went the other way from Upton Park. 'I think Bill Nick's gone barmy,' Alan Mullery said to me off the record, a confidence I feel I can break more than 50 years on.

Bill told me privately that he was concerned that the Artful Dodger of the penalty area seemed to be showing more enthusiasm preparing for driving to Mexico in a 1970 World Cup rally than playing football.

I did warn you to fasten your safety belts earlier in this journey through Jimmy's life.

Chapter 11

The 1970 World Cup Rally adventure

OF ALL Jimmy's many adventures, the pottiest was when he decided to participate in the 1970 World Cup London-to-Mexico rally. He was always a mad-keen motorist, but he allowed his enthusiasm to run away with him when the *Daily Mirror* announced they were staging the rally, starting at Wembley Stadium and finishing at the Azteca Stadium in Mexico City on the eve of the World Cup finals in which England would be defending the title they won in 1966.

The following is a full and fascinating Ford Motor Company article to which I contributed.

I have lifted it from Jimmy's scrapbook because it graphically captures his extraordinary experiences in the one and only rally of his career:

'Tick-tick-tick … The engine of the Ford Escort turned over slowly. Inside the car, now stranded on the side of the road, Jimmy Greaves stirred, his head slumped against the dashboard. He looked down. His racing overalls, once covered in oil, were now splattered in blood, as was the car windscreen, which was cracked and split from the impact of the crash. Greaves checked himself for cuts. Fortunately, the blood was not his own; nor was it that of the driver, the rally champion Tony Fall. So whose could it be?

Tick-tick-tick …

As Fall also began to stir, Greaves started to make sense of the blur of the accident. He had been asleep, but was jolted awake by the sound of screeching brakes as a horse galloped out of nowhere in front of their car on this lonely stretch of Panamanian road. Too late. A ton-and-a-half of souped-up Ford Escort had met half a ton of horse at 100mph. The horse came off worse, its head ripped clean off as it flew over the car. It was like *that* scene from *The Godfather.*

Tick-tick-tick …

Both drivers were shocked, but unhurt. Shaking, they stepped out of the car to inspect the damage. The windscreen was a mess, but the dent in the bonnet was not too bad. Feeling nauseous, the pair set about wiping the blood from the glass before climbing back into the car and speeding off on their way again. They left the dead horse behind.

Greaves and Fall had been making steady progress in the South American leg of the 1970 World Cup Rally and were among the leading ten drivers, but this accident was to set them back in the race order.

Only two more weeks to go …

When Greaves, the 30-year-old Spurs striker and England international, announced he would be competing in a cross-continental rally in 1970, the football community scratched its head. That one of the game's most prolific strikers should take up rally driving as a hobby (imagine Michael Owen taking up snowboarding) was amusing. That he should compete in one of the sport's most gruelling events – the World Cup Rally – on the eve of the 1970 football World Cup tournament in Mexico was insanity.

The rally was the brainchild of Walton Dickinson, a race promoter with friends in the Football Association. The idea of a rally featuring every country participating in the World Cup finals and culminating in the capital city of the host nation was conceived at a dinner party. Within a month, the brainstorm was viewed as an excellent opportunity to showcase the motor industry, and sponsorship with the *Daily Mirror* was arranged.

Kicking off at Wembley and culminating in Mexico City, the rally was viewed as a unique sporting event: the registration of a few celebrity drivers assured the nation's interest.

Greaves's registration with Ford and the 30-year-old Fall (winner of the notoriously difficult Rally of the Incas the previous year) was initiated by the car manufacturer, whose main plant in Dagenham was located near Greaves's Essex home. Ford had been looking for a high-profile driver to spearhead their campaign and Greaves, who had friends at the plant, had proved ideal.

Fall was also keen to work with Greaves. "My carrot was a two-week holiday in the Caribbean with my wife, courtesy of Ford after the race had finished," he said. "Jim hadn't done any racing before this point, so Ford wanted me to get him through the race in one piece. I had to teach him what to do, so in reality I was the brains behind the duo and he was the name. They introduced us and we got on very well, but before we started planning for the World Cup Rally, we went on a short trip in the car to Yugoslavia to see if we could get on over a long period of time. It was here I realised just how famous Jimmy was. My first taste of his celebrity came just after we set off for Dover. We got to the docks and the car was mobbed as soon as people realised who was in it. Even the customs office emptied. When we finally got to Yugoslavia, we ended up at a hotel and as soon as he walked through the door the receptionist did a double-take, rang everybody he knew and the nightclub downstairs emptied as we were mobbed by football fans."

With training underway, Greaves's interest in the World Cup Rally was heightened by the frustration of being dropped from the Spurs side after a disappointing defeat in the FA Cup at the hands of Crystal Palace. Greaves also knew he wouldn't be travelling with Sir Alf Ramsey and the England squad, so this would be his route to the World Cup finals in Mexico. He also felt his game was losing its edge; it was a view shared by Bill Nicholson, the Spurs manager. "By this time, Greaves's reactions had slowed," Nicholson said. "Reflexes are the first thing to go in a footballer, and he relied heavily on them."

With the transfer gossip raging around the club, Nicholson turned his attention to finding a new striker, while Greaves fielded offers from Joe Mercer, manager of Manchester City, and Derby County's charismatic general, Brian Clough. In the meantime, Nicholson located his target: Martin Peters of West Ham United. Peters – a 1966 World Cup winner with England and a former international team-mate of Greaves – was likely to drain the Spurs coffers of about £200,000. Spotting the financial difficulties of such a move, Nicholson shrewdly set up an exchange deal involving Greaves moving in the other direction.

The West Ham deal allowed Greaves to focus his efforts on the motor race once again (manager Ron Greenwood was not concerned at his new signing's extra-curricular activities after Greaves had scored two goals on his debut against Manchester City), and with only two months of the football season remaining, Greaves's sights were set firmly on the World Cup Rally.

He would come to regret the decision to compete in that almost as much as the one to join West Ham.

On April 19, a balmy spring afternoon, Sir Alf Ramsey, the England manager, waved the Union Jack that signalled the beginning of the *Daily Mirror* World Cup Rally. Bobby Moore, the team's captain, had already cut up the Wembley turf and placed a slab in the boot of each of the 96 cars revving their engines on the starting-line. Twenty-five thousand spectators waved the racing fleet off. Bobby Moore was last to speak to Jimmy before the flag dropped, "See you in Mexico City for a pint, Jimbo," he said, little knowing how significant that reunion drink would become.

Greaves and Fall sat side by side in car number 26 – a black and white Ford Escort. Both knew the 16,245-mile journey across two continents and 25 countries would be arduous, but neither was prepared for the gruelling eight weeks ahead.

The plan was for Fall to take on the bulk of the driving responsibility, with Greaves assuming the role of navigator and taking the wheel when the terrain and twisting contours of the road weren't too demanding. Greaves had proved to Fall that he was a competent driver, and the pair were the bookies' second favourites at 12/1 (Prince Michael of Kent, who had also been signed up for the race in a fantastic publicity coup, was ranked as one of the outsiders at 20/1).

The cars set off, heading for Lisbon via Vienna, Sofia, Yugoslavia, Monza and northern Spain. It soon became apparent that, after only a few stages of the rally, the race was not going to be the enjoyable challenge for which Greaves had hoped. "We were going 55 hours in one stretch without any sleep as we navigated the toughest terrain in the world," Greaves said. "We were travelling at speeds of up to 100mph on mountain roads that were built with only donkey travel in mind."

The pair boarded the boat to where the next section of the race would take place: Rio de Janeiro and the South America leg. "We had a much-needed break," Fall said. "And the sponsors arranged for us to have a holiday in Rio. It was a great chance for us to let our hair down and we did a lot of what Jimmy would call relaxing."

Greaves said, "Seventy-one cars left for Rio for speed tests that took place during tropical floods, which made driving treacherous and dangerous. We sped through clouds of red dust and then along miles of flooded, cramped and bumpy roads. It was such a tough stage of the rally that at the end of it, only 52 cars were left."

With 10,000 miles remaining, Greaves and Fall negotiated the Argentinian Pampas, which challenged them with 1,000 miles of treacherous paths and tracks in the toughest stretch of the race. An average speed of 60mph was required here, but the thin air, on account of being at altitude, reduced the cars' engine capacity by half.

The drivers suffered, too. "It was difficult to breathe up there," Fall said. "A lot of competitors passed out."

Battered by the abrasive twists and the harsh elements, the cars themselves began to buckle. "We were 15,000 feet up in the Andes on a narrow, winding mountain road when we lost a rear wheel close to the finishing line," Greaves said. "We had already used our spare and we finished the stage with me at the wheel and Tony at the back, pushing. We lost a wheel again on the next stage, but it so easily could have been our lives. Tony was driving and I was navigating as we came down a steep and narrow mountain road. Suddenly, an old peasant woman crossed the road in front of us. Miraculously, Tony swerved the car past her and skidded to a stop on the mountain edge as a wheel axle broke. We were literally feet from death. I hardly dared breathe as my brilliant co-driver manoeuvred the car back into the centre of the road before we jacked it up and started urgent repairs."

The cars were finally on their way to the finishing line. Peru was the first stop on the home stretch and there the roads were lined with football fans who had watched Greaves score a hat-trick in England's 4-0 stuffing of Peru in 1962. By now, though, the seven-week stretch on the road was affecting the drivers' health. "Our skin was taking a real hammering," Fall said. "We hadn't eaten any fruit or vegetables for weeks. There was plenty of red meat – all you'd eat was steak – but the lack of vitamins was a real problem and we began to feel very ill."

Only 32 cars made it to the Peruvian capital, Lima, which had recently been devastated by an earthquake. Landslides and tropical monsoons plagued the journey through Ecuador before engine problems in Chile nearly ended Greaves's rally. "We broke down in the middle of nowhere," Greaves said. "But I finally managed to thumb a lift on a bus that was going back to the garage [they had passed one on the road]. Half an hour later I was walking back to Tony, who was wondering if I had got lost forever, with my hands in my pockets and head bowed. It was worse than the feeling of being sent off the field. The bus had gone the opposite way to the direction I wanted. Shows what a good navigator I was!"

Only 23 cars completed the race. One cyclist, a driver and a rally official had lost their lives along the way. Greaves and Fall had finished in a creditable sixth place, with the Finnish partnership of Mikkola and Palm taking first place. "Jimmy Greaves has earned the admiration of the motoring world," Graham Hill, the former Formula 1 world champion, said during the medal ceremony. "It is an outstanding achievement for him to finish so high in a field against some of the greatest rally drivers in the business. The rally puts unparalleled demands on the durability of both men and machines. It takes guts and a lot of driving ability to get through."

Greaves was equally astounded to have made it through the event in one piece. "If I had realised how hard the race was going to be, I doubt I could have summoned up the courage to face it,' he wrote in his autobiography *This One's On Me*. "Those rally drivers are amongst the toughest and most fearless sportsmen I have ever met. There were times when I felt physically sick over the demands of the race, and several times I wanted to quit, but there was no way I was going to let Tony down."

I was in Mexico to greet Jimmy at the end of the marathon rally, covering the World Cup finals for the *Daily Express*. I had never seen him looking so exhausted yet elated that he had managed to complete what he described as the toughest challenge of his life. He appeared to have lost a stone and was drawn and haggard-looking.

Jimmy and main driver Tony Fall celebrated their sixth-place achievement by jumping fully clothed into a swimming pool at the sprawling, luxury 1,000-room, single-storey Camino Real hotel where I was staying. Enthroned on a chair that had also been tossed into the water, Jimmy proceeded to drink himself paralytic as if in practice for the approaching five lost years. 'I conscientiously followed the rule of the road: "Don't Drink and Drive,"' he told me. 'The only alcohol I consumed during the rally was while we were on the boat from Lisbon to Rio after we had tackled the mountains of Serbia in the European half of the event. Oh yes, and we had a bit of a lash during our drop-off in Rio.'

Alf Ramsey, who had flagged off the rally drivers in London six weeks earlier, was with the England team that had recently set up camp in Mexico, awaiting his captain, Bobby Moore. Jimmy, along with the rest of the world, was incredulous that his new West Ham team-mate and former England room-mate had been accused of stealing a bracelet in the Colombian capital Bogota. Having just been released from his Bogota imprisonment, Moore was holed up in an embassy house in Mexico City to avoid the attention of the world's media.

Deciding Mooro would welcome the company, a sobered-up Jimmy made up his mind he was going to visit his close pal. I did some detective work and discovered the address of the embassy house where Bobby was holed up. We drove there in a cab and found security guards blocking the front. I helped Jimmy shin over a side wall into the grounds of the house.

He was intercepted by the wife of the ambassador, who showed him out of the house with the instructions that he should make a conventional entrance. Jimmy knocked at the door and was shown back in. He later reported, 'Mooro almost dropped his lager in surprise when he saw me coming into his room, and he was even more surprised when I asked him where he'd hidden the bracelet!

The ambassador's wife almost fainted.'

While Bobby emerged as the best defender of the tournament, Jimmy showed no interest in the finals and met up with Irene in the Caribbean for a sunshine holiday. He had driven himself to exhaustion.

Chapter 12

Reminiscing with the Real Mackay

AN INTERLUDE here while I dig out a Q&A feature Jimmy and I produced when we were in harness for *The Sun* back in the 1970s after Dave Mackay had followed Brian Clough as Derby manager. A recovering alcoholic, Jimmy had just started out on his TV and media career, and Dave had that season lifted the league championship.

Here's the great Mackay talking about his career to his biggest admirer Greavsie, with me as the privileged observer and note taker:

Did you always want to be a footballer?
Not just a footballer, a Hearts footballer. They have always been my favourite club. When I was just a kid, I used to walk three miles there and three miles back to get to watch them play at Tynecastle, and I was so small I could nip under the turnstile and get in without paying. My one dream was to play in the maroon and white shirt.

You're the most competitive bloke I've ever known. Were you like that at Hearts?
As you know, whether I'm playing football, golf or tiddlywinks, I *have* to win. I used to be the smallest player on the pitch and to win

the ball I had to tackle twice as hard as anybody else and I never got out of the habit. Even now I'm retired, my players fear me in six-a-side kickabouts because I only know one way to play and that is to win. My two brothers also played for Hearts, and the three of us had a reputation for being ultra-competitive. Fitba's a man's game.

Yes, you used to kick lumps out of us in the Tottenham gym. But you were about much more than power and strength, Dave.
I like to think I could be as accurate with my left foot as the great Danny Blanchflower was with his right. I made a few goals for you, Jim, with my passes. I was lucky to play for a Hearts team that put the emphasis on skill and then joined a Tottenham side that played pure football because that was the way manager Bill Nicholson wanted it. Anybody thumping the ball without thought got a right mouthful.

Which was the greatest team you played for?
Well, obviously the Tottenham team that won the Double in '61, but the Hearts side with which we won the Scottish championship ran them close. I skippered the team that banged in a British-record 132 league goals that season. Even you, Jim, didn't rattle in that many! You made our Spurs side even better when you signed from Milan, and we deserved to be European champions in your first season but were robbed in the semi-final against Benfica by some diabolical refereeing decisions.

How difficult was it combining National Service in the army with your football?
I got off lightly. There was no war to worry about and I had a sergeant major in the Royal Engineers who was a football nut. He used to make sure I got home every weekend to play for Hearts, provided I got him a ticket. I also played for my regiment in

midweek and was as fit as a fiddle. I did more running about on the pitch than square bashing.

You won only 22 Scotland caps when players with half your ability got picked many more times. Why was that?
I played in the days when the selectors considered you something of a traitor for taking the English pound. A lot of Anglos were often ignored. I was always proud to play for Scotland, and if you mention the 9-3 game, Jim, this interview is over. That still hurts to this day. It was a freak result and is the only game people seem to remember me playing at Wembley.

The worst thing for all of us in those 1960s was losing dear John White.
Yes, I still well up when I think of it. He had asked Cliffie Jones and me to play golf with him but we turned him down because there was a lot of rain around. He went out on his own and got hit by lightning. It was a tragedy that affected everybody at the club, particularly his best mate Jonesie and me. I had been responsible for him joining Spurs because I'd played with him for Scotland and told Bill Nick that he had to sign him. He was a magnificent footballer, a real players' player who always put the team first.

Breaking your leg twice and then coming back to lead Tottenham to the 1967 FA Cup earned you the nickname of the Miracle Man.
Well, it was something of a miracle really when you think of the mess my leg was in when Noel Cantwell did me at Old Trafford. I'm not going over old ground, but you saw it, Jim – one of the nastiest tackles ever! Then I got it broken again in a reserve match and for a while it looked as if it was curtains. But I was determined to play again, and that was a marvellous Spurs team I captained at Wembley. You and Gilly (Alan Gilzean) were two of the best striking partners I ever saw. Poetry in motion.

You looked a giant on the pitch, Dave, and people would never believe me when I said I was taller than you.

How many bets did we win in pubs when we'd challenge people to guess which of us was taller? You beat me by half an inch when we stood back to back. Those were the days when any pressman joining us for a drink were told one, everything you hear is off the record, and two, make sure you get a round in.

Talking as somebody who is a recovering alcoholic, we certainly used to hit the old hooch back in our playing days.

Aye, we were a good drinking club, that's for sure. You and Gilly could really knock it back. I don't encourage my players to booze like we did. For us it was a sort of bonus, but now players are sensible enough to know that they should only drink in moderation. It's a classic case of 'Don't do as I do, do as I say'. I'd come down on them like a ton of bricks if they drank like we did.

Remember that game when the ref sent you off and you talked him out of it?

For all my reputation for being a tough guy, I was never, ever sent off and I was not going to let the referee spoil my record when I knew he was making a mistake. It was in a cup tie against Bristol City and that little so-and-so Johnny Quigley kicked me up in the air. All the ref saw was my retaliation and he said, 'Off, Mackay.' I grabbed hold of Johnny and marched him to the ref and he was honest enough – or scared enough – to tell the ref what had happened, and he let me off.

The fans loved the way you used to always kick the ball miles in the air and trap it as you ran out for the start of a match.

It started off as me showing off, but then it became something of a superstition, and I also did it to let the opposition know I had a bit of skill. A lot of people thought I was all about tackling. But I could play a bit. You will confirm, Jim, that I could beat all of you at keepy-uppy and I can still lob a two bob bit into my top pocket.

There's that famous picture of you grabbing Billy Bremner by the scruff of the neck that proves your competitive nature.
I hate that bloody picture. It shows me in a terrible light. People see that and think what a bully I must have been. But I was just putting young Billy in his place. I had not long come back after breaking my leg a second time and he jumped in with a reckless tackle. He and I have always been big mates and roomed together on Scotland trips. That was just a moment when I felt I needed to give him a bit of fatherly advice about watching his tackles. We often laugh about it.

When you at last won the Footballer of the Year award in 1969, you had to share it with Man City's Tony Book. Did that spoil it for you?
No, I was just proud to have won even if it was a joint award. Tony Book is a smashing bloke and he had an outstanding season. I would have been choked if I had gone through my career without getting the award because I never had false modesty and knew I deserved it. The fact that you never got it, Jim, is a joke.

I was shocked when you signed for Derby because you told me you were going home to Scotland.
That was the plan. I was all lined up to go back to Hearts as player-manager when I got a call from Brian Clough. He locked me in Bill Nicholson's office and said he was not going to let me out until I'd signed for Derby. He is the most persuasive guy I've ever met and he convinced me I could still play at the top level.

You changed your style completely when you moved to Derby.
Cloughie knew my legs had gone and told me just to use my positional sense and guide young Roy McFarland at the heart of the defence. Brian wanted me for my leadership qualities and I slotted in comfortably, more as a conductor than the old-style competitor. Others did the running for me and I just kept motivating them with the odd tackle and a flourished fist. I think opponents were frightened of my reputation, not realising that I was nothing like the player I'd been at Tottenham. But it all worked very well and I was nicely paid.

Now you've taken over from Cloughie as Derby manager and have won the league championship. Do you remain a Cloughie fan?
Of course, he is a master and I've been lucky to play under three of the greatest managers ever in Tommy Walker at Hearts, Bill Nick and then Cloughie. I have learned so much from the three of them. They are completely different personalities but have the same fundamental belief that football is a game of skill. The principles I hold are the same as when I first started out with that wonderful Hearts side.

What was the best advice you got from Cloughie as a manager?
That I should burn his desk! That's what he did to Don Revie's desk when he took over at Leeds, and when he came here to do some transfer business he said I should set fire to his desk because it gets rid of the stench of the old regime.

With a gun to your head, who would you say was the most important influence on your career?
Without question, my wife Isobel. She is the perfect football wife. Knows when to encourage and when to shut up. Without her, I would not have been half the player or half the manager. She is

my strength and I'm not saying this only so she'll let me off the shopping tomorrow so I can play golf. I'd have loved to have been a golf professional. Now there's a life, almost as good as being a footballer.

That interview from nearly 40 years ago gives the perfect insight into Dave Mackay the football man. He was a hero for all seasons.

A few years later, I created a television series for ITV called *Who's the Greatest?* in which celebrity advocates put the case for who were the top sportsmen in a series of head-to-head battles. The verdict was decided by a jury of 12 members of the public, with ace commentator Brian Moore as the distinguished judge.

Jimmy was featured against the leading striker of the day, Liverpool's dynamic Ian Rush, and after hearing the case for each player – put by comedians Ted Rogers for Greavsie and Stan Boardman for Rush – the Welshman won by seven votes to five. 'Should have been 12-0 to Greavsie,' veteran manager Bill Nicholson told me in an exclusive interview at his Creighton Road N17 home during his later role as Tottenham president. 'Jimmy was the greatest scorer of them all. I've never seen a player rival him for putting the vital finishing touch. While others were still thinking about what to do, whoosh, he would just get on and do it. He would have the ball into the net in the blinking of an eye and then amble back to the centre circle as casually as if he'd just swatted a fly. A genius.'

Bill's mind was now filled with action replays of golden goals from the boots of our mutually favourite footballer, Greavsie. Not the rotund, funny one on the telly. This was the 10st 7lbs lightning-quick, darting, dribbling, twisting, turning and passing the ball into the net Jimmy Greaves, the Artful Dodger of the penalty area, a pickpocket who snaffled more memorable goals than many of us have had hot baths. 'He never gave me a spot of trouble, you know,'

Bill continued, now thinking aloud rather than talking direct to me. I need not have been there. He was wandering around a precious past, and did not need any prompting or interruption. 'Even when it came time for us to part company, he knew in his heart he'd lost his appetite for the game. People who didn't know what they were talking about sometimes described him as a bit of a faint-heart, but in all the years I watched him I never ever saw him shirk a tackle. And I'll tell you what, there were at least ten goals that should have been added to his career total. Time and again, he would be flagged offside simply because his movement was too quick for the eye of the linesman.

The hardest of all to take was in the 1962 European Cup semi-final against Benfica here [Bill waved a gnarled hand at the wall in the direction of nearby White Hart Lane] when he scored a perfectly good goal that was ruled offside. That broke all our hearts. We might have beaten Jock [Stein] and his great Celtic to become the first British team to win the European Cup. Jimmy had two great partnerships for us, first with Bobby Smith, who provided lots of muscle in making openings for Jimmy, and then with Alan Gilzean, one of the most elegant forwards I've ever clapped eyes on. Greavsie and Gilly together were like poetry in motion. I was hoping for a third one when I put Jim together with Martin Chivers, but by then he was only giving half his attention to the game. He was quite the businessman off the pitch, and that took the edge off his appetite for the game.'

‘ But even with half his concentration, he was still twice as good as any other goalscoring forward. It hurt like hell the day I decided to let him go in part exchange for Martin Peters. But as a manager, you often had to do things that hurt you inside but were necessary for the team and the club. Martin was another wonderfully gifted footballer, but completely different to Jim. Alf [Ramsey] described him as being ten years ahead of his time, and I knew exactly what he meant. He was an exceptional reader of the game, a bit like Danny and dear John White, and knew where to be before anybody else had spotted the gap.

Nothing's changed. The ball is still round and the game is still all about positioning. If you're not in the right place, then you're not going to be able to do the right thing. Positioning, positioning, positioning. The three Ps. Now Jimmy always knew where to be to make the most of a goalscoring opportunity. It came naturally to him. You couldn't teach it. Quite a few of his goals were tap-ins, and people said he was lucky. He made his own luck by being in the right place at the right time. '

There was always mutual respect between Jimmy and Bill, and when the club gave him a long overdue testimonial match Greavsie was first to volunteer to make an appearance, even though by then he was into his heavy drinking phase. Jim:

' Bill and I had a sort of father-son relationship. We had been closer than most players and manager since he spent a lot of time in Italy trying to sign me. Never once had a cross word with him. A few sulks on both sides, but not what you could call a serious row. I respected his football knowledge, which was second to none, but we never met eye to eye on what my role should be. He would have liked me to tackle back and become a defender when the ball was in Tottenham's half, but the way I saw it that would have meant me not being able to do my job properly, popping the ball into the net. Surely that is what the game should be all about. Scoring goals.

Bill used to let Eddie Baily do the "bad cop" bit and dear old Ed and I had some great slanging matches. People used to hear us having a good old ding-dong and get the impression that we hated each other. But Eddie was a Cockney geezer like me and for us a row was quickly settled by a handshake and a peace-making pint. Then it would be all off again the following week when Eddie – spokesman for Bill – would be on at me about my defensive responsibilities.

I had a lot of respect for Ed, even though at times I struggled to show it because he had a tongue like a claymore and never stopped cussing and cursing from the sidelines. Remember, I had watched him when I was a kid from the Tottenham terraces and he couldn't half play the game. Could land a ball on the proverbial sixpence from 30 yards. We would have got on great as players, but by the time he became the Spurs coach he had become really spiteful with his verbals. Bill was happy to let him be the hard man, but the messages he gave were, I know, from the boss. "Mark your man, Greaves!"

I wasn't happy at the way Bill handled my departure from Spurs, but let's be honest, he was spot on with his reading of me. I had definitely lost my appetite for the game, but I just wish I had told him that I was not interested in moving to West Ham. He caught me on the day we were moving house, and I didn't have my thinking head on. If I had been thinking straight, I would have followed Dave Mackay's advice and joined Cloughie at Derby. He would have given me the kick up the arse I needed. But I wanted to be near my businesses, which were taking off. I have 20/20 hindsight and now know that I should have taken my boots to the Baseball Ground, but at the time my judgement was blurred.

Lovely Joe Mercer also got a message to me urging me to join him and my old drinking pal Malcolm Allison up at Maine Road. Blimey, there was not enough Bollinger in Manchester for Big Mal and me.

Any way, off I trundled to Upton Park, where Ronnie Greenwood sweet-talked me into signing for West Ham. I had known Ron from my England Under-23 days when he was coach of the team, and always respected him, even though he could bore you to tears with what I considered tactical mumbo-jumbo. I joined West Ham in a bit of a daze and without giving the move the full consideration it deserved. It was very unprofessional of me, and I hold my hands up that I was entirely to blame. It was ridiculous fans having a go at Bill Nick. His main responsibility was doing what was right for Spurs. And, at that moment in time, I was not right for the club. The thought of playing – and drinking – with my best mate Mooro obviously had appeal, and I knew that I would have a class striking partner in Geoff Hurst, my old England sidekick. Geoff and I were never in each other's pockets, but we liked and respected each other. So I signed for West Ham. Now, looking back, I realise I had made another cock-up. Nice one, Jim. **'**

Chapter 13

Hammered with the Hammers

JIM HAD drunk for fun at Tottenham. At West Ham, it became more than a pasttime. Suddenly, drink was a necessity. Hammers manager Ron Greenwood knew that he liked a glass or three, but convinced himself he could rekindle his appetite for the game. He had been England Under-23s coach when young Jimmy was first making an impact and saw him at his blistering best. Ron knew he needed to appease the West Ham fans when he agreed to let Martin Peters go, and bringing Greavsie to Upton Park made him a hero in their eyes.

At Tottenham, the opposite was true. Many Spurs fans vowed they would never watch Tottenham play again and some openly admitted crying the day it was announced that Greavsie would be leaving for their despised near neighbours round the North Circular. Alan Mullery, Jimmy's old team-mate for club and country:

‘ We were completely gobsmacked when we heard that Jim had gone. It was great to have Martin joining us, but it seemed madness to let go the greatest British goalscorer I'd ever seen. I honestly thought Bill had lost it. Sure, Martin was special, but it sent a shudder through the club that we'd lost Greavsie. Bill should have put an arm around his shoulder and talked him round into trying to find his old form. Imagine if we'd had Martin *and* Jim operating together. Even playing badly, he was twice as good as most strikers. It was like watching a car crash involving a best friend as Jimmy went into his drinking phase. He cut off from us all and none of us realised how bad it had got until the newspapers got hold of it. It was as if a member of our family had landed in the gutter. The way he pulled himself together was nothing short of a miracle. Later on, I loved watching him on the box with the Saint. They were a great double act. I wonder how things would have mapped out if Jim had stayed at Tottenham. I'll never forget some of the goals he scored for us. I was so proud to have played with him and to be able to tell people that I was in the same team as a footballing genius. There will never be another like Jimmy Greaves. What a player! What a great bloke! The day he died, I don't mind admitting I cried. '

Jimmy's arrival at West Ham was greeted with incredulity by the football world, but when he scored two goals on his debut on a rain-soaked pitch against Manchester City at Maine Road, everybody thought Greenwood had pulled off the coup of the century. Jim:

' I was so thrilled with my debut that I insisted on wearing my West Ham shirt on the train journey home. Blimey, I'd never done that in all my years at Tottenham. Perhaps I started the replica football shirts craze! There were not many supporters wearing them back then and clubs had not cottoned on to how big a money-spinner it could be.

Sadly, banging in two in my debut and scoring in our derby at Spurs were just about the only highlights I enjoyed before losing myself in the bottle.

For somebody with what was slowly but surely becoming a drink problem, I could not have gone to a worse club than West Ham. They had a drinking school there that could have taken on the old Bell and Hare crew of Tottenham and possibly drunk them under the table. It would have been a close match and would no doubt have gone into extra time.

The regulars in the Hammers school were Mooro – like Dave Mackay, the king of the barstool – John Cushley, Brian Dear, Frank Lampard senior, John Charles, Harry Redknapp, Jimmy Lindsay and, occasionally, Geoff Hurst. I was quickly accepted into the school. I not only prided myself on my drinking capacity but also on always paying my way.

The difference between that West Ham team and the Spurs players I had left behind was that Tottenham could really turn it on where it mattered – on the pitch. I found that, with the obvious few exceptions like Mooro, Hurstie and young Billy Bonds, West Ham were heavily populated with mediocre players. That may sound tough but it is fact. And I must be honest and admit that in my time at West Ham, I could be placed in the mediocre bracket. They have little to thank me for apart from a handful of goals that helped save them from a relegation that at one stage in the season looked a certainty.

I had always promised myself that the moment I stopped enjoying my football, I would quickly hang up my boots. And from the start of that 1970/71 season with West Ham, I was thoroughly miserable about West Ham's game and my contribution to it. Even as early as the September of the season, I had seriously considered packing it in. That was after a terrible 4-1 defeat at Newcastle. Ron Greenwood told Mooro and me that he was considering resigning and my reaction was that if he went, I would go as well.

I was sickened and disgusted at the way the West Ham board – in particular Ron Greenwood – handled the Blackpool situation. They fined the four players involved in the late-night drinking and dropped us, and did it in the full glare of publicity. The story was plastered all over the front pages as if we had been guilty of the crime of the century.

We deserved to have disciplinary action taken against us but it could easily have been done privately. I was particularly nauseated by the treatment Bobby Moore got. No player has given more loyal service – and top-quality service, at that – than Bobby did to West Ham. Ron Greenwood allowed them to cut off his legs, while he got off without anybody mentioning that the defeat at Blackpool was mainly down to his stupid tactics. He was a master chess player with his tactical planning but sometimes forgot that footballers are humans, not robots.

I remember a classic training session at West Ham when he had us all wired up, so that he could give us instructions from the touchline. As he was into full flow with his complicated orders, the groundsman at the Chadwell Heath ground ran his tractor over the main microphone line and cut off Radio Greenwood in its prime. I think it was several hours before all we players stopped laughing.

This day apart, I was no longer enjoying my football and I was getting into an agitated state, but found that once I had got a few drinks inside me my concern and worry drifted away.

In my last few months at West Ham, I began to shift beer in bigger quantities than ever. After training at Chadwell Heath, I would go to Jack Slater's pub opposite Romford Greyhound Stadium and drink right through until closing time. Most evenings, I would prop up any number of bars near my Upminster home. Suddenly, football didn't matter to me any more. All I was interested in was drinking. Once I had five, six or seven lagers in me, I would get a click in my head and the world would seem a rosy place. '

I have already described the depths to which Jimmy sank, but I now want to concentrate on the climb back up that earned the astonished admiration of everybody who had watched his descent into alcoholism.

It all started with him being given a platform in *The Sun* by sports editor Frank Nicklin, a dynamic journalist who was the main driving force in the paper's remarkable rise as a tabloid after Rupert Murdoch had taken over as the bulldozing boss.

My fondest memory of Frank is when he and Fleet Street sports agency giant Reg Hayter were jointly running the El Vino's cricket team. These two loveable reprobates were inseparable at the bar and on the cricket pitch (always standing together at slip). Frank was notorious for picking sub-editors or reporters for *The Sun* who could play cricket to a good standard.

Back in the days when I was helping to establish Jimmy Greaves as a columnist, I negotiated for him to join *The Sun*. Frank was almost as interested in the fact that Jimmy had been a first-class wicketkeeper as he was in what he could bring to the paper with his football celebrity and insights.

We are talking the early 1980s and Frank put the arm on Jimmy to join the El Vino's team for a charity match somewhere in deepest Derbyshire, Frank's home county.

By then, Greavsie was becoming a huge star in the Midlands because of his regular appearances on ex-Hayters man Gary Newbon's Central TV sports show. His catchphrase 'It's a funny old game', had caught on and was hung on him at every opportunity, even though Jimmy insisted that I ghosted it into his mouth and that he never actually said it. Comedian Harry Enfield picked up on it and started using it for one of his characters, a Greavsie soundalike. He was stuck with it.

Jimmy and I drove to Derbyshire from Essex for the charity cricket match, a round trip of nearly 250 miles. Because of motorway hold-ups, we were in the car together for more than seven hours. In the middle of it all, Jimmy went in to bat for the Hayter/Nicklin team and was bowled middle stump first ball. As Jimmy trudged back to the pavilion after his golden duck, Reg Hayter – who had a distinctive stutter – said, for all to hear, 'It's a f-f-f-funny old game.'

Two punchlines to the story: Driving back through London, Jimmy's BMW – with me in the passenger seat – was smashed into by a London bus. I had to separate a fuming Jimmy from the bus driver.

A few days later, Jimmy received in the post the local Derbyshire newspaper. The huge headline running across seven columns in the broadsheet read, 'GREAVSIE FLOPS WITH A DUCK'.

'Eff me,' said Greavsie, 'that's a bigger headline than I ever got for anything I did on the football pitch.'

Yes, a f-f-f-funny old game.

The platform in *The Sun* set the ball rolling for Jimmy's broadcasting career. First Central TV and TV-am followed by *Saint and Greavsie*, and all the time people who had known the drunken Jim were waiting for him to fall off the wagon. Jim:

‘ I knew all eyes were on me and those who had seen me at my rock bottom were convinced I would be back on the booze. Let's be honest, it was odds-on that they would be proved right. I had to go through all the withdrawal symptoms but it was Irene who kept me straight. She had seen me at my worst and quite rightly kicked me out. With me not knowing what day it was, she took power of attorney over my businesses and sorted out that mess. Somehow, she also found time to become a qualified nurse while bringing up our four kids. She deserved a gold medal. Yes, quite a girl, my Irene. '

Chapter 14:

Rising with the Sun

THE FIRST thing I did to help put shape and purpose back into Jimmy's life as he came out of his alcoholic mist was to negotiate a weekly slot in the top-selling *Sun*, a hard-hitting yet humorous column I ghosted in my new role as a freelance. It was easy to sell him to the paper's sports editor Frank Nicklin, a larger-than-life character who loved Jim and had newsprint for blood. He took Jim on at a then whacking £200 a column on the understanding that batsman/wicketkeeper Greavsie would play for his El Vino's cricket team. Remember that £200 was more than he earned in a week at the peak of his football playing career.

Let me say right here and now before I strangle myself with my halo that I was helping myself as well as Jim. I had tunnelled my way out of the *Daily Express* and was now earning my bread and butter as a television scriptwriter for *This Is Your Life* and as a boxing PR for the major British fighters managed by my closest friend Terry Lawless, including world champions Jim Watt, John H. Stracey, Maurice Hope, Charlie Magri and the irrepressible Frank Bruno. All were Greavsie fans and Jim loved going to the Royal Oak gymnasium in Canning Town to meet them. It made him feel wanted again. Every footballer I've ever known enjoys being around other sportsmen, tasting the dressing-room atmosphere and banter and the club camaraderie. They miss that as much as the action when they have retired. There was this spirit and ambience in buckets at the Royal Oak, and Jim breathed it in as if taking a much-needed drink.

Terry Lawless in particular was a big influence in helping Jimmy rediscover his self-belief. A born philosopher and motivator, Terry was used to dealing with champions and their doubts and fears – and they all have them, believe me. He convinced Jimmy he should be walking tall; he was a footballer like no other and a man people looked up to for what he had achieved for club and country. 'You're my hero and I know thousands of people share my opinion,' he told Jim one day when we were in a West Ham cafe killing time. 'One thing's for sure, you will never find the answer to any problems in the bottom of a glass, only more problems. Get your head up, Jim, and be proud. You are a master.'

That's how Terry used to talk to his boxers and make them feel special. Now he had Jimmy feeling like a champion again. Terry introduced him to his latest heavyweight hope, a youngster by the name of Frank Bruno. Who would have thought that ten years later they would play side by side in Jimmy's final football match, a testimonial at Southend United for his son Danny?

He started to get his confidence back, driven by the promise from Irene that provided he stayed sober he could make regular visits to see his four much-loved children, Lynn, Mitzi, Danny and Andy. 'Drunk,' said Irene, 'and you will get the door slammed in your face.' He was close to getting his life back together but still needed new challenges to take his mind off the booze.

Jim dabbled with selling insurance as an associate with Abbey Life, and under the tutelage of Paul Revere teamed up with dutiful daughter Lynn and reliable Malcolm Rowley in a policy-selling sideline. But his *Sun* column had made him itch to be heard and I knew just the man who could open doors for him.

A television sports columnist at the time, I was tipped off that Central TV (then still ATV) were hunting for a football pundit, and so I rang our old friend Billy Wright, the former England football captain and Arsenal manager, who had become their head of sport. I had been Billy's ghostwriter when he was in charge at Highbury and wrote a couple books with him. I suggested Jimmy would be ideal for his Midlands television team, but Billy – who had famously been given a chasing by Jimmy in his last season of league football – was wary of his reputation as a drunk. How ironic that down the line Billy's wife, Joy, of Beverley Sisters fame, would quietly approach Jim to ask him to help Billy with his drink problem!

At an urgent editorial meeting, Billy was persuaded by producer Tony Flanagan, presenter Gary Newbon and executive Trevor East that Jim was the right man for the Birmingham-based job, even though he would be a Cockney operating in the heart of the Midlands. 'I would stand out like a sore bum,' said Jim, deliberately avoiding 'thumb'.

It was the indefatigable Tony Flanagan who did most to talk Billy round to getting Jimmy on board. He made Billy read the column I was ghosting in *The Sun*, in which Jim and I had set out to deliberately shock with views that were aimed at puncturing egos and making people laugh. Gary Newbon played a recording of Bernie Stringle's *Just for Today* documentary and said to Billy, 'He looks comfortable in front of a camera. Let's go for it.'

So it was that Trevor East – who was to become vastly influential in the satellite TV sports world – telephoned Jim and offered him the position of resident pundit on the Central TV flagship football show *Star Soccer*. To the amazement of all of us, he turned it down.

In truth, he was frightened of it. 'I don't want the responsibility,' he told me privately. 'I got away with waffling on that Berny Stringle programme because it wasn't live and they could edit out

RISING WITH THE SUN

my mistakes. Imagine what the critics would do to me if I fucked up live on air. They'd be saying, "Greavsie's on the piss again."'

All this coincided with Jimmy being allowed back not only into the family home but into the bedroom. He had passed Irene's strict 'sober-or-else' examination, and they carried on with their marriage as if the divorce hadn't happened. Irene and my now sadly late wife Eileen became close friends and the Greaves-Giller bond was cemented.

Jimmy, battling against withdrawal symptoms, was still low on confidence and it was Irene who became his rock and guiding light. A very special lady, and a great advertisement for the East End, where we both grew up, it was Irene who astutely made Jim see the sense of joining Central TV.

Gary Newbon, the hugely popular front man for the Central TV sports team, said:

‘ We were disappointed Jimmy gave us a knock-back and were urgently seeking an expert pundit to sit alongside me when Jim phoned us back. "Is it too late to change my mind?" he asked in that distinctive, almost whining Cockney voice of his. "I've had a word with Irene and she says I've got to get off my arse, get up the M1 and take the job." This showed just what an influence Irene had on him. He would always admit he was half the man without her.

Signing him was the best decision we made. He worked with us for nearly 20 years and often said it was the most satisfying time of his life, and that included his football career. None of us knew just how witty he could be. I remember early on he said on air of Italian hardman Marco Tardelli that he was responsible for more scar tissue than Harefield Hospital. That's when I realised we had discovered a diamond. Somebody who could offer expert football punditry and make you laugh at the same time. Rare as hen's teeth. And when you analyse it, it was all coming from a man who had been there, done that. Nobody played the game better than Jim, and nobody could match his blistering wit on TV. Many people watched him thinking what a funny bloke he was, without any idea that he had been one of the greats of the game.

I'm glad you're doing a warts 'n' all book because Jim wouldn't have wanted you painting him as some sort of angel. He could be stupidly stubborn and we had some real wars behind the scenes and even occasionally on camera. Jim was often argumentative to the point where you wanted to strangle him, and he would never concede an inch. But he didn't bear grudges and we'd shake hands and get on with the job, and once that red light glowed on the camera he was a master communicator. There'll never be another like him. '

Soon after he cut his television teeth in the Midlands, I saw an opening for Jim that would give him a national platform and again I had the perfect contact.

Several years earlier, Greg Dyke had been a stringer journalist selling page fillers about Brentford to me on the *Daily Express* as 'Dyke of Uxbridge'. He disappeared off my radar screen to remerge as 'Dyke of LWT', masterminding the groundbreaking *Six O'Clock Show* with the Greaves-like Danny Baker after earning himself a BA in politics as a mature student at York University.

Next, he was brought in – along with Roland Rat – as saviour of the ailing TV-am, the breakfast television station that was buckling on the brink of bankruptcy. I approached him with the suggestion that Jimmy could join his team as the resident sports pundit. Greg called us to a meeting at TV-am headquarters at Egg Cup Towers at Camden Lock, and this is how the conversation went (Jimmy was suited and booted for his job interview, while Greg was dressed all in blue denim with an open-neck shirt, looking more like a country and western singer than the high-powered boss of a TV station. He was also sitting on a desk rather than in a chair.):

‘ You definitely off the piss, Jim?’

'As definite as I can be. Been dry for several months and have no intention of going back to my bad habits. Just must never take that next drink.'

'You'll feel at home in television. There are more pissheads in our business than in football club boardrooms.'

'That's a lot of drunks. I've often said that football clubs are run by a cabinet – the drinks cabinet.'

'Got disappointing news for you, Jim. I've appointed Mike Morris as our sports correspondent, with young Richard Keys as his deputy. But I think I've got just the job for you. What d'you know about television? The programmes, that is.'

'Well, I watch the box until the dot goes off the screen.'

'Just the job. You can be our TV-am television critic. ’

And that is exactly how Jimmy's TV-am career started. He was paired with brilliant showbiz journalist Joe Steeples, who did all the research and suggested what themes to take. In no time, Jimmy was matching the rodent puppet Roland Rat as the station's most compelling star with opinions and comments that crackled. He worked alongside the sunny, ultra-professional presenters Anne Diamond and Nick Owen, two of his former colleagues from Central. Nick recalls:

‘ Jimmy made for riveting television. None of us were quite sure what he was going to say, including I suspect

Jimmy himself. He never worked from an autocue, so everything was coming off the top of his head. Jim could be an awkward cuss because he would never rehearse and there were quite a few battles with the producers off camera. But he was sizzling in front of the camera and made a great career for himself, which was extraordinary when you think what he had earlier achieved on the football field. I recall hesitantly asking if he would mind having a word with a close friend of mine, who was drinking himself towards an early grave. Good as gold, he went out of his way to help him with advice that turned his life around. He did it all quietly and without ever becoming the big I-am. I greatly admired him, both as a supreme footballer and as a TV colleague. Everybody loved Jim. '

So suddenly Jim had a foot in two TV camps. This is how he recalled those early days on the box in an article we wrote together while he was climbing the television ladder in his new career:

' The first person I was introduced to by the garrulous Gary Newbon on arriving very nervously at the ATV studios in Birmingham was the football reporter who would be working on the *Star Soccer* show with us. He was a young, fresh-faced journalist called Nick Owen, who had recently arrived in television after collecting a BA honours degree in classics at Leeds University. In the nearby newsroom, a pretty presenter was preparing her script ready for the local round-up of news. She was Anne Diamond. The three of us had no idea that we were destined one day in the future to come together with an as yet unborn television company, and in circumstances of high drama and often high farce.

Next on the tour of my new stamping ground, I was reunited with executive sports chief Billy Wright, my first captain when I made my England debut during what seemed a lifetime ago. I played with Billy in the last three of his 105 international appearances for England in the days when he was the blond idol of football. He had skippered England across an incredible stretch of 90 matches, and had been the Black Country rock on which Wolves had built a legend of invincibility during their golden days of the 1950s. At the end of his distinguished playing career, Billy had wrestled unhappily with management at Arsenal before going into television management, where you don't have to collect points every week to satisfy directors and spectators.

Somebody unkindly reminded Billy that at the back end of his career I had got lucky and banged in five goals against him for Chelsea when Wolves were rated the mightiest club around. Dear old Billy then told this story against himself, "I played hundreds of matches during my career, captained England and won 105 caps, skippered three championship-winning sides and lifted the FA Cup. But the only three things I seem to be remembered for are skippering the side beaten by the United States in the 1950 World Cup, being beaten all ends up when Puskas scored a magnificent goal in Hungary's 6-3 win at Wembley, and continually tackling Jimmy's shadow when he nipped in for five goals against Wolves in my last season as a player."

"It's a funny old game, Bill," I said.

Billy showed a few years later that he had not lost the iron will that made him such a great footballer and magnificent ambassador for the game and our country. He managed very quietly to beat the sort of booze problem that would have cut down lesser men. It was his greatest victory, and I know that his lovely wife – Joy of the Beverly Sisters – was delighted to get her old Billy back after making a quiet approach to me for some confidential advice. I had become the go-to man for people with drink problems.

I appeared on Billy's *This is Your Life* tribute programme with the Saint, and while I made some tongue-in-cheek remarks about him rather than the usual syrupy comments, I was full of admiration for the way he had got himself together and was once again the shining hero. Well done, Bill, old pal.

The surprise fly-in guest winding up the show was legendary Russian goalkeeper Lev Yashin, who had stopped three certain goals from me at Wembley in 1963 in England's match against the Rest of the World. What a shock it was to see how time had treated him. He looked ravaged after what had been a Billy-style battle with the bottle, and the price he had paid was having a leg amputated. Within a couple of months of the programme, the greatest of all goalkeepers had died.

My first couple of appearances as football analyst on *Star Soccer* were worthy of a Monty Python sketch. If there was a wrong camera to look at, I looked at it. If there was a time when not to speak, I spoke. If there was some grammar what was to be mangled, I mangled it. I was in awe of the way Gary Newbon and Nick Owen read their autocue scripts with a casual ease. It made me realise just how naive I was about television. I had always been one of those viewers convinced that [the] people looking out at me from the 20-inch screen were talking directly to me with a full grasp of what they were saying. I marvelled at how they were able to remember everything and talk with such authority while being watched by an audience of millions.

But I quickly learned when I was on the other side of the camera that most of them are nodding and smiling at a screen that automatically reflects their words that have been carefully scripted before they go on air. Just thinking about the autocue, and the possibility of being asked to use it, made me break into a sweat.

I need to back track here to explain my fear of the autocue. When I left Kingswood secondary school at the age of 15 to start my football apprenticeship with Chelsea in the spring of 1955, I went against the advice and wishes of my schoolteachers. I had just been made head boy of the school, and I was considered a good candidate for advanced education despite the fact that I was a tortoise when it came to reading. It used to take me twice as long as anybody else to plough through a text book, but I still managed to scramble through for good all-round results in my exams. Sport took my main concentration, and when I found out that I would be too old to gain Essex schools representative honours at cricket during the summer term, I decided to accept the offer to join Chelsea and I left school at Easter.

My parents were delighted with my progress as a footballer, particularly as my lovely old dad was able to cop a hush-hush backhander of 50 quid in Irish notes in return for me agreeing to sign for Chelsea. Happy days! I had a brother and sister, Marion and Paul, both bright enough to get teaching diplomas, but all I had to show for my schooling was a final report that I could read only slowly.

In those days, nobody had ever heard of dyslexia. Dixie Dean, maybe. But dyslexia? It sounds like some sort of genital disease deserving of a Government health warning. It was Irene – who else? – who worked out that my problem was word blindness, and she has helped me and encouraged me to overcome it by slow, painstaking reading. But even now, I can get words back to front when I try to read quickly. So that is why I was terrified of the autocue. I am much happier making keyword notes for myself, jotting down one word or a short phrase that will bring to my mind an entire sentence. I would not recognise a split infinitive if you served it to me on a plate, but I do try to avoid cliches like the plague. I know that I continue to occasionally murder the Queen's English, but – let's be honest – the royal brigade sometimes trample on Greavsie's English with their hizes instead of houses, lynges instead of lounges and pynds instead of pounds. Okay, yah?

Gary Newbon protected me like a mother hen, and I have him to thank for steering me through my early appearances on *Star Soccer* and the Friday evening preview programmes. I was convinced I was going to be politely asked to leave after my first few weeks, and I kept open my options to stay in the insurance business with oldest daughter Lynn as my organiser.

The big mistake I made in my first couple of shows was trying to ape the likes of Jimmy Hill and Malcolm Allison, discussing tactics and technique. What I was trying to say went over my head, let alone that of any viewer. Anybody who knew me in my playing days will tell you that I am to tactics what Richard Nixon was to tape editing. I have always talked about the game in simplistic terms. It's a simple game and is complicated only by coaches who disappear up their rear end with their hocus-pocus that baffles players and leads to so much of the dull, sterile play that we witness today.

In my third appearance, by which time I had started to conquer my nerves, I was relaxed enough to talk about the game exactly as I would if I was standing on the terraces. There was an obvious offside goal that was allowed to stand, and I said, "Blimey, if I'd scored that one I would have kissed the ref. And if I'd been in the opposing team, I would've told the linesman where to stick his flag."

It just came out naturally. Gary Newbon laughed out loud and the technicians on the studio floor were also falling about laughing. I knew I had found my level. Try to make the viewers laugh while informing them. Much better than lecturing and pontificating.

From then on, my television career was up and running and I found out just what a powerful medium it is. I could not walk anywhere in the Midlands without being mobbed by people wanting to pump my hand. I had known nothing like it, even when I was knocking goals in at the peak of my playing days. I don't say this in praise of myself but just to illustrate the reaction you get when you become a regular on the small screen. I was determined not to become affected by the sudden adulation that dwarfed anything I had known as a player, but there are plenty of people in television who will tell you that it went to my head.

Even the press were nice to me. "Jimmy Greaves has brought something almost unheard of to football punditry – a sense of humour," said the *Sunday Times*. "Greavsie is the cheeky chappie of TV sport who has brought a rare and much-needed smile to the sad face of soccer," said *The Sun*. "He is irreverent, savagely honest, often hilarious and sometimes bordering on the irresponsible, which makes his act compulsive viewing and certainly more entertaining than the football that he is analysing," said the *Mail*.

I never used to read reports of the matches in which I played, but I did read the television critics – not because

I was seeking praise but so that I could learn from any constructive criticism about a world that was foreign to me. There was the occasional kick in the shins ("Jimmy Greaves sounds as if he has taken elocution lessons from Alf Garnett"), but on the whole I came out of it unscathed and I was encouraged to step up my sort of "voice of the people" approach to football. Looking back at video tape recordings of my early appearances, my face appeared as miserable as an untidy grave, and I was glad of the advice of Central fishing expert Terry Thomas, who told me, "Loosen up and smile, Jimmy. You've got a smile that lights up the screen. People don't want to switch on and see you looking like an undertaker."

So I started smiling along with the wisecracks, which prompted one sports page critic, who thought I was treating football with less reverence than it deserved, to write, "Why doesn't Greaves go the whole way and put on a clown's suit? He was one of the all-time great footballers, but now all he can do is poke fun at the game to which he owes so much."

This particular writer, who reported many of my matches, obviously did not get to know me. Even during my playing days, I used to send up the game and the people in it who I thought were taking it too seriously. My casual attitude used to drive theorists like Walter Winterbottom, Alf Ramsey, Bill Nicholson and Ron Greenwood up the wall. I will always maintain that football should be fun, and if the coaches who have got a stranglehold on the game would only loosen up and let the players express themselves as entertainers, our soccer – both at international and domestic level – would be all the better for it [ends boring football lecture].

Once I had the reputation for being funny, my job became tougher and I was conscious of *trying* to be funny instead of letting any wisecracks come naturally. But in those early days on *Star Soccer*, I thoroughly enjoyed myself. I quickly settled into a routine at what morphed from ATV into Central Television, and felt at home at the office where there was the sort of dressing room type of camaraderie I had known as a player. Gary Newbon became my good friend and I became his trusted confidant even though I used him unmercifully as the butt of many of my jokes. Once while on air, I held up a book that I was going to present to him. It was called *The Fat Pig's Story*. Within a couple of years we were calling each other much worse than that, and meaning it.

I had not lost my thirst for drink and I became known as "the tea boy" at Central because I planted myself by the tea-making machine and got through at least 20 cups a day. I told Gary that I preferred coffee and he thoughtfully had a coffee machine installed in the office for me. Sadly, there would come the day when he would have willingly made it an arsenic machine. "Make us a cup, Greavsie," became a familiar cry at Central as everybody – from executives, presenters, secretaries and crew – used to queue waiting for me to provide them with tea or coffee. It also became part of my routine to go out every Saturday evening to the Cheung Yin restaurant to get a massive takeaway order for the team working on the late-night *Star Soccer* show. This went on for months until we got a written complaint from the head of security saying that leaving the remains of our Chinese food in the office had led to an invasion of mice. We were ordered to stop bringing the food into the office. I sent a spoof reply back to the security chief that read,

"We shall be reporting you to the European commission for mice rights. By banning the Chinese takeaway binge, you are depriving our children of nourishment. Be nice to the mice!" I signed it Mickey and Minnie Mouse.

I was not popular with everybody at Central. I arrived one Friday evening for the preview show and after parking my car went to pat the head of the car park attendant's dog, which responded by biting me. From then on, I called it Norman Hunter.

My first season with the *Star Soccer* team went so well that I was given a larger canvas, and I started to contribute a regular feature called *The Greaves Report*, in which I took an off-beat look at sport. I played tennis with my fellow left-hander John McEnroe (who was a real charmer and nothing like his superbrat image), faced Bob Willis bowling flat out (I actually managed to see a couple of the balls), wrestled with Kendo Nagasaki (and found out a whole new meaning to horizontal hold), played bowls, croquet, tried arm wrestling (but quickly gave it the elbow), went fishing, motor cycled with Barry Sheene, actually got Sebastian Coe to stand still for a chat, hit double tops with Eric Bristow, played squash with Jonah Barrington and won a charity camel race by a head from Grand National hero Bob Champion.

I also gave the first out-of-the-ring television exposure to an up-and-coming young heavyweight called Frank Bruno. I drove him up to Birmingham in a powerful Mercedes owned by his manager Terry Lawless. On the way, I explained to Frank that I wanted him to put the gloves on and spar with me in a local gymnasium while I interviewed him.

The sparring session would have made a great sketch for a comedy show. Frank is six inches taller than me and

I was having trouble getting past his long arms to ask my questions. In those early days in his career muscular Frank was weighing about 15 stone, and I had ballooned up from my playing days weight of 10st 7lbs to around 13 stone. I was a welterweight masquerading in an out-of-condition heavyweight's body. Director Syd Kilby's plan was that I should "fight" my way inside Frank's reach and put a question each time I got to close quarters. Syd didn't realise the effort and energy you use just when sparring, particularly against a giant like Bruno. Each time I fought my way close enough to ask a question, I was breathing like a wounded bull.

I would start the interview and then the sound man would interrupt and say, "All I can hear is Greavsie's heavy breathing." "You could sell the soundtrack for a bleedin' blue movie," I said between gasps for air.

After about six tries, it was left to Jim to fix it. I told director Syd Kilby to forget about the sparring, and I said to Bruno, "I'll tell you what, Frank, you rest against the ropes in the corner and I'll interview you there."

A pity the cameras didn't follow us back down the motorway when we left Birmingham. We stopped off at a service station for a bite to eat and we had the place in uproar. I kept going up to the biggest, toughest lorry drivers I could find and challenging them to a fight. Then I'd point at Frank and say, "I think you should know that I'll be bringing on a sub."

The biggest laugh of the day was on me. Frank filled three trays with food and I was left to pay the bill.

We had a return match a year later and that was even funnier, even though my eyes water at the memory. By then, I was doing a regular enjoyable stint on the *Saturday Show* hosted by Tommy Boyd and Isla St Clair. I had learned from our first meeting in front of the cameras and this time I rehearsed the interview with Frank before our "live" sparring session. I worked it out with him that I would ask a question and then lightly hit him with three pulled punches. Bang, bang, bang.

Then Frank would reply and hit me with three light punches. Bang, bang, bang.

We got a nice rhythm going at rehearsal. Question – bang, bang, bang. Answer – bang, bang, bang.

Then we went "live" with the interview in the middle of a ring in the studio and Frank suddenly froze with the sort of camera fright that many, me included, had experienced before him.

I asked my first question and lightly hit Frank with three punches. He replied and lightly landed his three punches. I asked my second question and he replied, and we gradually got into the rhythm. By the time of my fifth question Frank began to relax, but somehow managed to get out of synchronisation.

I asked my question – bang, bang, bang. Instead of replying as we had agreed, Frank landed three punches that were twice as hard as usual and caught me completely unawares. My knees buckled and I fell forward into Frank's arms with my head spinning and water streaming from my eyes.

The studio crew were all folded up laughing off camera as I somehow managed to get through the interview. I got myself locked into a close-quarter clinch rather than risk taking any more out-of-time punches.

My first breakthrough on to network television came during the 1982 World Cup finals when I was invited to be a member of the ITV panel under the chairmanship of Brian Moore. The World Cup panels had first been introduced during the 1970 finals when the likes of Malcolm Allison, Derek Dougan, Pat Crerand and Bob McNab became household names by mouthing off about the lads sweating it out on the pitches in the heat and thin air of Mexico. I detested their pontificating, and thought they made right wallies of themselves. Now here I was becoming one of them.

So I took my opinions on to the ITV panel under the conscientious control of Brian Moore, one of the best pros in the business and as contrasting to me as it is possible to be. Mooro is sober, refined, articulate, organised, well-informed, in total control of his thoughts and deeds – an out-and-out perfectionist who is a credit to his profession. We have a mutual respect for each other even though I sometimes manage to get up Brian's nose with my casual, laid-back attitude. As chairman of the World Cup panel, he was in charge of a posse of outspoken football rebels, including George Best, Jack Charlton, Mike Channon, Denis Law, Ian St John and, the big daddy of the pundits, Brian Clough. Somehow Mooro kept us under some sort of control as we attempted to turn the World Cup into a foot-in-mouth tournament.

It was like a game of musical chairs in the studio, with panellists queueing for places on the set to condemn, crucify, compliment and occasionally cheer the players and managers struggling for success in Spain. It was easy to play a blinder in the studio. I managed to pick eventual winners Italy from the first day as the likely champions, and could have eaten free meals for life in England's multitude of Italian restaurants, where every waiter and every chef is a soccer nut.

The craziest thing of all was having George Best sitting in the studio in London with us watching his former Irish international team-mates progressing to the quarter-finals. They would have done even better had they had the sense to select George, who was looking trim and fit following two seasons in the USA. Bestie is the greatest footballer of my lifetime, and I include the likes of Pelé, Di Stefano, Puskas, Eusebio, Maradona, Cruyff, Matthews and Finney in that assessment. Even if he had been half fit, he would have been worth his place in the Irish squad and it was beyond my comprehension that they had ignored him.

I had a lot of time to talk to George, who is one of the nicest blokes you could wish to meet. Like me, he has had problems with booze and has occasionally fallen back into the arms of the bottle. We agreed that the then Tottenham star Glenn Hoddle and United skipper Bryan Robson were the only modern-day English footballers who would rate in the class of the great players of our era, and we were both of the opinion that all coaches should be locked in a huge stadium where they could bore each other to death with their tactical theories. The biggest change in the game since finishing our league careers was, we decided, the emergence of 'personality' managers. They had become bigger than the game and were better known than the players, which we agreed was a bad thing for football.

The biggest of the personalities, of course, was on the World Cup panel with us – Cloughie – but both George and I were of the opinion that his saving grace was that he could really manage and was able to put action where his mouth is. Cloughie was subdued with his views in comparison with previous television appearances, but was still the man viewers switched on to see and hear.

I was allowed the last word on the 1982 World Cup and almost gave Mooro a heart attack when I said, "These finals have all been about long balls, short balls, square balls, through balls, high balls, low balls, and to you, Brian, I would just like to say it's been a [deliberate pause] pleasure being here on the panel."

My stock shot up after my World Cup appearances and I was lucky enough to get a good press nationwide. My performances came as a surprise to most people, who did not realise I had been serving an apprenticeship in the television game with Central. I knew I must have made an impact because suddenly the demand for interviews and personal appearances quadrupled. I had also made my mark with the chiefs of ITV Sport and I was rewarded with a regular spot on *World of Sport*, linking up "live" with Ian St John in *On the Ball* from my base in Birmingham. This laid the foundation for what was to become the *Saint and Greavsie* show.

And while this was all going on, the forces of fate were working to bring Anne Diamond, Nick Owen and me together in the unlikely setting of Camden Lock. We were about to have indigestion for breakfast. ❜

Chapter 15

The TV-am Soap Opera

JIMMY AND I collaborated together on 20 books and scores – the operative word – of newspaper and magazine articles. None was more harrowing and hilarious than his recounting of his experiences at TV-am, which needs a history lesson on the arrival and survival of the station on our screens in the early 1980s. This was how Jimmy recalled the incredible experience to me in an interview 30 years ago:

‘ If a scriptwriter were to put down on paper the off-camera events and shenanigans at TV-am since the company's birth, he would have a soap opera to match *Dallas* or *Dynasty*, a farce suitable for the *Carry On* series, great drama of Shakespearian proportions and, finally, a story of an incredible triumph against all the odds. TV-am or not TV-am: that was the question when I arrived in May 1983 just ahead of the London Electricity Board representative, who gave the ultimatum that if the electricity bill was not paid within half an hour, he would cut off the supply to the studios. TV-am came that close to a total black-out.

I got a ringside seat for the greatest TV show on earth thanks (or no thanks) to my pal Norman Giller, who told new chief Greg Dyke that I was the ideal man to present a hard-hitting sports opinion column of the air. Greg was newly arrived from LWT with the simple brief to save TV-am from the knacker's yard in the wake of the "Famous Five". With the eccentricity that accompanied his career, Greg appointed me the TV-am television critic. "All I ask of you is that you do it with a bit of humour. No over-the-head highbrow stuff. We're looking to go down market."

"That's very flattering of you," I chuckled. "You can't get much more down market than me. "No offence, Jim," said Greg, who had so much energy pouring out of him that they could have plugged him into the mains and not had to worry about an electricity bill. "I want us to become *The Sun* of the air, not the toffee-nosed *Telegraph* like the other lot made it."

The "other lot" were the TV-am all-star founders who had become flounders as the channel headed towards bankruptcy. The "Famous Five" who had won the franchise were Michael Parkinson, David Frost, Angela Rippon, Anna Ford and Robert Kee. Esther Rantzen pulled out at the last minute "to concentrate on motherhood".

Within minutes of Greg giving me the job, Michael Parkinson, one of the survivors of "the other lot', walked into the office. He and his wife Mary were holding the fort on air before going off to Australia for a summer break. "Jimmy's joining us," said Greg.

"Marvellous," said Parky. "Our sports coverage could do with some beefing up."

"He's going to be our television critic," said Greg.

"Oh, I see," said Parky, his eyes clouding over. "That's, uh, very interesting."

Greavsie becoming the television critic for *Good Morning Britain* must have made as much sense to him as Freddie Trueman reading the news. As one of the founders of TV-am, Parky had been under enormous pressure in the previous few weeks and looked shell-shocked and in need of that trip Down Under.

Parky had been a leading member of the ambitious TV-am consortium which was awarded the lucrative breakfast television franchise by the Independent Broadcasting Authority in December 1980. From day one, these giants of the television world were drowning in a sea of inefficiency and egotism.

I switched on for the launching of TV-am on the morning of 1 February 1983. There was the magnificent aerial shot of hundreds of people forming the *Good Morning Britain* opening title (so good that it survived all of TV-am's revolutions), and then there was the familiar face of Frostie. "Hello, good morning and welcome," he said. It was a nice, warm, friendly start and from there on it was downhill all the way.

Items were being presented as if they were carved in stone and brought down direct from Mount Sinai. It was all too heavy and formal and I, along with thousands of others, quickly switched over to the BBC, where Frank Bough and Selina Scott had been comfortably established for three weeks with their *Breakfast Time* show.

Within a month, the "Famous Five" had an audience that had dwindled to 300,000 and by the middle of March they had so few viewers that the programme was officially zero-rated. BBC's figures had gone up to 1.6 million and among the scores of jokes buzzing around was that TV-am were going to change the name of their programme from *Good Morning Britain* to *Is There Anybody Out There?*

It was no laughing matter for the 'Famous Five' and with advertisers reluctant to spend any money, there was suddenly a serious financial crisis looming. Peter Jay resigned and was replaced as temporary chief executive by Jonathan Aitken MP.

In April 1983, Angela Rippon and Anna Ford departed in such a blaze of publicity that it's a wonder Egg Cup Towers didn't burn down. Angry Anna Ford faced rival cameras and said, "There's been a great deal of treachery going on behind our backs." She then got some sort of satisfaction by throwing a glass of white wine in Jonathan Aitken's face during a private party. All that was missing was JR and his stetson and the well-oiled Sue-Ellen. Jim:

'Greg Dyke, described as a "37-year-old whizz kid", took over as editor-in-chief and I was among his first signings along with keep-fit expert "Mad" Lizzie Webb and weather wise Wincey Willis. My old Birmingham side-kick Nick Owen, who had joined the original TV-am team as a sports presenter, was about to be promoted to full-time couch duty while Parky was in Australia, with Henry Kelly joining as a co-presenter. The enthusiastic Mike Morris would step into Nick's sports shoes, with a young sports reporter called Richard Keys coming in as his deputy.

Dykie then made his two most inspired signings. "You worked at Central when Anne Diamond was there, didn't you," he said to me one day. "What d'you think of her?"

"Very pretty, very professional," I said. "One of the best presenters I've seen."

By then, Anne had joined the BBC in London, and a week later Dykie announced that he had signed her for the TV-am team. "I didn't want to come," she said later. "I was very content at the BBC and at that time TV-am was a laughing stock. But Greg called me a coward and said I was frightened of what was the last great television challenge.

It was the force of his personality and his sheer enthusiasm that persuaded me to give it a go."

I was less impressed when Dykie announced that he had also signed a small felt puppet answering to the name of Roland Rat. Dave Claridge, who had a big hand in the 'orrible rodent's rise from the gutter, brought Roland to TV-am to entertain the younger viewers.

Thanks largely to Greg Dyke's policy of concentrating on "popular" television, TV-am started to close the gap on BBC's *Breakfast Time* and in less than a year we had overhauled them in the ratings. But our self-congratulations were rather muted because everybody was giving the credit to Roland bloody Rat for increasing our share of the audience. One rival across at the Beeb said, "It's the first time a rat has come to the aid of a sinking ship."

I preferred to think the improvement in ratings was due to the excellent presenting standards being set by Anne Diamond and Nick Owen. They had a good "made-in-Brum" chemistry between them, and their interviewing technique made guests relax and come up with fascinating answers to questions that were probing without being prying

My job on the sofa was made much easier by the back-up work of top show business journalist Joe Steeples, who did all the research for me and selected the clips of programmes that I was previewing. In January 1984, our news output was given a boost by the arrival of that master of newsreaders, Gordon Honeycombe.

As well as *Good Morning Britain* was doing in the ratings war, the channel was losing money in a spectacular and worrying way. It was pouring away like blood out of a gaping wound. I was having to wait weeks, sometimes months, for my fees and full-time staff members had to agree to take "voluntary" pay cuts. Losses had spiralled to £12 million a year, and Camden Lock was running deep with rumours that the station was only weeks, perhaps days, from being closed down.

Timothy Aitken took over from his cousin, Jonathan, as chairman of the ailing company, and Greg Dyke moved on to new pastures after just over a year of miracle working. Most of his ideas were winners, and the only time he was threatened with a staff mutiny was when he had the presenters reading out the bingo numbers from the newspapers. They will tell you that it was the lowest spot in their television careers.

Greg could point with understandable pride to the fact that by the time he quit, he had built up the audience from 200,000 to around 1.5 million. This was the foundation on which the company was to build its success out of the wreckage of near disaster. Greg later became the boss of London Weekend Television, where he had first made a major impact as producer of the innovative *Six O'Clock Show*. It was Greg who masterminded the ITV takeover of league football, putting together the idea for the imaginative package of "live" matches. Even now, I bet he misses our regular games of indoor football with a Sellotaped paper ball in the TV-am corridors. We miss his Matthews-style runs (Jessie Matthews, that is) and his kisses and cuddles whenever he scored. Fortunately, it was not very often.

A new force in the slim, immaculately groomed shape of Bruce Gyngell was about to blow like a hurricane through the TV-am corridors of power. If he wanted to play with the ball, we would have to change to Aussie-rules football.

The amazing "Pink Panther" of the antipodes was about to pounce, and TV-am would never be the same again.

If there is a more enterprising, energetic and eccentric man in the world of television than Bruce Gyngell, then I have not come across him. From the second he waltzed like a fire-breathing Matilda into Egg Cup Towers, he was what is known in modern jargon as a "hands on" manager. He came in as managing director, but soon had his hands on every control button in the building, and this triggered a "hands off" reaction from Greg Dyke, who made his exit shortly after Gyngell's arrival. Greg was soon followed by director of programmes Mike Hollingsworth, whose power struggle with the Aussie invader made the egg cups rattle on the TV-am building.

It was Mike who finished up on toast (a sort of ego on toast) and he was soon on his bike to more challenging fields. Just to complicate matters, Mike and Anne Diamond had started a raging romance that has since been blessed with two well-publicised babies. At one stage it got to the point where the gossip columns were heaving with stories that Gyngell had ordered Anne to marry the father of her children or quit. But I knew that old Brucie would be too canny a character to lose his trump Diamond, the queen of the TV-am pack. It was all much more dramatic and spellbinding than any television soap opera.

Anne – Lady Anne, as I dubbed her – knows she is superior at her job, and makes sure she gets the best possible deal for her talent, which possibly leads to some off-screen jealousy. She knows how to stand up for herself, and proved it in an electric interview with old Labour warhorse Denis Healey, who was sitting on the sofa in the summer of 1987 alongside former Tory Defence Secretary Michael Heseltine. TV-am viewers saw just the start of the drama when Anne questioned Healey on newspaper stories about his wife Edna having paid to have a hip operation rather than going on the NHS.

Healey's florid face went purple, and he accused TV-am of "a classical dirty trick" by inviting him to speak about the Venice economic summit when they really wanted to quiz him about his wife. He then went OTT by asking Anne, who was plainly pregnant, where she planned to have her baby. She stood her ground, and rightly protested that she was a journalist not a politician and that she was merely asking questions about the day's news.

During the commercial break, Healey brought gasps of astonishment from everybody in earshot when he ripped into Anne with a volley of abuse.

He then tried to storm off set, forgetting that he was still connected to his neck microphone cable that was wound around the leg of the sofa. It was like a scene from a Frank Spencer comedy as he struggled to extricate himself.

Political editor Adam Boulton was just off camera, and as Healey went past him in a rage he poked him heavily in the chest and made some less-than-complimentary remarks about TV-am.

Michael Heseltine took great delight in confirming all that had happened to a posse of newspaper reporters, scoring political points in the build-up to the general election. And, of course, every headline was marvellous publicity for TV-am.

I rated Anne Diamond and Nick Owen the best double act in the world of television interviewing. They had the knack of putting studio guests at their ease and could smile like angels while putting loaded questions that drew the best answers for their viewers. Roland Rat jumped overboard in 1985 and swam across the channel to the

BBC. We missed the little rat, but this allowed the potty but talented Timothy Mallett the chance to make a name for himself as presenter of *Wacaday*.

TV-am finally lost out in a bidding war with GMTV in 1990 after a Government change of franchise legislation, and Gyngell was criticised for revealing that Margaret Thatcher had written a private letter to him sympathising that his company had lost out.

The Wizard of Oz had been let down by the Iron Lady.

I often used the TV-am sofa as a soap box, and my tongue occasionally towed me into trouble. I had the meteorological office gunning for me in the autumn of 1987 when I described all television weather forecasters as "useless ginks". I was in the studio the day after they had failed to warn us about a hurricane that ripped through the South East, causing serious structural damage and destroying thousands of trees. I took my temper out on lovely TV-am weathergirl Trish Williamson, and said on air that she "should be bloody well sacked".

I didn't mean it, of course, and it's been good to see her progress to the job of forecaster for the national ITV weather team, but I would still rather rely on my own judgement looking at the sky than listen to some of the codswallop coming from the so-called experts. The more sophisticated they become with their computers, the farther out they seem with their forecasts.

The nearest that I've ever come to thumping somebody on the TV-am set is when Mike Smith suggested I was a small-minded bigot. His verbal dig came during a Camden Lock sofa discussion about a mess of an LWT show called *Trick or Treat*. I made the honest observation that I objected to the Saturday evening programme being shown at a time when

Scanned from Jimmy's personal scrapbook, his proudest moment with Spurs as a member of the triumphant European Cup Winners' Cup team in 1963: left to right back: Jimmy, Maurice Norman, Bill Brown, John White, Bobby Smith, Tony Marchi; front: Terry Dyson, Ron Henry, Danny Blanchflower, Peter Baker, Cliff Jones.

Jimmy celebrates a 1967 goal with three of his favourite team-mates, Dave Mackay, Cyril Knowles and the other half of the G-men, Alan Gilzean.

Parading the FA Cup with 20-year-old Joe Kinnear after the 1967 FA Cup Final victory over Jimmy's old club, Chelsea.

This was a joke as Jimmy swigged from a giant bottle of champagne after the 1967 FA Cup Final victory over Chelsea. A few years later he would have tried to empty the bottle.

Jimmy smokes in the dressing-room after a victory at the Lane. This was common in football, and the likes of Tommy Harmer and goalkeeper Reg Matthews took a puff at half-time.

Jimmy continued his happy habit of always scoring in his major debuts with two goals for West Ham against Manchester City at Maine Road in March 1970. This is the first, whipped past goalkeeper Joe Corrigan on a rain-soaked surface.

By the time Jimmy got to West Ham he was already a businessman off the pitch, setting up a packaging and travel company with his brother-in-law Tom Barden.

Jimmy loved this grainy picture from his scrapbook because it captures the fun he liked to have on the football pitch as he dances with his best mate Bobby Moore in the middle of a tense First Division tussle.

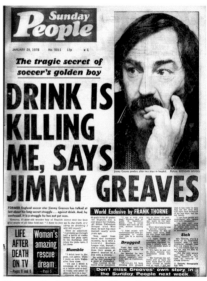

At the wheel of his 1970 World Cup London-to-Mexico rally car, Jimmy spent most of his time in the navigator's seat alongside crack co-driver Tony Fall.

The exclusive Sunday People *front page* story by Frank Thorne in 1978 that first revealed Jimmy had a major drink problem.

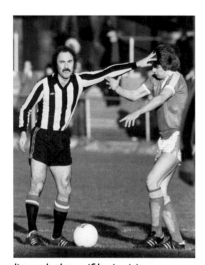

Jimmy looks as if he is giving a rugby hand-off while playing for Barnet, still in his drinking days. Later in the match he lost his temper and was shown the red card for dissent.

Brothers Danny (left) and Andy Greaves, who have always been fiercely proud of their dad even though they had to live in the great man's shadow.

The final match of Jimmy's career and with boxing idol Frank Bruno as his shooting partner. They played together in son Danny's testimonial match at Southend in 1990 when Jim was 50.

Anne Diamond and Nick Owen, the TVam presenters Jimmy rated the best double act in television ... until Saint and Greavsie came along!

Saint and Greavsie became national treasures with their irreverent and innovative show.

Jimmy and Ian St John knew they had made it when they became Spitting Image dummies.

The viewing public loved Jimmy, and he collected several TVTimes *awards* as he transcended the world of football.

The quiz show Sporting Triangles *was launched in 1987, with Nick Owen (second left) as the* presenter and Willie Thorne, Tessa Sanderson and Jimmy as the rival captains.

Jimmy joined Ian Botham on a leg of one of his great charity walks, and they later played alongside each other in the Ron 'Chopper' Harris testimonial match at Stamford Bridge.

While collecting his 1966 World Cup medal from Labour Prime Minister Gordon Brown at Downing Street in 2009, Jimmy might have mentioned that he was right of Stanley Matthews.

One of Jimmy's favourite photographs, taken in 2005, aged 65 and ten years ahead of his stroke.

The Royal Mail honour Jimmy with a postage stamp. 'That will take some licking,' he said.

Harry Kane greets the man whose Tottenham goalscoring records he is trying to beat.

Surrounded by family and friends, wheelchair-bound Jimmy visits the new Tottenham Hotspur stadium. It was a few yards yet a world away from the old White Hart Lane.

children were obviously among the viewers. *Trick or Treat* was jointly hosted by Smith and a flamboyant character called Julian Clary, also known as The Joan Collins Fan Club. My objection, and I was talking as a concerned grandfather, was that the gutter-style innuendo in the programme had no place on the screen during early evening television time. The tatty quiz show had already received destructive publicity for employing porn stars as hosts.

There are plenty of high-powered people in the world of television who will tell you that Greavsie's no saint. In fact, I can sometimes be one of the most awkward cusses I know, and if I was a programme producer I would hate to have to deal with me. I've got a sort of cuddly, cheeky chappie image with the viewers, but the only part of me some TV bosses would like to cuddle is my windpipe.

Maybe it's a throwback to my days on the bottle but there are some who consider me a sort of Jekyll and Hyde character. There's the wise-cracking, relaxed guy you see on the TV screen, while off camera I can – just very occasionally – be a bit of a misery guts with a touchpaper temper.

I make this honest admission, so that the people with whom I have fallen out can perhaps try to understand that I don't mean to lose control of my temper. It's just that I've got a fuse that is so short that it needs only a spark to ignite it, particularly if I feel hard done by. When I lose my temper, I say that it's the O'Reilly coming out in me. O'Reilly was the name of my ancestors on my mother's side, southern Irish folk with magic in their tongues and, so the legend goes, wildness in their ways. It's from them that I have inherited my runaway tongue and my volatile temper (and perhaps what was my drinking habit). A typical case of my temper zooming past boiling point came in the autumn of 1984 when I was in trouble for threatening to thump a milkman. We were trying the country life in a 15th century farmhouse that we had bought in the depths of Essex at Lindsell, near Great Dunmow. I was sitting with my feet up in my study when I heard a commotion coming from the drive leading up to the farm. I ran out to find Irene and my sons, Danny and Andy, in tears and screaming at the milkman, "You've killed our dog."

"What the hell's going on?" I shouted.

"The milkman's run over Wincey," sobbed Irene.

We had named our collie after TV-am weather girl Wincey Willis.

I called the milkman every name under the sun (or even the *Mirror*) and told him in no uncertain terms to get off my land. All dog lovers will know how I felt, and when the milkman showed no remorse I went for him with a verbal volley that concerned him to the point where he reported me to the police.

The incident was so upsetting that we decided to jack in the good life in the country and move back to the village world or Little Baddow. We had just forked out 15 grand on a new roof, and I lost thousands on the sale while everybody else in the country was making massive profits on selling their homes.

That was par for the course for me. We've had a couple of dozen homes and I have rarely shown a profit. The classic was when I bought a beautiful place in Cornwall. It was in an idyllic setting, with a mix of river and country views. Our first Saturday there, I had to do a show at Central. The traffic was so horrendous that I got to the studio with just minutes to spare. As soon as I came off air, I telephoned Irene and told her to put the house on the market. We always used to say afterwards that we were the only people who ever went on holiday to Cornwall and took all our furniture with us. '

I had taken on the role not only of Jimmy's ghostwriter but also his representative, a job at which we quickly realised I was not the most efficient. The end of this arrangement came the day I told him I had booked him into an after-dinner speaking assignment at a sports club in Bognor Regis. I used to travel with him, introduce him at the speaking engagements and make sure he was not tempted to take a drink in the days when he preached the Alcoholics Anonymous doctrine that 'one drink was too many and 20 not enough'.

Jimmy would always drive and on this particular day as I settled alongside him in the passenger seat, he asked me what address we were aiming for in Bognor Regis. I looked at our booking confirmation and discovered that I had got Regis right, but it was Lyme Regis down in West Dorset not Bognor Regis in West Sussex. I was only 75 miles out, and Jimbo was not best pleased. That meant a real ear bashing and I can call a procession of witnesses to confirm that he could unleash a vicious volley of the verbals when feeling aggrieved.

Without an agent to guide him, Jim was rudderless and made some terrible misjudgements, such as putting his name to a scam in which tea-drinkers were assured it would help them lose weight. He was also threatened with lawsuits after an up-and-over door that he endorsed proved less than reliable. His later involvement in a golf course project hit him heavily in the pocket. 'Got well and truly bunkered,' he said through gritted teeth.

The man who could pick his way through any defence often struggled to judge the character of people, and like so many sports stars before and after him he was taken for a ride by conmen out to part him from his money.

While trying to run his own affairs in the 1980s, he got involved in a screaming match with Central TV executive Andy Allan when negotiating the renewal of his contract, and on Andy's advice got himself a proper representative in the shape of experienced theatrical agent Barry Brown. He knew the difference between Lyme Regis and Bognor Regis!

Jimmy became a popular fixture, along with Chris Tarrant and Lenny Henry, on the Saturday morning kids' programme *Tiswas*, swapped jokes with Tommy Boyd on *The Saturday Show* and was a team captain on the quiz show *Sporting Triangles*, pitched against another former footballing master, Emlyn Hughes. Jim and Emlyn were from different generations and never liked each other from the moment the former Liverpool skipper was poached from BBC's *A Question of Sport* without Jim knowing a thing about it before his surprise arrival in the Birmingham studios. Their rivalry came to a head when Jim was instructed to wear a special sponsored Sporting Triangles sweater in which he knew Emlyn had a financial interest. It became a 'Sweatergate' bust-up, and led to Jim and his good mate Gary Newbon having verbal fisticuffs that seriously threatened their friendship.

While this was going on, rumours whooshed around the Midlands that Jimmy was back on the booze. It was reported that he had been seen smashing down the door of a Birmingham nightclub in a drunken rage. Many were quick to believe it until we got to the bottom of the mystery by identifying Jimmy lookalike actor Michael Elphick, of *Boon* fame, as the out-of-control drunk who was involved in the nightclub incident. The lesson Jimmy learned from this was that people were expecting the worst from him.

One side effect of Jimmy's years lost to the bottle was that he had developed a short temper. He had little or no patience and the man who had been a pussycat as a footballer was now likely to erupt over anything he could not control.

There was violent evidence of this when he got involved in what he described as his 'car crash television' experience. He successfully anchored a low-key Midlands-only chat show that got such great ratings that ITV decided they wanted it to go on their national network. It was decided to give the programme a huge budget and they brought in veteran London television scriptwriter/producer Roy Bottomley to supervise the show. It was to be called *Greavsie's Gaff*, with the viewers seeing Jimmy interviewing guests in what was supposed to be his kitchen at home but was so obviously a studio set. It quickly became known as Greavsie's Gaffe.

I had worked with former *Daily Sketch* tabloid reporter Bottomley on *This Is Your Life* and knew he was the sort who would irritate Jim. He was a skilled journalist and scriptwriter, with a cutting tongue and a swaggering little man's Napoleonic complex. Bottomley decided to turn Jimmy's almost quaint little chat show into an all-singing-and-dancing celebrity affair. It was the last thing Jimmy wanted, believing his local chat show had been a success because he concentrated on interviewing unknowns who had interesting things to say. 'None of them were plugging their next book or film,' he told me, 'and they were not in the studio because they had long legs and big tits.'

Roy's shows were so complicated and crowded with B-list guests that Jim reluctantly had to use an autocue, and because of his dyslexia read his lines in a monotonous way, knowing that people behind the camera were sniggering when he mispronounced words.

It got to the point where Jim blew a gasket and had Bottomley up against a wall threatening to do him grievous bodily harm.

Once again, rumours swept the Midlands that he was back on the sauce. The national chat show was justifiably caned by the critics and it left Jim with a lasting suspicion and fear of the autocue. 'I died on my arse,' was Jimmy's honest assessment.

Chapter 16:

Saint and Greavsie

IT WAS John (Brommers) Bromley who launched the ground-breaking *Saint and Greavsie* show in his role as head of LWT Sport in the autumn of 1985. He watched the down-the-line exchanges that Jimmy had from Birmingham with London-based Ian St John in the Saturday *On the Ball* segment and his Fleet Street-trained ear told him this was box office.

Ian had been an idol on Merseyside when playing in harness with Roger Hunt in the Bill Shankly-inspired Liverpool side of the 1960s. He had impressed with his broadcasting skills when finishing runner-up in a BBC TV 'Find A Commentator' competition, and he took over as anchorman of *On the Ball* from the master Brian Moore.

Brommers had first made an impact as a football journalist with the *Daily Herald* and *Daily Mirror* at the same time as his near-neighbour Greavsie was starting out on his football adventure. Now, as a television executive, he knew gold dust when he saw it:

‘We were putting the *World of Sport* programme to bed after a 20-year run and I was looking around for ideas to replace it. I was listening in to *On the Ball* with Ian St John and Jimmy Greaves talking down the line to each other like a couple of mates having a natter at the bar. Ian casually referred to Jim as "Greavsie" and Jim delightfully called Ian "Saint". "That's it!" I said aloud to myself, "Saint and Greavsie" – and the show was born. I told them we wanted them to talk about football just as they would if sitting side by side in the dressing room. No mumbo jumbo. Just talk to each other like the old footballers you are. It worked a treat, and suddenly people found themselves laughing out loud while also getting the latest football gossip and news. I had known Jim since he was taking his first professional kicks and we always looked on each other as old mates. Ian was a sharp footballer on and off the pitch, and I was always bumping into him at celebrity functions, so I knew he had star quality. They went together like fish and chips. I had become a matchmaker. **'**

The only person who needed persuading that it was a good idea was Greavsie. As usual when a plan was first put to him, he had self-doubts and would instinctively kick it away. Jim:

' When it was first put to me, I was very wary. Co-presenting a national network show seemed a huge step up. Remember, I still considered myself a recovering alcoholic. It seemed like only the day before yesterday that I had told the world that drink was killing me. I had tremendous respect for Ian as a player with Liverpool and Scotland, but in those days I never really knew him as a person. He always seemed surrounded by showbiz types. Jimmy Tarbuck remains one of his closest pals – and, to be honest, I got the impression he was a bit of a flash git.

He was coming back into my life after suffering some hard times trying to establish himself as a manager and coach. His coaching ability was highly regarded in the game, particularly at Coventry and Sheffield Wednesday (where he was big Jack Charlton's right-hand man). He put his head on the block as manager at Portsmouth and still carries the scars of an unhappy ending to his managerial career when he was axed without having really been given a proper chance to show what he could do. Football's loss was television's gain. But did I want to take the gamble of working alongside him? Two virtual novices together. A Cockney and a Jock? Could it work?

I voiced my concerns to my Central TV team-mate Gary Newbon and he said I should grab it with both hands. "You'll kick yourself if you turn it down," he said. "A national TV programme is something we all aim for. You've proved with your *On the Ball* banter that you and the Saint have got a natural rapport. Go for it."

Irene was making similar positive noises, and so I agreed with Brommers to give it a go. If anything was going to drive me back to the bottle, this was it. I was taking on what all recovering alcoholics are warned to avoid – extra pressure.

It took Ian and the producers and directors time to get used to me. I was not your conventional television presenter. I hated rehearsing and left all the nuts and bolts to the Saint. Live television needed to be spontaneous, and if I was going to throw in my wisecracks and asides they needed to be off the cuff and not sounding as if I had been practising them.

The way Ian and I worked on the show was exactly how l used to play football. I left the Saint to do all the hard graft – reading the autocue and setting up all the inserts – while I just concentrated on slipping in and out of the action with hopefully funny one-liners and considered comments on the main items. The Saint and I were very lucky in having imaginative editors at the helm in Bob Patience and then Richard Worth, and we had excellent input to the show from ITV team members of the time – notably Martin Tyler, Alan Parry and Jim Rosenthal (now all true legends of the sport-talk game).

We set out to entertain and explain, in that order. We didn't think the vast majority of our viewers wanted us blinding them with science about what is only a game. There were too many people disappearing with a flash and a bang up their own exhaust pipes when talking about the game as if bringing the tablets down from Moses (and I don't mean hurdler Ed Moses).

If Ian and I did have to get deadly serious about things, we had 78 caps between us to prove that we knew what we were talking about. Our bright and breezy approach meant we had to take a lot of stick from some serious sections of the media who thought that we treated football too lightly. "Saint and Greavsie are a couple of jokers who have managed to take football down to the level of a second-rate music hall act," wrote one quality paper scribe. Each to their own. **)**

The ITV lawyers used to have kittens when Jimmy was live on air. He rarely stuck to a script and he could blister the furniture with some of his views. Referees were always a favourite target and he once went an insult too far and finished up having to apologise in court after suggesting the match referee was trying to get himself in the history books by sending off a player for the publicity it could get him. Jimmy found out the hard way that you should never make an opinion sound like a statement of fact, advice that I freely pass on to all those keyboard warriors who infest the world of social media. Think before you type.

Saint and Greavsie became such a massive hit for ITV that the budget was increased to give the boys a break from the straitjacket of the studio. Jimmy played golf with the Spanish magician Seve Ballesteros and he and the Saint memorably visited Donald Trump in his New York penthouse, where the future President of the United States was talked into making the draw for the League Cup, then known as the Rumbelows Cup. It made for priceless television, with Jimmy comparing the luxurious Trump Towers with the office of Aston Villa chairman Doug Ellis. The Donald grinned into camera, convinced Jimmy was being complimentary.

Jimmy's greatest coup was to get into the ring with then world heavyweight champion 'Iron' Mike Tyson. It made a lasting impression on him:

‘ It was one of my most memorable television interviews for our *Saint and Greavsie* show. At the time, Tyson was being billed as the "Baddest Man on the Planet". I met him in his training camp tucked away in the Catskill Mountains in New York, where he was preparing for his world title defence against Michael Spinks in Atlantic City.

He trained in a small gymnasium above the cop shop in what was a one-horse town. As I watched him belting sparring partners around the ring as if they were punch bags, I got the feeling that I would not want to tango with Tyson, let alone tangle with him. I honestly felt that I was in the presence of a being from another planet. The first thing that struck me about him was his cliff wall-face of a body, and in particular a neck that looked as if it might once have been a smoke stack on a tug. But it was not just his physical appearance that was so impressive and also intimidating. He had an aura about him that was almost electric, or even nuclear.

Back in the mid-60s, I had met Muhammad Ali when he was in London training for his second fight with Henry Cooper. He too had an aura, but it was one that brought a smile to your face. Tyson brought a chill to the heart. With Ali, you felt you were in the company of a great entertainer as much as a great sportsman. With Tyson, the feeling was more of being close to an unexploded bomb. I got a close-up sense of his strength and power when I climbed into the ring to chat with him in front of the television cameras.

He gave me a riveting 15-minute interview during which he playfully patted me in the ribs, and left a small bruise that I wore like a badge of honour. Mike sounded like a surgeon about to perform a cutting operation as he showed me how he went about mounting a body attack. "The main target area," he said as he pushed me into a corner of the ring under a mock (thank God) assault "are the liver, the kidney region, the heart, the floating rib and the abdomen".

Tyson peppered his conversation on camera and off with boxing facts. He's a genuine fan of his sport, and a walking record book on its history. I've never spoken to anybody quite like him. He is an uneducated man from the dead end of Brooklyn, yet talked to me like somebody who has swallowed a dictionary. He wouldn't win any prizes in the academic world, but has street sense of Mastermind proportions.

Mike and I had a long off-camera chat as he was changing in the locker room. One thing I can reveal is that the most impressive part of his anatomy was never seen in public. I'll leave it to your imagination! Let's just say he could have swept the gymnasium floor without a broom! Yet he had a surprisingly high, almost effeminate voice and a slight lisp.

I asked him what it was like to land a knockout punch, and he replied, "Better than the greatest orgasm you could ever have."

He told me he'd never forgotten that he'd come from the streets. "I go back to my old neighbourhood a lot," he said. "It does me good to remind myself where my roots are. Man, they are the toughest streets on God's earth. Everybody has to fight just to survive. I go to prisons and drug rehabilitation centres just to give people hope. It makes you want to cry to see old friends who failed to beat the trap into which they were born."

He later, of course, got to know the inside of prison for real. He got put away for rape, which pretty much destroyed his image and made commentators reach for the old saying that "you can take the man out of the ghetto, but you can't take the ghetto out of the man". '

Jim and Ian lived at opposite ends of the country and so were never in each other's pockets. They liked and respected each other, and were not one of those double acts poisoned by backstage hatred. If we could have bottled the Saint's spontaneous laugh in reaction to Jim's ad-libs, we would have something to cheer everybody up. It was so infectious that the cameramen and floor managers used to fall about laughing off camera. I asked the Saint to give his honest assessment of Jim for a tribute article on his 65th birthday in 2005:

'As a goalscorer, none better. Quick as a flash and the ball was in the back of the net before defenders even knew a chance was on. As a bloke, one of the funniest men I ever met in my life, but he could also be a pain in the arse. He used to cause murders off camera in our programme-making days, all because he refused to rehearse or wear an earpiece.

Jim never knew what was going on in the control box. He could be the most stubborn man walking this earth, but I loved the guy. We had great chemistry right from day one. The difference between us was that I was organised and wanted to be on top of every second of each show, while Jim was laid back and gave the impression of not caring – but deep down I know that he did. When they wrote the *Odd Couple*, I think they must have had we two in mind.

I didn't really get to know Jim properly until we started working together on *Saint and Greavsie*. I marvelled at the way he pulled himself together after all his problems with the hooch. When we first started meeting in the green room before shows, I would go along with him and order a Coke until one day he said, "For gawd's sake, Ian. I know you're a Scotch and Soda man. Don't feel you have to hold my hand. I've kicked the sauce, and that's it. Don't worry about it and drink what you want." It was always Coke, water or better still coffee or tea for Jim right the way through our seven-year run. What discipline!

I was sitting in the stand at Wembley with Liverpool skipper Ron Yeats the day England won the World Cup in 1966. Everybody thought we two Jocks wanted England to lose, but we had our mate Roger Hunt playing and Gerry Byrne and Ian Callaghan were in the squad. I was amazed that Alf could not find a place for Greavsie because he was easily England's most potent striker, but I guess the scoreline proved him right. But it was one hell of a gamble. I know Jim was choked not to play, but he always insisted in our private chats that it had nothing to do with his later drink problem.

We were both dead lucky when Brommers had the idea to put us together. It gave us both a great platform and a good living, then they chopped the show as quickly as they had decided to put it on. In no time at all, Jimmy reinvented himself as a stand-up comedian and after-dinner speaker. You can only admire the man. Nothing puts him down for long. '

The end for *Saint and Greavsie* came in 1992 when ITV lost a bidding war for the new Premier League matches to the fresh kid on the block, Sky Television. It was Greg Dyke of all people – he set light to Jimmy's TV touchpaper when boss of TV-am – who pulled the plug as head of LWT. The final programme was broadcast from Sweden during Euro '92, Greavsie wearing a Viking helmet and with the giggling pair singing 'This Could Be the Last Time' as they cycled off into the distance in a buggy as the final credits rolled. It *was* the last time.

They were brought back by Setanta Sports executive Trevor East for a one-off *Saint and Greavsie* during the build-up to the 2009 FA Cup Final between Chelsea and Everton, and that was it for football's Morecambe and Wise apart from the occasional personal appearance and after-dinner dates.

'We couldn't even talk on the phone after Jimmy's stroke,' said the Saint. 'If I could speak to him I'd say, "Wasn't it fun? Thanks for the laughs."'

Jimmy sobbed the day Ian lost his fight with cancer, aged 82, in March 2021. He could not express himself, but I know that he would have wanted to say that he loved the Saint. In his mischievous way, Jim would have said, 'Not a bad bloke, for a Jock!'

And can't you just hear the Saint's contagious laugh?

Saint and Greavsie. The Untouchables.

Chapter 17

Safe as the Banks of England

NOW FOR something completely different (apologies to Monty Python). My next assignment after ghosting Jimmy's *This One's On Me* book was a commission to work with goalkeeping great Gordon Banks on his autobiography *Banks of England*. Took me ages to come up with that title! For one of the chapters, I reunited Gordon and Jimmy. Since their last meeting, Gordon had lost an eye in a car crash and Jimmy had got, well, smashed.

I now hand the reins over to Gordon (sadly no longer with us; remember this was back in 1980 and Jimmy was in the early stages of his comeback):

‘We had not seen each other for a couple of years and I was expecting the worst after all the harrowing stories I had heard and read about his drink problem. But as he came towards me, moving through the crowded London hotel foyer with his familiar balance and economy of effort, I was pleasantly surprised. Jimmy Greaves looked a million dollars.

I had found it hard to believe when he had confessed publicly to being an alcoholic. He had certainly liked his drink in the days when we were England team-mates, but there were players with bigger consumption who had not suffered the nightmare Jimmy had lived through.

As we shook hands with a warmth that suddenly evaporated time and cemented our old friendship, we took instant stock of each other. Jimmy wasted no time in getting his sharp Cockney wit to work. "Just think, Gordon," he said, "since we last played for England together you've become one-eyed and I've become pie-eyed!"

It was the old Greavsie smiling up at me. Mischievous, impish. A loveable little sod. I wanted to cuddle this sweet man who had given me and millions of football fans so much pleasure and fun over the years. We were together in a Park Lane hotel to talk over old times.

I needed help to revive old memories for my book and who better, I thought, than Greavsie, who just happened to be one of the greatest things on two feet during my playing career. We had shared so much together both on and off the pitch during the high summer of our playing days. Now, with a tape-recorder between us, we looked back on the good old days and – sad to say – some not-so-good.'

GB: The first time we were together, you bugger, you made me look a right bloody idiot.

JG: That must have been about 1959 or 60. You had been called up to the England Under-23 squad for the first time.

GB: That's right. We were training at Stamford Bridge and the press photographers wanted an action shot of me for their files. I asked you to kick the ball to me, so that I could make a save. As you approached the ball, you dipped your left shoulder and I dived to my right and then you slipped the ball into the other corner of the net. The photographers fell about laughing.

JG: That was 20 years ago. Twenty years. Seems like only yesterday, and you know what a lousy day yesterday was. I remember we had two nicknames for you. One was Fernandel because you looked so much like the rubber-faced French comedian. The other was Sugar. You were always impersonating that entertainer who pretended he was drunk. What was his name?

GB: Freddie Frinton. He used to sing 'Sugar in the Morning' with a bent cigarette in his mouth and his top hat over his eyes.

JG: You used to have us in fits taking him off and staggering about as if you were drunk out of your head. So we called you Sugar. It might have been more appropriate if I'd done the drunk act!

GB Actually, Jim, I admire the way you've stood up and faced your problem. It took a lot of courage admitting to the world you were an alcoholic.

JG: It was the only way to beat the disease. I knew that with everybody's eyes on me my pride would help me conquer the problem. When I was asked to write an autobiography, I decided to hang my skeleton out for public viewing.

GB: I really used to envy you, did you know that, Jim? You seemed to have everything going for you. I admired the way you were able to cut off from your playing career to concentrate on building up a successful business. Everything seemed to come so easily to you on the football field and I thought all was perfect with your businesses and your marriage.

JG: I pissed it all away, Gordon. It got so that the booze became like a monster. To be honest, I'm lucky to be alive. But then, you've hardly had roses all the way since we last played together.

GB: You can say that again. But like you, I've had to come to terms with it. Out of the wreckage, we can salvage the self-satisfaction that we have both been able to help others because of the nightmares we've experienced. I'm sure your book has given hope to a lot of people with the drink problem. Likewise, I've been able to give encouragement to many victims of accidents who have lost an eye. Particularly youngsters. Many parents have asked me to write to children who have lost the sight of an eye to tell them that they can still lead ordinary lives.

JG: Something I've learned from the hell I've been through is that you can achieve anything you want provided you are single-minded about it.'

GB: Exactly. I made up my mind I was going to play again and I did. Admittedly, it wasn't in top-grade football, but at least I got another couple of seasons in when everybody had given me up as finished.

JG: I could have wept for you when I heard about your car smash. In fact, I went on a bender when I read about it. I was close to rock-bottom with my drinking at the time and remember wondering why life had to he so cruel. Then, some time later, it was all over the newspapers that your marriage was in trouble and that made me feel really morose.

GB: Aye, Jim, that was obviously a terrible period in both our lives. But that marriage business was blown up out of proportion. We've got it all back together now and everything is fine.

JG: I hope you're putting that in your book. Your readers will enjoy hearing some good news for a change!

GB: I've skated over it. I like to keep my private life private.

JG: But if you're doing an autobiography, surely you've got to tell it as it is.

GB: My book is about Banks the footballer. I think people identify with sportsmen by what they achieve on the field rather than what they do away from the game. My wife Ursula and I were really hurt by all the malicious stories that were flying around during our moments of difficulty.

JG: Well, surely your book gives you the opportunity to put the record straight.

GB: I wouldn't want to subject Ursula and our kids to all that again. I've admitted I became bloody difficult to live with after my accident. It was a really traumatic time for me trying to re-adjust and for a short spell I guess I went off the rails.

JG: You wouldn't be human if you had not had some [sort of] psychological reaction after what happened to you.

GB: I got myself sorted out in America. It was just a question of getting away from domestic pressures for a while, so that I could think everything out. I caused Ursula a lot of misery, but she was strong enough to cope with it and to understand that I was going through torture after what happened to me in the car crash. My kids were smashing. They arc quite grown-up now and I really enjoy being at home with them.

JG: Well, all I hope, Gordon, is that you let this tape go into the book verbatim. I'm sure people will admire you for the way you've managed to hold everything together despite all the problems. And I know what you mean by the enjoyment you get from being with your kids. Now that I've kicked the bottle, I spend all my time at home with Irene and the kids and we get on marvellously together. I call them kids! Lynn, my eldest daughter, has just got married.

GB: Robert, my eldest, is talking about marriage. God, Jim, we could be grandfathers the next time we meet!

We took a rest from our taping session to share a pot of coffee for two. Jok r Jim couldn't resist a gag at his own expense. 'At least it's cheaper drinking with me these days, Gordon,' he said. 'A couple of years ago, this reunion would have cost you a bottle of vodka!'

As Jimmy poured the tea, my mind was weighing up what he had said about 'telling it as it is'. How much should a sportsman strip himself for his public?

At the time of my domestic squall and also immediately after the car crash, both Ursula and I could have capitalised by accepting big-money offers to tell our stories. But it is just not our way. We both believe that people in the public eye deserve their privacy. Our marriage was strong enough to survive the sort of strains and stresses that have broken many others. I had a brief fling at about the time of going to America that brought me unwelcome and unsolicited publicity. It was over very quickly, but for quite a while there was a dark shadow thrown over our marriage because of the uncalled-for exposure.

But it could not break the bond of love between my family and myself, and once I had completed my contract in the United States I could not get back quickly enough to them. Despite some of the spiteful things that were written and said by outsiders at the time, Gordon Banks is a home-loving man. I admire the way Jimmy has had the guts to bare his soul, but there are some personal things that I prefer to keep to myself.

My thoughts were interrupted by the sight of Jimmy almost choking over his coffee cup with laughter. 'What have you remembered?' I asked, switching the tape-recorder back on.

JG: Do you recall asking my advice about a transfer in 1967 when Leicester put you up for sale? There were two clubs in for you.

GB: That's right. Liverpool and Stoke. I asked you which one you would select.

JG: It's just come back to me what I said to you at the time. My advice was that you should go to Stoke because Liverpool were a finished force. With foresight like that, I should have been a BBC weather forecaster.

GB: That's right, you big pillock. Liverpool were such a finished force that they have since won every bloody thing in sight. Still, I've got no regrets about the move I made. Stoke were a great club to be with. They could play some cracking football and socially I would have to say they were the top club in the country. You would have had a ball with us, Jim.

JG: Yes, you had a good drinking school there. I've had lots of good nights out with you and my old mate George Eastham.

GB: George was with us that night we nipped out for a drink before the match in Portugal.

JG: Alf [Ramsey] went potty. We thought we'd got away with it when we crept to our hotel rooms at about two o'clock in the morning without being spotted. But Harold Shepherdson had been to our rooms and put our passports on each of our beds.

GB: What was the name of that bar we were drinking at?

JG: The Beachcomber. They had all those exotic drinks, remember? We got stuck into a drink called a Zombie. It was a rum-based drink with a real kick.

GB: That was the place with the alligators in the tank. Ray Wilson kept lobbing chunks of ice out of the ice bucket at them.

JG: Nobody said a dicky bird to us the next morning, but when we got to Lisbon for our last training session, Alf said in that exaggerated posh voice of his, 'I think there are seven gentlemen who wish to see me.'

GB: He was fuming. He said he would have sent us home if he'd had enough players in the squad. And he would have done as well. Alf was the most loyal bloke walking this earth if you gave him 100 per cent, but anything less and he could cut you dead.

JG: A myth has been allowed to grow up about Alf and me. People think we hated each other, when in fact we got on quite well.

GB: Well, you and Mooro used to take the piss out of him something rotten, always mimicking his strange, strangled accent.

JG: He went to elocution lessons to try to get rid of his Cockney tones. Should have asked for his money back. He was always putting aitches where they shouldn't have been and Mooro and I used to crease up. I remember sitting alongside him at a banquet when he said to the waitress, 'I don't want no peas, please.' It became a catchphrase behind his back.

GB: We all felt for you when Alf left you out of the 1966 World Cup Final team. You didn't say much, but we all knew you were sick.

JG: What could I say? The team had played magnificently against Portugal in the semi-final when I was injured. Alf had to decide whether to change the team and it was quite understandable when he stuck with a winning side. It was the worst thing that happened to me in my career, missing that final. I got well sozzled that night. Anyway, Gordon, that's enough about me. This is supposed to be your book. I've got some statistics here that will interest you. According to the record books, I played 23 league games against you and scored 13 goals.

GB: That should be 14 goals. Do you remember that fantastic shot of yours on the turn up at Leicester when you were in your early days with Spurs? I didn't get a sniff of the ball as it flashed into the net. It was right on half time and we thought the ref had whistled for a goal, but then he said he'd blown for half time and refused to allow the goal. All you Spurs players went berserk, and no wonder, because it was a belter of a goal.

JG: How about that penalty I scored against you at White Hart Lane?

GB: It was the craziest goal ever allowed. There was hardly any grass around and I had gone back inside the goal to wipe all the muck off my hands ready to face the penalty. You, you sod, side-footed the ball into the other corner of the net while I was bending down and the twit of a ref went and gave a goal. What made it worse was instead of telling the ref he was wrong, even my own team-mates were falling about laughing.

JG: You chased him all the way back to the halfway line arguing and all you got for your trouble was having your name taken in those days before yellow and red cards.

GB: He wrote my name down in his little black book, and I told him where to stick it. I don't think I've ever been so angry on a football pitch, but I've done nothing but laugh about it since. It was hilarious – but not at the time.

JG: Here are some more statistics, Gordon, which incidentally come from my well-researched book. Ends commercial! You and I played together in 20 matches for England between 1963 and 1967 and were on the losing side only three times.

GB: Our first defeat was against Scotland in our first game together. That bugger Jim Baxter took control of the game and scored both their goals. I thought he was going to become the greatest Scottish player of all time, but he didn't maintain the standards of that game.

JG: It's no secret that Baxter had my trouble. He preferred a glass in his hand to a ball at his feet. But what a player when he was at his peak! He was as smooth as silk and all style and skill. They murdered us in midfield, where they had Dave Mackay and John White as well as Slim Jim Baxter. The only midfield trio to match them was the one we had in the Spurs side of the time – Danny Blanchflower, Mackay and White.

GB: They were a bit special. Just my luck to come up against them on my international debut.

JG: I thought your international career was finished the next month. Do you remember, we played Brazil?

GB: Of course, I bloody remember. How could I forget that free kick of Pepé's? It did a circular tour of the penalty area before going past me into the net.

JG: I've never known Alf get so boiled up over anything. He kept saying over and over again that he had warned you to watch out for the bender. In fact, he went on so much about it that in the end every time he mentioned it we would fall about laughing behind his back and make faces at you.

GB: I still insist that no ball has ever bent as much as that one. Alf wouldn't have it, though.

JG: Let's be honest, Gordon, you were positioned *behind* the wall instead of to the right of it.

GB: Now don't you start, Greavsie. Even now, I can hear Alf saying that in my sleep. I wondered if he would drop me for it, but I kept my place for the first tour match against Czechoslovakia.

JG: That was the game when Alf told us we had to get back to the hotel immediately after the game. I was elected spokesman and had to ask if it would be all right for us to go out for a quiet drink before going back. He gave me that piercing look of his and said, 'If you must have a drink, you can go back to the fucking hotel and have it.'

GB: Alf didn't swear very often, but when he did you knew he meant what he was saying. As I remember it, we *did* go straight back to the hotel that night and Alf and all the officials joined us in a big party to celebrate what had been a great victory.

JG: Everybody felt like death the next morning and we had to fly to East Germany. It was a diabolical flight because we had to go through the Berlin corridor at about 3,000 feet and the plane was pitching about like a rowing boat in a storm. I was sitting with Bobby Moore and he said all straight-faced, 'We'll be all right because the England doctor will look after us.' He pointed across the aisle and there was Doc Bass [Dr Alan Bass] laid flat out with a wet, iced towel on his forehead and looking as green as the Wembley turf. It was a mixture of a hangover and the flight. Mooro called out, 'Is there a doctor on board for the doctor?'

GB: Wasn't it in East Germany that Alf took us all to the pictures to see what he said would be an English film?

JG: It was an English-made war film and Alf said it would be in English with German sub-titles.

GB: That's right. When the film started, it had all been dubbed in German. We started having a moan at Harold Shep, who kept saying,

'In about five or ten minutes' time, they start speaking English.' When they did start speaking in another language, Russian I think it was, they put sub-titles up in German. With that we all got up *en bloc* and walked out of the cinema.

JG: Talking of doing things *en bloc*, d'you remember when we were sitting on the touchline watching Brazil play Argentina in Sao Paulo in 1964? The crowd started pelting us with rubbish and Alf gave the shortest tactical talk of his life, 'Run, lads.'

GB: I was sitting next to Alf and his actual words after a juicy apple core had splattered against his back were, 'I don't know about you, gentlemen, but I'm fucking off!'

JG: Do you realise, Gordon, that we were on the losing side in our first and last matches together for England and each time it was against the Scots?

GB: The second time was in 1967. We lost 3-2 at Wembley. It was our first defeat since the World Cup and the Scots had the cheek to claim they were the world champions.

JG: I've got painful memories of that match. I got a knock on the ankle that put me out for two weeks. Jack Charlton broke a toe and moved up to centre-forward and Ray Wilson was a hobbling passenger for most of the game. I got some terrible stick in the press for my performance, but if they had seen the state of my ankle after the game I think they might have been more sympathetic.

GB: I could never understand why Alf didn't recall you after that match. He said a couple of years later that you had *asked* not to be selected.

GB: Alf had that all wrong. I would have loved to have got my England place back, but Alf had misunderstood a conversation we once had. He had been getting into the habit of calling me up for training with the squad and then not picking me for the match. You know me, Gordon, I was hardly the world's greatest trainer. Anyway, I told Alf that unless I was going to play, I preferred to give the training get-togethers a miss. He interpreted that as meaning I didn't want to play for England any more.

JG: Remember the last time we played together before your accident?'

GB: You mean in that Mickey Mouse 5-a-side tournament in Toronto.

JG: That's the one. You, Mooro, Big Jack and I were also in the patched-together team. It was a real take-the-money-and-run job. Anyway, I went further than just play, and got my travel agency involved in the tournament being staged world-wide.

GB: You always were the one for a business opportunity, Jim.

JG: Well it blew up in my face. The tournament idea flopped and I was left with a bill for thirty grand. I didn't feel too grand. I had to fly back to Toronto on my Jack Jones and argue with a Mafia-type bloke to get my dosh back. I think that little episode helped me lose myself in drink.

We stopped taping while Jimmy ordered another pot of coffee. 'I'm hooked on this stuff now,' he said. 'I drink gallons of tea and coffee, but at least when I wake up the next morning I don't have a hangover and I know exactly what I did the previous day.'

You could not tell by looking at him the hell he had been through. He was elegantly dressed and appeared prosperous. Since we had last played together he had grown a thick, Mexican-style moustache and his hair was well groomed in the modern bubble-cut fashion. I noticed that he smoked heavily, but even in his playing days with England he had liked a cigarette or a pipe.

People who had not been lucky enough to see him at his peak missed the pleasure of watching a genius at work. I always used to enjoy playing against him because it was such a challenge, and if you were beaten by him (which I often was), then at least you had the consolation of knowing a master had put the ball past you. We continually chatted to each other during games and Jimmy used to tell me exactly where he was going to place his shots. Often, of course, he was bluffing and he would have me diving the wrong way.

As he sat there, coffee pot in hand, I wondered what his modern-day transfer value would be if Trevor Francis could fetch £1 million. It seemed a good point at which to switch the tape recorder back on.

GB: If Trevor Francis is worth a million, Jim, I reckon you would have been worth at least twice that at your peak.

JG: Careful, Gordon. People will read that and think we have formed a mutual admiration society. Funnily enough, I was just going to say to you that if Phil Parkes is worth half a million, then your value would be something in excess of £3 million. I don't mean that as a slight on Phil, because he is an excellent goalkeeper, but I have never seen anybody to match you for class and consistency.

GB: This is getting embarrassing. Let's change the subject. Would you like to be playing in today's game or were you happy to have had your peak when you did?

JG: Obviously I would like the money they are earning now, but I wouldn't want to swap eras. I think you and I were lucky to have played when we did. I am sure the game was more enjoyable for players and spectators, particularly in the late 1950s and early 1960s.

GB: I agree with you. Goalkeepers got little or no protection from referees when I first came into the game, and the likes of Bobby Smith and Nat Lofthouse thought nothing of trying to batter you into the net. But you accepted it as part and parcel of the game and just took it in your stride. Now I think if anything goalkeepers are *over*-protected and consequently they are not learning the physical aspect of the game. It's definitely not as entertaining for spectators to watch.

JG: The last time I played with you, Gordon, was in a Goaldiggers match for the National Playing Fields' Fund. It was some time after your accident and Jimmy Hill had arranged a game against a team of European All Stars at Birmingham. Bobby Robson was playing in midfield and you – if you'll pardon the expression – were having a blinder, stopping everything that came at you. Bobby turned to me and said, 'If Banksie is one-eyed, then all I can say is that the First Division has a load of blind goalkeepers.' After the match, he told me he was going to try to sign you for Ipswich, but nothing came of it.

GB: That's the story of my life since the accident. Promises, promises. I got really disillusioned trying to get back into the game. Clubs just didn't want to know me. I don't know if they think I've lost the power to think as well as to see out of one eye, but some clubs didn't even have the decency to reply to my job applications.

JG: It's astonishing how many of that 1966 World Cup squad are now out of the game. Ronnie Springett and Peter Bonetti were the other two goalkeepers in the squad. They are both out. The full-backs were George Cohen, Ray Wilson, Jimmy Armfield and Gerry Byrne. They're all out.

GB: Even Mooro is out of the game. It's madness. Surely the Football Association could employ him in some capacity. All that knowledge going to waste. I would have jumped at the chance to have taken over the England youth team after Brian Clough and Peter Taylor had said they were no longer interested. But I didn't get a look-in.

JG: Nobby and Jack Charlton are managers, but they are the only two unless you count Geoff Hurst, who's involved with the England team and with Chelsea. So out of 22 players, 13 of them are no longer connected with the game at top level. Ron Flowers, Roger Hunt, John Connelly, Terry Paine, George Eastham and even Bobby Charlton are not involved in the league scene.

GB: Only Norman Hunter, Ballie, Martin Peters and Ian Callaghan are still playing in the league. I wonder if any of them will get the chance to manage or coach a top club? Or have they got disillusionment to come like so many others who were in that 1966 squad?

JG: I've never wanted to get involved in the game as a manager. There are too many pressures for my liking. You are answerable to too many people, most of whom don't know what day it is. You have to satisfy not only your players and directors but also the fans and the media. If you're lucky, you might find a few minutes each day for your family. That's not for me. It would be enough to drive me to drink!

GB: Then how do you see your future, Jim? I love being involved in football and want to try to give back all the things that I have learned about the game. How can you live without it?

JG: At this moment, I'm collaborating on a series of novels about the game. I've got the writing bug and feel there is room in the book world for a sort of Dick Francis of football. He writes superb thrillers about the racing world. I'm sure there is a big audience who would like to read entertaining novels about the *real* football world. I am taking it really seriously and have even learned to touch-type.

GB I look forward to reading your books. How about writing a novel about a one-eyed goalkeeper who becomes a star in the United States?

JG: Come off it, Gordon. That would be too far-fetched!

As I watched him walk jauntily away through the crowded hotel foyer, weaving easily past people as if they were not there, the years melted away and I could see a little white-shirted imp conjuring his way through defences for goals that had even the opposition applauding in appreciation.

Jimmy Greaves. They don't make them like him any more.

This interview was taken from *Banks of England*, published by the long-gone Arthur Barker Publishers. Gordon passed away in February 2019 aged 81, two years before Jimmy, also 81.

We will not see their like again.

Chapter 18:

The Cloughie connection

ONE OF the first calls Jimmy got when he started out as a columnist with *The Sun* was from the most controversial yet charismatic character in football, Brian Clough. 'Hey, young man,' he said on the telephone from his Nottingham Forest office, 'I just want you to know I'm here to give you any help I can. If you don't accept my offer to come up here and interview me, I'll come down there and kick you right in the goolies. Got it? No fee required.'

This was Cloughie's way of helping out an old mate. They had been pals since playing together for England in 1959. Twenty-one years on, Brian was the manager of the back-to-back European Cup winners and Greavsie was a recovering alcoholic. I went along to operate the tape recorder and also for a reunion with Cloughie, who had given me his first interview when he took over as boss at Derby County at the start of breathing fire into the East Midlands soccer scene.

Their conversation makes fascinating reading and emphasises just how much the game has changed:

JG: Do you remember our first game together for England back in 1959?

BC: Remember it? Hey, I can still feel it and taste it as though it were played yesterday. It was against Wales at Cardiff and the forward line was John Connelly, you and me, Bobby Charlton and my Middlesbrough colleague Edwin Holliday.

JG: You and Holliday were both making your England debuts.

BC: Correct. We were both Middlesbrough lads by birth but as different in temperament as it's possible to be. I was a bag of nerves and desperate to do well among all you household names, but Edwin seemed completely unconcerned by it all. I remember that he arrived without his boots and his mam brought them down by train and delivered them at the ground 25 minutes before the kick-off. That would have destroyed me, but Edwin casually sat down and started changing the studs, whistling away as if he didn't have a care in the world. That was my introduction to the atmosphere of international football.

JG: Our match fee was 20 quid, which was also our weekly wage.

BC: I would willingly have paid to play for my country. Same as now, I'd manage them for nowt.

JG: You were outspoken, Brian, even in those days.

BC: You call it being outspoken. I call it having an opinion.

JG: I remember you being worried about who was going to give you the ball.

BC: Dead right I was worried. There I was stuck in the middle of the two biggest names in the game – yourself and the master, Robert Charlton – and I couldn't see who was going to pass to me. We were all receivers rather than givers. When I pointed this out to team manager Walter Winterbottom, he said, 'Just go out there and inter-change and then go and strike for goal.' He made it sound as easy as putting jam on bread. He gave the same spiel to Len Shackleton years before and Shack said with an innocent look on his face, 'What side of the net would you like me to put it, Gaffer?'

JG: We drew 1-1 and Walter picked the same attack for the match against Sweden at Wembley 11 days later.

BC: My second and last match for England. The mix was all wrong and I was the one who got the chop. Lost it 3-2. That result is carved into my heart. Something happened in that game that should have put me in the *Guinness Book of Records*. The ball hit the underside of the bar and I somehow managed to sit on it on the goal line. It was trapped under my unmentionables and I couldn't move to put it in the net. I sat on it so long it's a wonder I didn't hatch the bloody thing.

JG: Thinking back to when we were youngsters just coming into the game, we had some marvellous players to inspire us. I'm thinking of the likes of Matthews, Carter, Mannion, Lawton, Lofthouse, Finney, Shackleton. Where have all the great individual players gone?

BC: It's much more of a team game now, young Jim. Coaching has had a lot to do with the disappearance of really creative players. Too many coaches are frightened of genius. They don't know how to handle it. So they take the easy way out and destroy it. I'm not against coaching but bad coaching is a criminal offence. It's a sad fact of life that there are more bad coaches than good ones, and they are the people who set out to destroy rather rather than create.

JG: Who was your favourite of those glittering stars of our youth, and could he fit into today's football?

BC: I would have to plump for Tom Finney. He was a real master and a marvellous ambassador for the game both on and off the pitch. I will always remember my first overnight stay with an England squad. We were in a posh hotel and I was a kid from the sticks, completely overawed by the surroundings and the big-name players. I was having a breakfast of bacon and baked beans and was so nervous that I tipped the lot on to my lap. There are a lot of people who would have made capital of that and made my life a misery by taking the mickey. But that nice man Finney helped me clear myself up and quietly arranged for the hotel to clean my trousers. They were the only pair I had with me and I was so green that I didn't even realise you could get things cleaned and ironed in a hotel.

JG: Footballers can be really cruel with the mickey taking. But Tommy's always been the first gentleman of the game.

BC: I always stamp on anybody taking the mickey out of a club mate. When Roger Davies first signed for Derby, he had to take some unmerciful ribbings from established first-teamers. It got out of hand until I threatened that if anybody else took the mickey out of him, I would give them a whack on the nose. Another time here at Forest, Garry Birtles was going through it because I kept beating him at squash. I put a notice on the board saying that anybody wanting to take the mickey out of Garry's ability on the squash court should challenge me for a £10 sidestake. The mickey taking stopped.

JG: We've deviated a bit here, Brian. Can you talk a bit longer about Tom Finney?

BC: A bit longer? I could talk all day about that man. He could play in any forward position. People seem to remember him best as a winger, but don't forget that in the later stages of his career he switched to centre-forward and he was brilliant. Took all the knocks without complaint and tormented the hell out of defenders with sheer skill. Bill Shankly played with him for years at Preston and said that Tom could run through any defence while wearing an overcoat and a pair of wellies. If he were just starting in today's game, he would have no trouble at all adjusting simply because there's no substitute for skill.

JG: There are not many skilful youngsters coming through in the game today. Are you concerned about the lack of talent?

BC: Hey, Jim, the trouble with you is since you switched to this writing and broadcasting lark, you've joined the army of pessimists. Let me tell you that English football is like a diamond mine. There are lots of shining talents around. They need cutting and polishing and putting in the right setting, but if you look after them properly they will dazzle. The game is in a healthy state despite what the obituary writers might say. We can all go forward together with confidence about the future provided a few attitudes are changed.

JG: What is needed to lift our football out of its present slump?

BC: There's an easy answer. A successful England team. Ron Greenwood carries a lot of responsibility. He's got a team together that will get us through to the 1982 World Cup finals and then we need to do well in Spain. If we shine in Spain, it will reflect in our attendances at home.

JG: Are you optimistic of our chances of making a strong challenge for the World Cup?

BC: Provided Ron picks our best team, yes.

JG: That sounds an odd thing to say.

BC: Well, let me tell you, young man, that while I may have a reputation for shooting my mouth off, you would be amazed at the amount of listening I've done over the years. Two men I listened to more than most were Harry Storer and Bill Shankly, and they both gave me the same advice: 'Always select your best team.' That statement will no doubt baffle the laymen, but you would be surprised how many managers don't, for various reason, pick the best possible team that is available to them.

JG: Bill Nicholson said exactly the same thing to me last time I interviewed him. 'Always pick your best team.'

BC: Well, Bill certainly knew what he was talking about. One of the all-time great managers, and what a gentleman. I always picked his brains at every opportunity. If you're going to pick brains, Jim, always pick the best. Just like selecting a team. If I were in your boots, I'd be picking the brains of that lovely man Brian Moore. He really knows how to work a camera.

JG: Have we got the players to make us a world power?

BC: Without question. There are plenty of those diamonds I was telling you about in our game. It's up to the England manager to pick them and make them dazzle. It might hurt old pros like you and me to hear this said, Jim, but many of today's players are technically better than in our day. Better than me anyway, but you, of course, were a genius. And make sure you leave that on tape for your readers.

JG: Changing the subject quickly, do you go along with the growing belief that players are now taking too much money out of the game

BC: Football is just beginning to stabilise after the introduction of freedom of contract. At first, players went berserk asking for fortunes and managers and clubs went equally mad by agreeing to give them what they were demanding.

JG: And do you think it's now under control?

BC: I wouldn't go as far as saying that, but we at least now know what's to be done. Footballers must be made to understand the facts of life otherwise they will be putting clubs out of business. They will have to understand that if there's £20,000 coming in, they can only have £19,000 between them. If they take £21,000, that's bad business for their club and ultimately bad business for them because at that rate the club wouldn't be there for long. I think we're coming into a period in our game where common sense will prevail and greed will take a back seat.

JG: It's good to hear you in a buoyant, optimistic mood.

BC: Why shouldn't I be? When you look around here at the Forest ground with its new £2.5 million stand and the trophies that the club have won in the last few years, you have to be optimistic about what can be achieved in football. If Forest can do this, then there's hope for all clubs. We're only a little club y'know, but it's not stopped us thinking and acting big. That's the art of management. Taking decisions and putting your head on the chopping block for them. You're soon found out in this game if you try to do anything by halves. You can't hide. Every decision is there to be judged. Many clubs can have our sort of success provided they get their management right. That may sound conceited but it's an honest opinion. I'm always getting myself into hot water by speaking my mind, but our football might be in a better state if more people were more honest and direct with their opinions.

JG: D'you remember trying to sign me from Spurs before I joined West Ham?

BC: Bloody hell, I put out more smoke signal messages than those Indians in a John Wayne western. If you'd joined me at Derby, I'd have put five more years on your career, lots of money in your pocket and proper silverware and medals in your cabinet. That's the trouble with you soft southerners. Wander north of Watford and you get a nosebleed.

JG: If it's any consolation, I've tortured myself that I didn't follow up on your interest. You would have given me the kick up the arse I needed.

BC: No, James, what I would have done is put an arm around your shoulder. That's what you needed back then. Somebody to quietly coax you to play. You were the master, and I would have got you playing like you did in the old days before Alf Ramsey kicked the confidence out you.

JG: That's all in the past, Brian. I'm here to interview you about today's football. Do you think there's less honesty in the game these days?

BC: Let's say there's less sincerity. I look around the boardrooms and I see more sharks than there used to be. They are coming into the game for the wrong reasons, buying their way into clubs for image and appearances' sake rather than because they have a genuine love for football. Some of the dignity is going out of the game and I think that's sad.

JG: What advice would you give any young manager coming into the game?

BC: Be creative. Don't wear blinkers. Have opinions and really *manage*.

JG: If you were running our game, Brian, what changes would you introduce to improve it and make its future more secure?

BC: For a start, I would put you out of work with your Central TV job. I would ban television cameras from all grounds for a period of three years. A total blackout. There is no question in my mind that television is doing untold damage to our game. The weekend before last, I saw highlights and goals from nine FA Cup matches. Why should anybody bother to leave their armchairs when they know they can enjoy a bonanza on their television screen? We've sold it too cheap and it's costing the major clubs money in possible shirt sponsorship income. I want to see football banned from the TV screens for three years during which we in the game must work at getting people back into the habit of going to the grounds to see football in the flesh. Then, after the three-year ban, I would sit down with TV bosses and negotiate a sensible deal that would allow just one live 90-minute match to be shown, possibly on a Sunday afternoon. I don't like the filleted service that we get at the moment with edited matches in which only goals and controversial incidents are shown. Let's have just one game, warts 'n' all.

JG: I don't think your blanket ban would be popular with senior citizens and invalids who rely on their television sets for their football entertainment.

BC: They have my deepest sympathy and I would think proposals could be made to make entrance fees as cheap as possible for senior citizens. My heart bleeds for the people unable to leave their homes, but to be brutally honest our game will become a sick invalid unless we stop television luring so many of our customers away.

JG: You mentioned possible live coverage of a match on a Sunday afternoon. Are you in favour of Sunday football?

BC: Deep down, no. Barbara, my missus, says she'll walk out on me if regular Sunday football comes. It's the only day that sanity comes to our household and we can lead a normal, family life. That's important to me. But I won't fight against Sunday football if it is proved that this is what the public wants. I just won't campaign for it. Ideally, I would like to see Sunday summer afternoon football watched by families in shirt sleeves and colourful summer dresses. That would be utopia. But then what would happen to our family get-togethers at home and what would happen to Sunday cricket? As you can see, Jim, I'm fairly torn apart on the subject of Sunday football. It will be the public that decides whether it is to become a regular fixture.

JG: If you could make one law change to make football a better spectacle, what would it be?

BC: I don't think the laws need to be tampered with to any great degree. One thing I would like to see is for any offence in the penalty area to be punished with a penalty kick. Obstruction, dangerous kicking, spitting, back-chat to the referee, any misconduct. Make it a penalty. Those free-kicks in the box are a farce.

JG: Imagine that it's 1990. How do you see the game being played and presented?

BC: I don't think there will be that much difference in the way the game is played, but there will be a big change in the presentation. There will be a lot more razzmatazz with clubs going all-out to attract family audiences. I hope there will be a lot of all-seater stadiums and that hooliganism will be just a bad memory.

JG: What will Brian Clough be doing in 1990?

BC: I think you and I will be pushing each other around in wheelchairs, Jim. I just can't visualise that I will still be in management. The generation gap between me and the players would be too wide. I can still put them in their place at the moment by taking them on to the squash court and beating them. But I think that will be beyond me when I'm 55. Some cocky little 18-year-old will be able to say, 'Look at that silly old bastard!' I will have lost the gift of communication that's so important between a manager and his players. I can't have them calling me 'grandad'.

JG: Well, I think you will still need football, Brian. And football will definitely need you. If I were running football in this country, I know that by 1990 I would have you well established in the England manager's chair.

Eight years after this conversation, Jimmy got a confidential call from Brian's wife, Barbara, explaining that she was worried about her husband's reliance on alcohol. She asked if he could have a quiet word to try to encourage him to come off the booze. 'Brian has always respected you,' Barbara said, 'and I know he admires the way you had the character to defeat the curse of drink. You just might be able to make him see reason and accept that he is harming himself with his drinking.'

He revealed this to me following Cloughie's passing in 2004 at the age of 69. Jim:

'My agent Barry Brown rang me after I'd had a quiet, confidential word with Brian about his increasing reliance on alcohol. Barry was the reluctant go-between for a Fleet Street newspaper. "I am duty-bound to put the following offer to you," he said. "The *News of the World* is trying to stand up a story that Brian Clough has a drink problem. They say they know you've been talking to him and are willing to pay £25,000 for revealing what advice you gave him."

"Tell them I don't know what they're on about," I said. Ten minutes later, Barry rang back. "They've upped the offer to £30,000," he said. "The answer is still no," I said. "As far as I'm aware, Cloughie does not have any problem. Tell them to lay off."

I contacted his good pal, the TV commentator Brian Moore, to tell him to warn Cloughie that reporters were poking their noses into places where they did not belong. Mooro has had a long and close association with Cloughie, and I knew that he was genuinely concerned about the rumours that were scorching around the football world about Brian's drinking habits.

The reason I put on record the big-money bribe that was made to me is not to show what a goody two-shoes I was to turn it down but to illustrate the depth of interest there was in one of the most incredible characters British sport has ever produced. I was saddened and angered that Cloughie was never given the England manager's job. It should have been his when Don Revie deserted, but the chicken-hearted men who run our game did not have the courage to appoint him and played it safe by giving the job to "Reverend" Ron Greenwood. I spent my final dismal season under Greenwood's management at West Ham, and I can state with some knowledge that he was not in the same league as Cloughie.

He talked a good game, but was too much of a theorist. Ron used to go over the heads of many of his players with his tactical talks, and did not have the powers of motivation that are so vital for a manager. Cloughie was Churchillian in the way he could inspire a team by saying the right thing at the right time.

What he achieved at Derby and then more so at Forest was nothing short of miraculous. He was dynamic, driving, single-minded, perceptive, inspiring, controversial, stubborn, ruthless, courageous, energetic, tough, ambitious, egotistical – all these ingredients have gone into the cocktail character that, shaken not stirred, made Cloughie one of the most successful managers of all time. There is no question that he would have been the people's popular choice as manager of England, but the establishment always feared him as being too hot to handle.

Beneath the skin of the tough, uncompromising manager was a sensitive and loving family man. Brian was immensely proud of his profession and a quiet fighter for good causes. It was fitting that he cemented his legend in Robin Hood's Nottingham territory. I got the feeling that in another age Cloughie would willingly have robbed the rich to help the poor. He was continually doing charitable work without seeking publicity, and I know better than most that when you were in trouble he was ready to help without seeking anything in return.

It was one of the great football crimes that he was never given command of the England team. His decisive attitude could have sent a breath of fresh air right through our game, but the establishment were frightened of his magnetic attraction for controversy.

I suppose it's a case of history repeating itself. Robin Hood hardly endeared himself to the establishment!'

Chapter 19:

Stand and Deliver

WHEN ITV lost their football rights to Sky, Jimmy suddenly found himself unwanted on the box and this is when he reinvented himself and came up with Jimmy Greaves Mark IV. After the footballer, the drunk and the television star, we were now treated to the stand-up comedian. From 1999 up until his stroke in 2015, Jim performed on stage and together he and promoter/compere Terry Baker appeared in dozens of theatres around the UK.

Terry, a Hampshire-based disc jockey turned entrepreneur with the support and organisational skill of his wife Freda, saw the potential of Jimmy as a crowd puller:

‘ I had admired Jimmy as a footballer – who didn't? – and rated him one of the funniest men on television during his long run on *Saint and Greavsie.* I wanted to know all about his football experiences and was fascinated at the way he'd turned his life round after admitting being an alcoholic. It struck me that there were lots of people like me who wanted to know all about him, and so I put the idea to him of a theatre show. He was reluctant at first but I gently talked him into it and right from his first stage appearance he was an instant hit.

Just as with his football, he was a natural with a microphone in his hand. He could deliver a joke as well as any top comedian, and his anecdotes about his life and times meant he had audiences eating out of his hand. They loved him north, south, east and west. We called the show simply "An Evening with Jimmy Greaves", and we had sell-outs right across the nation.

He was the greatest British goalscorer there has ever been, so that in itself gave him lots to talk about because his many supporters wanted to know about his football adventures. Then he could tell tales about his life in television, and in particular stories about the people he had met while starring on *Saint and Greavsie*. As these included the likes of Donald Trump, Mike Tyson and Seve Ballesteros, he had dozens of riveting stories to share. I can't think of anybody in the world who could have matched his experiences, including of course having the character to beat the curse of alcoholism.

He was a born raconteur and would take a story and simply make it come alive. Perhaps it was the Irish in him, but he could really hold the attention of an audience with his tales of the unexpected. On top of his ability to make people laugh, he was a thorough professional and was never late for a show and was always impeccably turned out and mostly word perfect. If ever he did mess up a punchline, he had the ability to win the audience over by cussing himself and turning it into part of his act as if he had meant it. He had charisma by the lorry load. It was a real thrill and honour for both Freda and I to work with him for more than 15 years. I miss him like a brother. He was a diamond. '

After the restrictions of live television when he had to watch his language and his line of attack, Jimmy loved the freedom his stage shows gave him:

‘ People don't realise what a straitjacket you're in when working live in a studio, as Saint and I were for seven years. There were legal eagles hovering just off camera to make sure you didn't slander anybody, there was a floor manager shouting instructions given to him by the control room, you had to know which camera to look at and exactly where to be when talking or reacting to what Saint was saying. And all the time you had to act naturally and have your timing exact to allow for the VT inserts and the commercial breaks. Saint was much better at all that technical stuff than I was, but I was the one who was having to deliver the punchlines. On the stage, I am free to be myself and talk the people's language. I could eff and blind and not worry about the grammar book.

I have always hated it when so-called experts try to intellectualise what is the people's game. Complicating what is a simple sport is one of my pet hates. In the question-and-answer sessions refereed by Terry, I can bounce off the audience and say what I really feel without wondering whether I am upsetting the politically correct brigade. Even if I say it myself, we've had some terrific shows, particularly when I've shared the stage with the likes of George Best, Harry Redknapp, Stevie Perryman, Chopper Harris, Henry Cooper and the potty Gazza. Most of it has been much too hot for television! ’

Thousands enjoyed Jimmy's stand-up comedy act at his procession of gigs (and gags) across the nation. Here's a sample of his jokes:

'It's a fact that I went to Oxford and got a blue. And if some prat had not jogged my elbow, I would have got the pink and black as well.'

'I watched *Countdown* the other day with that beautiful Rachel Riley, and I have to tell you that I got aroused. First time I've ever got a seven-letter word!'

'I had a worrying goal drought once when I just couldn't put the ball into the net. It was the worst 15 minutes of my career.'

'Ron "Chopper" Harris told me he went home with a broken leg after a game for Chelsea. I asked who it belonged to.'

'George Best used to go missing a lot – Miss Canada, Miss South Africa, Miss Ireland, Miss World.'

'What d'you call a Scotsman in the closing stages of a World Cup finals? Referee.'

'England beaten by Iceland! Can you believe it? Next week they're playing Asda and then Tesco.'

'Saint and I were offered a job at Sky after ITV gave us the elbow. But we turned it down because Ian didn't fancy putting up those satellite dishes.'

Jimmy was also in demand as an after-dinner speaker. He became, let's say, quite rotund in his later years and used to get howls of laughter when opening his speech with the line, 'Good evening, fellow athletes.'

Just four days before his stroke in 2015 he went down to Exeter, where his old Spurs team-mate Steve Perryman was director of football. Steve, former Tottenham captain and 854-game holder of their club appearances record, recalled:

'Jim came to one of our legends dinners at St James Park and gave a speech as a favour to me. He was in fantastic form and got a standing ovation. He was both interesting and hilarious. I had appeared with him in many of his theatre shows and I had never known him funnier than this night. I couldn't believe it the next weekend when Terry Baker phoned to say he'd been rushed off to hospital after a serious stroke.

I played with Jim at the back end of his career with Tottenham, and I've never seen anybody to touch him for control of the ball, the ability to trick his way past defenders and then that trademark passing the ball into the net. He was a Rolls-Royce of a player. I went to his funeral with a lot of his old Spurs team-mates and we were unanimous in considering him not just the finest forward we'd ever seen but also the loveliest bloke. Jimmy was class from top to toe.'

Just weeks before Jim's Exeter visit, Terry Baker had organised a 75th birthday bash at Stevenage during which Jim was reunited with his old sidekick Alan Gilzean, and he gave a speech in which he was his top-nick sharp, sparkling, saucy self. To see the G-Men back together was hugely emotional for everybody who had enjoyed watching their partnership at Tottenham in the summer time of their lives.

Gilly had been hailed as the 'King of White Hart Lane' and was held in similarly high esteem at his original club Dundee, where he laid the foundation for a career celebrated on both sides of the border. None of us at the party, of course, realised that this would be the last time they would ever be together. Six weeks later, Jimmy was hit by his stroke and in 2018 Gilly suffered a brain tumour and passed on, aged 79.

During the Stevenage evening dripping with nostalgia, Jimmy and Alan paid tribute to each other. 'Gilly was one of the most talented footballers I ever played with or against. He was magical,' said Greavsie.

'Jimmy was simply the greatest goalscorer who ever pulled on a pair of football boots,' said Gilly. 'I would have paid to play with him. It was a privilege.'

As a mutual friend of both of them, I shared the top table at the birthday feast, and we recalled our memorable times of me chronicling the footballing feats of the G-Men on the pitch and enjoying their company off it – mostly at the bar. Jimmy would expect me to give Gilly a prominent place in this biography.

It is well documented how Greavsie hit the bottle. What had been less publicised is that Gilly could drink the lot of us under the table, but kept his habit away from the public gaze. While Jimmy had a sledgehammer, in-your-face style of humour, Alan was much more subtle and could cut people off at the legs with his dry delivery. He hated attention and just wanted to be left alone to get on with his life and his drinking. Over-the-top journalists like me made him cringe. 'It's just a game of fitba'', he'd say when I was going into excited hyperbole over one of his performances.

He was studiously laconic with his humour, deadpan in the style of legendary Scottish comedian Chic Murray.

Bill Nicholson, Tottenham's manager supreme, had cause to call him into his office one Monday morning. 'Alan, I've had a complaint from a supporter,' he said. 'He claims he saw you coming out of a nightclub at two o'clock in the morning.'

'Well, he's mistaken,' Gilly replied with that poker face he always had on the football field. 'I was going *into* the club.'

Sitting alongside me at Jimmy's birthday bash was Tottenham's former captain and another White Hart Lane idol, Steve Perryman.

He was trusted by the Gilzean family to release the news of Alan's passing in 2018, and when he rang this old hack I was deeply saddened.

'We've not only lost a great footballer and Tottenham legend,' Steve told me, 'but we've lost a great man. We all loved Gilly. There was nobody who did not have a soft spot for him as a feller, and we were all in awe of him as a footballer. He could make the ball talk.'

Worth repeating that I always described Alan as a Nureyev on grass, because he was so balletic. You could have set his movement on the pitch to music. He danced many a *pas de deux* with Greavsie and then with big Martin Chivers as his partner. What music the G-Men made together, with Alan providing the subtlety of touch with either foot and glancing headers that were his trademark. He happily took second violin to lead virtuoso Jimmy, but was a master soloist in his own right.

Gilly was an extraordinarily gifted forward who could thread a ball through the eye of a needle. He specialised in flick headers and was an intelligent positional player who often popped up in unmarked places that caught defenders napping. I am often asked what the pair of them would be worth in today's mad transfer market. Priceless! £200 million and rising.

Born in Coupar Angus on 22 October 1938, Alan first made a name for himself as a free-scoring forward with Dundee, winning the 1961/62 league title with them and helping the club reach the European Cup semi-finals the following season. He is as much idolised at Dens Park as he is at Tottenham.

Alan, married to a policewoman, arrived at the Lane in December 1964 as replacement for the bulldozing Bobby Smith. The contrast was stark, but he was every bit as devastating as the mighty Smith and he majestically earned the title 'The King of White Hart Lane'.

He and Greavsie went together like bacon and eggs and they were the most dynamic duo in the league for three or four years. Gilly won 22 Scottish caps and settled into another winning partnership with Martin Chivers when Jimmy moved on in 1970.

Alan wound down his exciting and often eccentric career in South Africa, and cut his links with football after a brief experience as manager of Stevenage and then working as a depot transport manager. He disappeared completely from the football radar, leaving behind Spurs stats of 343 league games (93 goals) and 96 cup matches (40 goals). His son Ian was a Spurs youth player and later scored goals for Dundee, just like his adored dad.

Sportswriter James Morgan produced a superb book on Gilly's apparent 'disappearance' called *In Search of Alan Gilzean*. It turned out he had moved to Weston-super-Mare when the transport company he had been working for in Stevenage relocated to Bristol, where he quietly got on with his organisational duties without ever boasting about his exploits as one of the finest footballers of his generation. After 30 years out of the spotlight, Alan returned to the celebrity circuit to get the acclaim his talent deserved. When I put the 'gone missing' stories to Gilly, he told me with that famous straight face, 'I always knew where I was.'

There will never be another like Gilly, a centurion on both sides of the border. I'll never forget the night the G-Men were reunited. A peerless pair.

Chapter 20:

Best of the Best

JIMMY AND I used to spend hours discussing our favourite teams and players, much of our conversation dictated by book and newspaper column deadlines. The one thing we always agreed on: that George Best was the greatest British-born footballer of them all. John Charles, Bobby Moore, Duncan Edwards, Bobby Charlton, Stanley Matthews, Tom Finney, Jim Baxter and Jimmy Johnstone used to get into the argument, but it always ended with George coming out as number one. Here's Jim talking about his favourite footballer, a view that I know he would have wanted me to include in this biography:

‘Simply the Best seems too glib and clichéd a description for George Best, but I am comfortable using it because it just happens to be totally accurate. George *was* simply the best British footballer of my lifetime, probably of anybody's lifetime.

OK, I admit to bias because George and I were close pals with much more in common than just our footballing careers. They have a lovely saying in Belfast – which you are likely to hear soon after touching down at George Best Airport, "Maradona great; Pelé better; George best."

That's better than anything I can coin. I'm choked just thinking about the loveable, cheeky sod. He used to take the piss out of me for giving up being pissed. I never, ever felt it my business to try to talk him out of his "have-booze-will-travel" existence. In many interviews, he would tell journalists with that mischievous grin of his, "Jimmy has chosen his way, I've chosen mine – and I know who's getting the most enjoyment out of it!"

How could I argue with that Irish logic? George lived his life like there was no tomorrow, laughing, joking, shagging, staggering and brawling through his middle age. Eventually, there was no more tomorrow. But I honestly think – no, I *know* – George would not have had it any other way.

George did everything by the bucketload. He played football better than almost anybody on the planet, he loved many of the women he bedded (which was on the Casanova scale), he drank more than was good for him but loved every drop, and he spent every penny as if money was coming out of a tap. It was George, of course, who famously said, "I've spent my money on booze, women and fast cars, the rest I squandered."

Everybody, the world and its brother, had an opinion on George. And d'you know something, he didn't give a monkey's about any of them. He lived his life the way he wanted to and – surprisingly, for somebody pictured so many times with an attractive blonde on his arm – he was happiest as a loner.

He once told me that his most contented times were spent sitting alone at continental-type cafés just watching the world go by. For all his exposure across front pages and on the box, he remained a shy man at heart.

George cared about other people that other people didn't care about. I will let you read that sentence twice to see that it makes sense.

I remember before one of our roadshows up in Leeds, we were sitting having a meal in a pizza restaurant when shuffling in came the vaguely familiar figure of somebody we suddenly realised had been a pioneering player when George was first making his name in the game.

It was Albert Johanneson, the black South African winger who had been a runner-up in the 1965 FA Cup Final with Leeds. He had gone on the skids after his retirement and had become yet another loser to booze.

I left George and Albert talking over old times to get prepared for the evening's show. Bestie, not for the first time, failed to turn up and later admitted that he and Albert had gone out on the piss.

"Well," said George, "I at least had the satisfaction of giving Albert one more decent night out. Nobody gives a fuck about him. He deserved my full attention for just one night."

That was the caring side of Bestie, who was an easy touch for hard-luck stories. But even "Generous George" became a little disillusioned when people would get him to sign all sorts of things "for sick friends and relatives" only to find them appearing on eBay a few days later.

When George was desperate for money after his liver transplant, his conscientious agent Phil Hughes persuaded him to have the trophies, medals and mementoes he had won and the shirts he had worn auctioned. Phil could not believe how little was left when he went to George's house. Most of those prized possessions had been given away, stolen or lost.

One thing that always amuses me is when people talk about George having had a short career. He actually played on for 11 years after his ten eventful seasons at Old Trafford. Sadly, many of the games were for teams not really worthy of his regal presence. It was like finding a Goya in a garage sale.

As a winger, George was like Stanley Matthews on steroids. He had mesmerising ball control, the speed of an Olympic sprinter over 20 yards and a deadly eye in front of goal. And he was recklessly brave. Any defender threatening him physical harm – and there were a lot of them in his peak years – was treated to the full monty. He would tease and torment them, risking serious injury as they kicked out trying to stop him. George rarely came off a pitch without having got the better of his marker.

They kept telling us that Pelé and Maradona were better players, but if George had performed in those highly skilled Brazilian and Argentinian teams, surrounded by gifted footballers, he would have been acclaimed worldwide as, well, simply the Best.

He used to be searingly honest on our roadshows organised by my agent Terry Baker when it came to the question-and-answer sessions with the audience. I used to wince sometimes, hoping there were no legal eagles in listening distance.

Here is a vetted version of some of our answers in the often blistering Best & Greavsie show. All the questions were pitched by members of the audience, and A1 Sporting Speakers entrepreneur Terry Baker acted as referee:

Q: If you two were starting out all over again as players, would you lay off the booze?

GEORGE: You must be pissed to ask that question! I would have done everything the same. I'm not one of those people who look back and regret things. I did what I wanted to do at the time and thoroughly enjoyed myself, and I'm still knocking it back. I would never have Jim's discipline to stop drinking and – hands up – neither would I want to.

JIMMY: I like to think I would have been more sensible the second time around, but there is so much money to be earned now that it must be difficult to avoid the high life. To be honest, I loved my drinking days and wouldn't change a thing, apart from the secret drinking I got up to in the silly last days. I've not touched a drop since 1978 and have become a boring old fart. That can never be said about George.

Q: How big an influence did Matt Busby have on you, George, and Bill Nicholson on you, Jimmy?

GEORGE: Sir Matt was like a second father to me and I had great respect for him. People said he was too easy on me, but he gave me several bollockings that almost brought me to tears. He was not the soft fella that was portrayed in the press. Sir Matt could be ruthless when necessary, but he had soul.

JIMMY: You will never catch me saying anything bad about Bill, even though he broke my heart when telling me that Tottenham didn't want me any more. He was as honest as the day is long and I owe him everything for bringing me back from Italy, where I was like a drowning man. Bill could talk the ears off a donkey but there was nothing he did not know about football tactics. He and Alf Ramsey were big rivals for the Tottenham job, and I don't think Alf ever forgave Spurs for favouring Bill as Jimmy Anderson's successor. They were both master coaches, who were suspicious of me because I was a maverick.

Q: Why did you and Bobby Charlton hate each other, George, and how did you rate him, Jimmy?

GEORGE: That's bollocks. We misunderstood each other, rather than hated each other. Bobby and I came from different worlds. He did not approve of my lifestyle and I was not over-impressed by his. What I do know is that I have got a lot of fun out of life. I'm not sure Bobby can say that. Have you ever seen him laughing? Let me say in front of all you witnesses that I rated him highly as a player, and it was a joy to have Charlton and Denis Law on my side. Three European Footballers of the Year together. It didn't come better than that. Even Real Madrid had only two of those!

JIMMY: Bobby is certainly an all-time great but he remains a mystery to me. I played with him at Under-23 and full international level across more then ten years, and I can honestly say I didn't really get to know him. Big brother Jack wore his heart on his sleeve and was as open as a book, but Bobby was always miserly with his thoughts. I envied Bobby's ability to bomb in those long-range shots, but I never saw him get carried away with excitement. Perhaps it was something to do with that 1958 plane crash that he survived. Blimey, I'd never have flown again if that had been me. The experience seemed to squeeze the humour out of him. But, no matter what you think of his personality, he was a great, great player. Best, Law, Charlton. It does not get better than that.

Q: With a gun to your head, gents, who was the greatest player of your generation.

GEORGE: In Europe, Johan Cruyff. He was magical when at his peak. On the world stage, I have to go along with the general view – Pelé just ahead of Maradona, but Alfredo Di Stefano and Ferenc Puskas were something special when playing together for Real.

JIMMY: Not just because he's sitting on the stage here with me, I'd vote for George every time. If only he had played in a World Cup finals, he would have been feted as the great player that he is. George is one of only a handful of players who could take a match by the scruff of its neck and win it on his own. I'd willingly have paid top dollar to watch him play. He was an Irish magician.

Q: Did either of you ever go on the pitch drunk?

GEORGE: I played with hangovers a few times, but I was a good enough professional to make sure I was fit to play in my Manchester United days. Mind you, there were a few games in the United States where I might have struggled to pass the breathalyser test.

JIMMY: I only took liberties at the back end of my career when I was playing with the likes of Woodford Town, Brentwood, Chelmsford and Barnet, but I was never near being legless. I was certainly never drunk during my league and England career. Barnet were marvellous with me. I would disappear on benders and they would cover for me by saying I was injured. At West Ham, I just played as if I'd been on the piss.

Q: Is it right, George, that you bedded seven Miss Worlds?

GEORGE: Total rubbish. It was only four. I didn't turn up for the other three.

JIMMY: And don't forget it was you, George, who said that you spent loads of money on wine, women and song, and squandered the rest.

Q: Were you caught in bed with a blonde on the afternoon of an FA Cup semi-final, George?

GEORGE: That's another lie. She was a brunette. Seriously, I was amusing myself with a lady in my hotel room on the afternoon of the 1970 FA Cup semi-final against Leeds. We were just talking and flirting when Wilf McGuinness, then the Manchester United boss, came knocking on the door like a maniac. I didn't see what harm I was doing. It was surely better to be relaxing, talking to a nice lady, than worrying about that evening's game.

JIMMY: Bill Nicholson caught me in a bed once – a flower bed. I was having a pee.

Q: This is a question for both of you. Did anybody ever threaten to break your leg while you were playing against them?

GEORGE: Only a few dozen times. They didn't realise it, but they just made me play better because I wanted to prove they did not belong on the same pitch as me. I know that sounds arrogant, but without that sort of confidence don't bother to try to play at the top.

JIMMY: We both played against the best hard men in Bites Yer Legs, Chopper Harris, Tommy Smith and Peter Storey, but they would not have lasted five minutes in the game if they had set out to deliberately break legs. I remember Tommy Smith calling me over once before a match against Liverpool at Anfield, and he handed me a piece of A4 paper. Typed on it was the evening menu for the nearby Liverpool infirmary. The Scouse fans used to throw him raw meat as the match kicked off.

Q: Are you jealous of the thousands of pounds today's players are earning each week?

GEORGE: No, it's their time and my advice is enjoy it while it lasts. I was a big earner throughout my career and have no complaints. Mind you, if Greavsie and I were playing now, I've no doubt we'd both be on more than £100,000 a week. Think of the booze that would buy!

JIMMY: I feel nothing but joy for them, but I worry that many of the foreign invaders are here just for the dough. I wish they would get more involved in knowing the history of the clubs for which they're playing. But hark at me, I couldn't wait to get out of Italy when I was picking up what was considered a fortune with AC Milan. All I hope is that they are getting the best advice on how to invest the money for the future. They can be made for life.

Q: What has been the lowest moment for each of you?

GEORGE: Getting sent to prison for drunk-driving and assaulting a policeman. I know I deserved it, but what good did it do anybody? I could have done something for the community, something like training under-privileged kids. But they wanted to make an example of me. As I was sent down, I turned to my solicitor and said, "I suppose that's the knighthood fucked." I even got hammered for that by the press when it became public what I'd said. Surely a sense of humour is the only thing that keeps people sane at times like that.

JIMMY: Mine was crawling to our dustbins and draining the remains of vodka from bottles that my wife Irene had thrown away. That was when I knew I had to stop drinking or finish up dead at a very young age. I was still in my mid-30s.

Q: How do the pair of you rate David Beckham?

GEORGE: Well, he can only kick the ball with his right foot, can't head the ball, can't tackle and doesn't score nearly enough goals. Apart from that, he's not bad. Actually, I've got to know him well and he's a smashing lad, but not a patch on Bobby Charlton as a footballer.

JIMMY: He's the pride of Essex, of course, or certainly East London. It's great to see the way he has conquered Old Trafford and he and his Spice girl have got a great eye for business off the pitch. One of the few players who rivals even you for good looks, George, but nowhere in the class of the greatest of all England midfield schemers, Johnny Haynes. And he could kick with both feet.

Q: Who were the hardest players you played against?

GEORGE: There were a squad of hit men in the days when Jimmy and I were playing. Every team had an assassin, a hatchet man whose one job was to try to stop the ball-players from running with the ball. Don't forget, they could tackle from behind then. We were not given any protection by the referees. I was kicked by the best of them, Norman "Bites Yer Legs" Hunter, Ron "Chopper" Harris, Tommy "Iron" Smith, Dave Mackay, Billy Bremner, and we had a good marker in little Nobby Stiles, who would have tackled his granny if Matt Busby had asked him to. But the hardest of them all was Peter "Cold Eyes" Storey at Arsenal. He seemed a real hard case to me. He used to prowl around the pitch almost grunting as he waited to chop anybody trying to get past him.

JIMMY: I'll go along with that. I could have a laugh with Chopper and Smithy, and even Bites Yer Legs could take a joke, provided his Big Brother boss Don Revie was not watching. But Storey was always a mean and moody sod, and I never warmed to him. He got a suspended sentence later on for allegedly running a brothel. He certainly had something of the night about him. Chopper has become a good mate and we have lots of chuckles over the games in which we tried to get the better of each other. I once pointed to the sky and told him there was rain on the way. As he looked up, I nipped away to meet a cross and scored against Chelsea. It was the only kick I had against him all game.

Q: If you could turn the clock back, gents, what major change would you make?

GEORGE: I would play on for Manchester United for another five years and break every record in the books. I think if Matt Busby or Alex Ferguson had been in charge,

I would never have stopped playing at the top so early. But let's say Tommy Docherty was not my sort of manager. I always thought he was more interested in his own image rather than the club's.

JIMMY: That's an easy one for me. When Bill Nicholson telephoned me on transfer deadline day and told me Ron Greenwood was waiting to talk to me at Upton Park, I would have left Ron talking to himself. It was the silliest move of my career.

Q: George, why did you go missing so much?

GEORGE: Well, wouldn't you have gone missing if waiting for you in the bedroom were Miss United Kingdom, Miss United States, Miss World?

JIMMY: The only misses that got me into trouble was missing chances in my last few games with Spurs. It convinced Bill Nick that all I was interested in was rally driving.

Q: George, people said you should have been ashamed of yourself when you turned up drunk on Terry Wogan's live television show.

GEORGE: It's the people around Terry who should feel ashamed. They plied me with booze in the hospitality room before the show started, knowing full well that I was getting drunk. They wanted me pissed when I walked on set. I have no doubt about that. Well, they got their wish and I was not proud of my performance that night. I don't think Terry was part of it. He was shocked when I walked on stage as pissed as a fart. It was his production team. I think they were struggling in the ratings at the time.

JIMMY: I cringed in embarrassment for you, George. It was obvious they'd done you up like a kipper. If it had been me, I'd have chinned Wogan but you are always a pussycat when you're boozed. My world of television can be just as bad as the worst of the Fleet Street tabloids and they spit you out when they've had their pound of flesh.

This final question was a rehearsed plant to set up the climax of the show: *What's the truth, George, about that story of you and a Miss World in a Manchester casino?*

GEORGE: It's been a bit embroidered, but this is the true version. I was playing roulette in a Manchester casino, got lucky and won £20,000. The girl who brought me luck that night was the Swedish Miss World, Mary Stavin. She was hanging on my arm as I cashed in my chips. She put a few wads in her handbag, and I stuffed the rest in my jacket and trouser pockets. Then we got a chauffeured limousine back to the five-star Manchester hotel where we were staying.

As the wizened little Irish night porter let us in, I tipped him 20 quid to bring a bottle of chilled Dom Perignon up to our room.

Mary, in a see-through negligee, was just coming out of the bathroom and the 20 grand was spread over the bed when the porter arrived with the bubbly.

As he put the tray on the bedside table, the porter asked a little nervously, "I wonder, Mr Best, if you'd mind a fellow Ulsterman putting a personal question to you?"

"Fire away," I said, peeling off another tenner from the stack of money and handing it to the old boy.

"Well, I was wondering," said the porter, "just where did it all go wrong?"

When George passed on in November 2005, a light went out on the football stage. I played against him, I drank with him, I laughed with him, I liked him a hell of a lot and I never ever pitied him. George chose his path and did it his way right to the last.

Yes, he was simply the best. ❯

Chapter 21

The 50-year milestone

GOING THROUGH my files, I came across the following Greavsie commentary on life as he passed his 50-year milestone. I am certain you will find it fascinating, a man who was a national treasure taking stock back in 1990. This is Jimmy talking, not knowing there were another 31 years still to come. He and daughter Lynn were concentrating on selling life insurance just in case the TV world crashed around his ears, which it did just two years later when Greg Dyke pulled the plug on *Saint and Greavsie* because Sky had established a monopoly on televised Premier League football.

‘ Now that I have reached the dreaded half-century – my 50th birthday passed without celebration on 20 February 1990 – I have to say about my life as I often say about my money, "Where has it all gone?" The one thing that I cannot get used to is the speed with which life races by. Was it really 12 years ago when I hit rock-bottom as an alcoholic, scrambling on my knees alongside a dustbin in the early hours of a winter's morning? I was trying to recover a bottle of vodka that Irene had thrown away in a desperate but hopeless attempt to stop me drinking.

Where did the first half of my life go? Was that really me who they used to call the "Goalden Boy" because of the ease with which I was able to pump the ball into the net? It must have been because I've got a yellowing newspaper cutting with a banner headline shouting "GOAL KING GREAVES". I have just blurred memories of it all and I feel as if I have been on the outside looking in at somebody else's life.

What I say to outstanding modern players like Gary Lineker, Paul Gascoigne, Bryan Robson, Ian Rush and John Barnes is, as the old song goes, "Enjoy yourself – it's later than you think." Suddenly, and I promise you that it's in a blinking of an eye, you will find your careers are over. What you must do is recall the past with pride, suck every experience you can out of the present and make sensible plans for the future.

You might think this is Greavsie the insurance salesman talking, but I cannot stress strongly enough to today's players the need to get the best possible guidance on how to invest their money while their earning power is at its peak (and, unashamedly wearing my insurance hat, I will be happy to give "best advice" to anybody who contacts me). I occasionally see old footballing mates – internationals as well as the bread-and-butter players – on their uppers and there is little sadder than the old footballer with nothing to kick around but his memories. As I said to George Best when I was struggling to adjust to retirement, "They shoot horses, don't they. So why not shoot old footballers?"

"Have another drink," said George. "And while you're about it, make mine a large one."

Bestie. What a character. What a player. What a man. What a boozer!

[George died following a liver transplant, aged 59].

You will find me in philosophical mood in this trip through what has so far been a hectic second half to my life. There is nothing like galloping middle age to concentrate the mind on making sure you avoid committing any more mistakes in the minefield of life. I have trodden on quite a few mines in my time, but luckily I have remained in one piece.

What I missed most of all when I stupidly retired from football at 31 was being centre stage. Thank God (and Gary Newbon, Trevor East, Bruce Gyngell, Nick Owen, Anne Diamond, Bob Southgate, Bob Burrows, Bob Patience, Bob Hall – so many Bobs – John Bromley, Roy Bottomley and Uncle Tom Cobblers and all), television put me back in the spotlight. All right, sometimes you cannot tell the difference between the real Greavsie and my Spitting Image puppet, but at least I'm up there getting my fat face and refined voice noticed. I promise you that there is nothing more frustrating than being an exhibitionist without a platform. It's like being a pianist without a piano or a painter without a canvas. Or an alcoholic without a drink.

I'll be the first to admit that I have been a jammy sod to have got another showboating career going for me, while many of my old footballing pals have had to settle for mundane jobs. This is why I stress the importance of forward planning for today's big-earning footballers.

One day – and one day soon – they will discover that the oil well they have struck has dried up. When they have fired their final shots, they will find that there is room for only a handful to continue to make a living out of the game in the managing/coaching field. And the likes of the Saint and I, giggly Emlyn and Bob "The Headmaster" Wilson will not easily give up our studio seats (mind you, there's always a good chance that my TV bosses might kick me out to make way for somebody a little easier to handle).

I am building up to a lecture because I am concerned about the stories I hear about many of our current leading players. They have not learned from my mistakes and are, so I am reliably informed, hitting the bottle in spectacular style. They might think they have got it under control, but suddenly – and it creeps up on you like an invisible snake – they will find it is they who are under the control of the demon drink.

There is an established England international player who I am told gets paralytic after most matches, and the kitty for the drinking school that he leads is the equivalent of what I used to earn in a week as a First Division footballer. I've been down that road, lording it at the bar after matches and contenting myself that I would be able to run the booze off in training. But please, lads, take it from me – and pin this on the dressing room noticeboard – BOOZERS ARE LOSERS.

Maybe they see me on "the box" and think that I have done all right for myself despite swimming in alcohol during and immediately after my playing career. What they haven't seen is the torture that I went through in the days when I was being haunted by the dreaded DTs. You have no doubt heard of James Stewart and his imaginary friend Harvey, a giant rabbit, when he was playing the part of an alcoholic. Well, in my nightmares, I was accompanied by an anything-but-friendly giant in a suit of armour. He used to threaten to crush me in the desperate days when my drinking was out of control. In my sober moments, I was able to identify him as the foot-tall figure in armour that decorates our fireplace to this day. But in my drinking fits he used to look eight foot tall and was a terrifying sight as he came menacingly towards me and I found that I was being strapped to a hospital bed to stop me from doing myself an injury when my drunken rages were pushing me to the edge of suicide. I am not reliving these memories for the sake of sensation (I've had enough sensation to last me a lifetime, thank you). I am recalling the horrors that I went through in a sincere attempt to try to convince any of today's footballers – anybody, for that matter – that they should drink only in moderation.

It is not necessarily the heavy drinkers who get themselves trapped by the illness of alcoholism. I was not the biggest drinker in my school. Bobby "Old Hollow Legs" Moore could drink me under the table. So could indestructible Dave Mackay and Alan "Make Mine A Double" Gilzean. And I was always running a bottle of champers behind Malcolm Allison when we used to hit the London clubs (and I don't mean Arsenal, Spurs etc). But all four have come through their boozing without bruising.

I had lower resistance to the advance of alcoholism and by the time I realised the danger, it was too late. I was trapped in that nightmare world in which one drink is too many and 20 is not enough. To all those footballers – people from any walk of life – who are saying, "It couldn't happen to me", think again. It can happen to you unless you drink sensibly. The moment you have to have that next drink, you are in trouble.

To all footballers, my message is: please take it easy. There is nothing wrong with a pint or two as reward and relaxation after a match or a tough training session. But know when to say no to the next round. I have had the stories from enough sources to realise the extent of the drinking – and even some drug-taking – on the footballing circuit. It honestly worries me and if this article pulls up any of the lads and makes them control their drinking, then old Greavsie, recovering alcoholic, will be delighted.

I have always been a political animal (right of Genghis Khan, old leftie Greg Dyke would say). But while I am a Tory with deep socialist roots, I would not hesitate to switch my allegiance to the party that can promise to make the environment number one on their manifesto. Now that I am well into the second half of my life, I want to encourage the powers-that-be to create a better world than the one I entered in 1940. When I was born in East Ham, a maniac with a toothbrush moustache was preparing to unload his bombs on London. I had entered a world at war. Now my grandchildren are being born into a world losing a war against pollution.

Before I bow out, I would like to see the world a better place. For the sake of my grandchildren, and their children, and their children's children. If we are not careful, there will not be a world for them to inherit. I think there is a lot of worrying coming my way. It's a funny old life.

I hear rumours of a Super League on the horizon. That will be interesting because for sure the Football League needs a kick up the pants. It is being run by people stuck in the past, and only England winning the World Cup in Italy this summer can save their crumbling empire.

Much of my future energy is going to go into building up my insurance business with my daughter Lynn, who has got her mother's practical mind, thank goodness. Just 12 years ago, I did not think I had a future. Now I want to encourage people to build for it with wise investment and winning policies. One thing I will not be doing is becoming a member of the "smart set".

In the summer of 1989, I was voted one of Britain's seven scruffiest men. I was in good company. The other "seedy" six – according to the Mr Harry menswear chain – were Terry Wogan, Jeremy Beadle, Kenny Everett, Gorden Kaye, Nigel Lawson and Neil Kinnock. Scruffiness makes strange bedfellows! I like to think of myself as casual smart. I have always hated wearing ties and would like to strangle the man who invented them, using a Windsor knot, of course. I am happiest in an open-necked shirt and a sweater (provided it's not endorsed by Emlyn Hughes).

In the second half of my life I must find as much time as possible for Irene, the lady without whom there would – for me – be no television career, no books, no insurance company, no future. I owe her everything and I have got to try to make up for the years of happiness that she lost because of my slavery to the bottle. That's the worst thing about alcoholism. It is those nearest and dearest to the alcoholic who suffer the most. Somehow, I must find a way to make amends. Somehow. '

That was Jim baring his soul in the spring of 1990. England reached the semi-finals of the World Cup in Italy and he starred on the ITV panel, each day wearing a different T-shirt with a topical tabloid headline about the tournament. I got the T-shirts printed by an Indian stallholder on Pier Hill at Southend and had them biked up to Jimmy in the London studio. 'Now Is The Hour for Beckenbauer' was our last one on the day of the final, won by Der Kaiser's Germany. I thought it was a clever idea, but my much-respected colleague Patrick Collins in the *Mail on Sunday* accused Jim of dumbing down the coverage.

ITV's official monitors reported that people were switching over from BBC 'to see what Greavsie's headline said'.

We were literally making the headlines.

Within two years, the major clubs had broken away to form the Premier League. Ironically, it triggered the end of Jimmy's terrestrial TV career when Sky bought the rights to screen the new product. His insurance business failed to take off and by the end of the decade he was earning his living as a stand-up comedian.

Yes, a funny old game.

Most of all, Jim felt guilt about how his drinking period imploded on his wife Irene and their four children Lynn, Mitzi, Danny and Andy. It tortured him that he was not there for them at a key time in their lives. He opened up to me during the publicity build-up to eldest son Danny's testimonial match when he was coming to the end of his career with Southend United in 1990.

> ‘ My kids were at their most impressionable age when I was really hitting the bottle. I should have been there like my dad was for me, showing Danny and Andy how to be two-footed and running Lynn and Mitzi to their social events. But I was out of it and left Irene to carry all the responsibility. I was caught in a vicious circle, hating myself for letting them down and drinking to hide my shame.
>
> I have since tried to make it up to them and am always there for our kids and their kids. I need them to know that I love them and will do anything to make up for any psychological damage I may have caused. That is the worst thing about alcoholism. It hurts the people you care about most.
>
> Danny has been unlucky with injuries, otherwise I think he would have made a big impact as a player. He has a good

footballing brain and understands tactics much better than I ever did. But everybody who ever wrote about him started their article with "Danny Greaves, son of ..." That was a terrible weight on his shoulders.

As for Andy, he has been blessed with a personality that will light up any room. I've got no worries about him making it in life. My two girls, Lynn and Mitzi, are both beautiful and confident young ladies who, thank goodness, take after their mum with their sensible approach to life.

They appear to have come through the ordeal that I caused unharmed, but who knows what they really think deep down. It can't be any fun watching your dad rolling drunk and out of control.

Then there's Irene. What I put that lovely lady through is beyond description. She always used to tell me I was two people. Sober, the love of her life. Drunk, a complete stranger who she despised. I also hated that drunk, but it was not until Irene blocked me from seeing the children unless I was sober that I finally came to my senses.

I owe Irene everything and if you could find a way of putting that into words for me, I would appreciate it.

I hope Irene has got the message. '

In 2009, after a long, nationwide campaign, Jimmy and the rest of the non-playing squad in the 1966 World Cup Final were at last awarded their medals. Irene decided not to be the plus-one guest at the Downing Street presentation by Prime Minister Gordon Brown and Jimmy instead took along his agent/manager Terry Baker.

How ironic that the Prime Minister and Jimmy got on famously because politically they were as far apart with their views as the length of the Wembley pitch. Put it this way, in football speak Jimmy would have worn the No. 7 shirt and Brown the No. 11. Five years later, Jim's medal was sold at auction for £44,000. Jim:

'It was pure economics. I needed the money for family requirements. I was in good company. Gordon [Banks], Nobby [Stiles]. George [Cohen], Ballie [Alan Ball], Geoff [Hurst] and our beloved captain [Bobby Moore] had all sold theirs. What's the point of having them sit in a bank safe because you're frightened of attracting burglars? Geoff Hurst was telling me how his place had been turned over a couple of times by thieves looking for his medals. Puts the fear of God into you. I enjoyed the ceremony at Downing Street and catching up with so many old mates. I told Norman Hunter that I came out in bruises just shaking his hand! Gordon Brown proved to be a lovely bloke to meet, and of course I took the opportunity to take the mickey out of Jock footballers. In truth, I think they have produced some of the greatest of all time, the likes of Dave Mackay, John White, Gilly, Jimmy Johnstone, Jim Baxter, Denis Law. Blimey, I could name dozens, and that Ian St John geezer could play a bit. But I wasn't going to give the Saint or any Scot the satisfaction of knowing that I was a secret admirer.'

So there you have it, an exclusive: Jimmy coming out as a lover of Scottish football and footballers.

Chapter 22:

The final years

SHORTLY AFTER his reunion with Alan Gilzean, Jimmy suffered his life-changing stroke. It came the very week that he and Steve Perryman were due, at long last, to be inducted into the Tottenham Hotspur Hall of Fame. 'Both Jim and I had for quite a while had issues with the organisers over the induction,' Steve said. 'But we had finally sorted it out and I was looking forward to sharing the honour with Jim. It was so sad that he was unable to be there for what was a proud occasion for both of us.'

Jimmy's last six years were torture. He had relays of carers visiting him four times a day, and he became a virtually mute companion, sitting in his wheelchair ten feet from his much-loved Irene seven days a week. Eldest son Danny did his best to keep his father's spirits up by having a large van converted so that they could get Jimmy's wheelchair in and take him on a weekly visit to an out-of-the-way pub for a breakfast, or to the barber's shop in nearby Danbury for a haircut and shave. Danny said: 'It was the least I could do to give Dad some feeling of normality, and it took the pressure off Mum for a few hours. Everywhere we went, there was a buzz when people realised Dad was with us. You could almost feel his popularity. With our loyal friend and driver Andy Keen at the wheel, we took him to the new ground at Tottenham and manager Mauricio Pochettino and Harry Kane made a fuss of him. Dad couldn't believe the new stadium. He was used to playing on mud heaps at White Hart Lane. We were thrilled when he got his MBE. Obviously we would have liked it to have been a knighthood, but at least he was being given long-overdue recognition for all that he achieved, both in football and broadcasting. As a family, we are very proud of all that he did on the football pitch and in the television studio and on the stage. A remarkable life by any standards.'

Harry Kane – the modern-day Greavsie at Tottenham – was thrilled to meet Jimmy on his visit to the new billion-pound Spurs stadium and then the ultra-modern training centre. 'It was an honour to share some time with a legend of not only Tottenham but of the game in general,' said Kane. 'I come from a Tottenham-mad family and he is a god with us. Jimmy's great achievements at Spurs and his goal record for club and country are certainly things that I aspire to. It's important that we continue to recognise the many great players in our history who have laid the foundations for what we're trying to achieve today. Jimmy's record speaks for itself. He was a master.'

Danish international Christian Eriksen made a special journey to the ground to meet Jimmy. 'The name Jimmy Greaves is famous throughout football,' he said. 'My father and first coach, Thomas, often talked about him as one of the greats. It is very sad to see him as an invalid and I just wanted to pay my respects. He has a very special place in Tottenham Hotspur history.'

After his stroke, Jim was placed in intensive care in the local Broomfield Hospital in Chelmsford and then moved to the private Wellington Hospital, within a six-hit of Lord's cricket ground. But cricket fan Jimmy could not have cared less. He was too busy fighting for his life.

I remember pushing him around the streets of St John's Wood in his wheelchair as a break from hospital, and a few hundred yards from the Wellington we went over the Abbey Road zebra crossing made famous by the Beatles. His speech by then had been reduced to grunts and he signalled me to put my ear close to his mouth, 'Beatles,' he said. 'Help!'

There was still the joker Jim inside him.

Lynn, his eldest daughter:

> ‘ I was working for a doctor at the time and he told me that the severity of Dad's stroke would have been too much for 95 per cent of people. He was amazed by his strength and determination to recover. We all went to his bedside to say our goodbyes, and it was six years before he finally let go. Mum had to carry the biggest load because he hated it if she left his side, and his face would beam whenever she came into the room. We gathered the family together and went to watch them get remarried at a very moving ceremony at a small local church. They had never really taken notice of the divorce papers. That was all a means to an end by Mum and it worked. You couldn't make it up. ’

Before his stroke, both Jim and I were seriously concerned about the number of his old playing pals who were suffering from various forms of dementia, with Alzheimer's the common denominator. We had planned a campaign to bring it to public notice, but got little encouragement from the football establishment. They were petrified of getting swamped with the sort of lawsuits from ex-players that have hit the NFL in the cash register for millions of dollars.

But all the evidence points to heading the ball causing dementia in later life, and we were looking for support for a move to ban heading, particularly for younger footballers. Our idea was that clubs should experiment with a game in which nobody could head the ball, and that each team would have two players wearing distinctive gloves. They would be designated punchers of the ball who could only handle in the opposition penalty area and only when the ball was above head height. Nobody else apart from goalkeepers could handle the ball.

It sound a goofy idea, but at least it would mean that footballers reaching their 60s and 70s would know their names. I would like the Football Association to consider trialling our idea in memory of the one and only Jimmy Greaves. If you think it's an idea worth trying, hands up.

Jim 'left the building' on 19 September 2021 aged 81 and was cremated five weeks later on 22 October during the Covid pandemic, with an invitation-only congregation of 200 family and friends. There were only family flowers and the public were invited to make donations to the Jimmy Greaves Foundation, with the money split between three of his favourite charities: Alcoholics Anonymous, the Stroke Association and the Dogs Trust. Jimmy was always a fanatical dog lover and what he missed most was the early-morning dog walks with the loyal Lester, named after the great jockey Lester Piggott, who was one of Jimmy's heroes.

I had a chat at the wake with Paul, Jimmy's brother. It was quite surreal because there he was with Jimmy's head on his shoulders but standing just over six feet. 'If Jimmy had had your height,' I said, 'he would have played centre-forward rather than inside right or left.'

'Jim's low centre of gravity was important to his game,' he said. 'I arrived after the war and Jim was already making a name for himself in schools football. By the time I left primary school, he was a household name with Chelsea. As a family, we were bursting with pride.'

Paul and sister Marion, who gave a beautiful reading at the funeral, both became head school teachers. Like all members of the vast Greaves family, they were as bright as buttons.

Jimmy used to mockingly say he had his brains in his feet. Don't believe it. He was one of the most intelligent men ever to brighten my path.

I just hope I have painted his portrait properly, warts 'n' all. Just as he would have expected.

I can hear him right now, 'Nobody's perfect, Norm.'

Put a ball at his feet or a TV camera in front of him and he got pretty damn close.

Chapter 23

Quote, unquote … The tributes

IN THE course of my football-chronicling career – reporting from 33 countries – I collected and collated many quotes for my newspaper articles and the 20 books I wrote in collaboration with Jim. Here is a cross-section of what Jimmy's playing peers, opponents and broadcasting colleagues had to say about him during the course of his playing and television adventures:

Ted Drake (1970)

I was proud to be Jimmy's first manager. He gave me a few grey hairs, but I've not seen a more effective teenage footballer in my life. When he was in the mood, he could take any defence apart. They could have put the Tower of London guards on him and he would have run them dizzy. Quick enough to catch pigeons and if there was half a chance you could put your house on him to take it. We had loads of brilliant youngsters at Chelsea, but Jim was head and shoulders above them all.

Sir Stanley Matthews (1980)

Jimmy did me the favour of playing in my testimonial game at Stoke, and he was also alongside me when I played my very last match in an exhibition in the Middle East when I was in my 50s.

He was a magnificent footballer with a deadly finish and the ability to beat three or four players in the space of a hall carpet. I would have loved to have had him to pass to at his peak. I was in the game a long time and did not see a better British goalscorer. He had that Cockney swagger and when at full pace could beat the best defenders.

Sir Walter Winterbottom (1975)
Jimmy was not quite the perfect forward because he would not listen to instructions, but I learned to let him play it off the cuff and there were few in his class as a finisher. He was a cheerful young man and good for team spirit. Not a team player but certainly one of the greatest individualists to have come out of the English football system. I would have paid to watch him play.

Danny Blanchflower (1964)
Jimmy is a poet in football boots and everything about his movement on and off the ball rhymes. You cannot teach anybody to be a Jimmy Greaves or a George Best. They are sent to us from the heavens and we should thank our lucky stars that we are around to enjoy them.

Bobby Smith (1998)
Jim and I have a laugh when we see what the players are earning these days. If he had been at his peak now, the bidding would have to start at £50 million. We had a great understanding. I used to knock 'em down, and Jim would knock 'em in. I am not boasting but anybody who saw us will confirm there were about three years when we were the best double act in the game. He was an unselfish player and was just as happy to see me banging the ball into the net. I was all power, Jim was all skill. Defenders just did not know how to handle us. I remember when we knocked nine goals into the Scotland net, with Dave Mackay and Denis Law spitting blood.

Jimmy got a hat-trick and I scored two. That was as good as it gets. Jimmy? Never anybody better.

Alan Gilzean (2015)

I felt the luckiest man on this planet to have Jimmy to play alongside me. The wee man was a magician and could take apart the tightest defence with brilliant dribbling, smooth acceleration and then the sweetest of finishes. He was an absolute joy to play with, and he was great company at the bar!

Tom Finney (1984)

There were some great goalscorers in my day like Tommy Lawton, Nat Lofthouse and Billy Liddell, but when Jimmy came along he was a sensation. He emerged near the end of my career but from day one it was obvious he was something special and there was nobody to touch him at his peak. He always seemed to enjoy playing against Preston and famously scored five goals in Chelsea's 5-4 victory over us. He was a magnificent player.

Jack Charlton (1990)

Jimmy was a little rascal who could always make me smile with his quick Cockney wit. I would rate him high in the world's top ten as a striker, certainly the best of the British forwards I played against week in and week out. You would think you had him wrapped up and then the little blighter would pop up out of nowhere with a blinding goal. He and our kid [Bobby Charlton] were magical together for England and every one of us in the '66 squad felt for him when he failed to make the final. He deserved to be on that stage.

Sir Bobby Charlton (1990)

There have been few better goalscorers in my lifetime. He was a natural, with wonderful technique and an instinct for always being in the right place at the right time. We played together over more than ten years and never had a cross word. He lived his style of life, I lived mine and we were careful not to make assumptions about each other. Let's just say he was a brilliant footballer who was untouchable on his day.

Ron 'Chopper' Harris (2019)

I am proud to say I was one of the few defenders who could stop Jimmy playing – well, for at least 89 minutes of the match. Then the little sod would give me the slip and grab a goal with his only chance. We often used to appear on stage together and Jim would tell the audience I was a bruise on his memory. I was allowed to tackle from behind in those days, and I always liked to let Jimmy know I was there. Once I was sticking closer to him than a second skin and he said, 'Chop, you'd come to the loo with me if I went for a shit.' I told him, 'No, Jim. But I'd be waiting for you when you came out.' I remember my first game against him, Chelsea against Spurs at White Hart Lane. I was still a teenager and he had just come back from Italy. Our manager Tommy Doc said, 'Don't take your eye off him for a moment, and don't listen to his chat.' The game was into its closing minutes and I had not given him a sniff of the ball. We were standing on the edge of the box waiting for a corner to be taken when he said, 'You've had a great game, son.' 'Thank you, Mr Greaves,' I said respectfully.' He scanned the gathering clouds and said, 'Looks like we could get a good soaking in a minute. Look at those clouds.' It was all said in conversational tone and I glanced up. In that split second, the ball arrived at his feet and he was away like a greyhound – and the ball was in the back of our net. Unbelievable. Let me go on record as saying he was the greatest goal scorer I ever marked. Take that how you like. Seriously, he was the best of them all.

Martin Peters (1981)

I once saw Jimmy score 11 goals in a schools match. To my mind, he will always rate as the greatest British goalscorer there has ever been. He was magical. I would have loved to have played with him at Tottenham, but how ironic that my hero moved to West Ham in the part-exchange deal that took me to White Hart Lane. Geoff Hurst, Bobby Moore and I all rated him the greatest. And what a lovely man, always ready with a wisecrack and looking to support the underdog.

Johnny Byrne (1980)

You can count on the fingers of one hand how many world-class goalscorers England have had, and Jimmy Greaves has to be number one on anybody's list. He has scored some of the greatest goals ever seen and is also there for the tap-ins. That's the sign of a great player, one who can be there at the right time to put the finishing touch. Jimmy is a good mate of mine so I am biased, but when anybody asks me who is the greatest goalscorer he is always the first one I come up with.

Sir Alf Ramsey (1985)

Jimmy probably cost me more sleep than any other player. He was a magnificent footballer, possibly the finest English forward of his generation. But he was not always a team player. I needed players who were disciplined to follow my instructions because that was important for the rest of the team. It was totally untrue to say that we did not like each other. We always got on very well and he was not only clever with his feet but with his tongue as well. It was nothing at all personal leaving him out of the 1966 World Cup Final. I simply did not wish to change a winning team, and I believe he understood that.

Denis Law (2010)

Both Jimmy and I felt we were prisoners in Italy. I was playing with Joe Baker in Turin and like Jimmy we got to hate their defensive style of football. It was wonderful to get back to the freedom of the English game, and Jim really filled his boots. No question that he was the greatest goalscorer England ever produced. I recall a match when he played for England against the Rest of the World, and he was the best player on the pitch by a mile. And don't forget the likes of di Stefano, Puskas and Eusebio were on the pitch. He scored the winning goal and would have had four but for Russian goalkeeper Lev Yashin. I scored the Rest of the World's goal and said to Jimmy at the end, 'You should have had a hat-trick. It's a bit easier than in Italy.' He agreed, and said, 'Anything is easier than in Italy.'

I used to tell the press I didn't like him and some people took me seriously. In truth, I had enormous respect for him and rated him one of the all-time great goalscorers. Why on earth wasn't he knighted?

Don Howe (1997)

I played in the England team in Peru when Jimmy made his international debut, and his goal was one of the few bright things on that South American tour. He became one of our all-time great forwards, and I remember us having sunburned tongues when he scored five goals against West Brom in a club game in his Chelsea days. When I went into management I often used to wish I had a Jimmy Greaves to call on, but that was an impossible dream. Jimmy was unique and he could literally make a goal out of nothing. I considered it an honour to be on the same pitch as him and it has been a delight to see all that he has achieved since hanging up his boots and beating the bottle.

Pat Jennings (2021)

I grew up thinking Jimmy was a genius because of the number of goals he scored against Northern Ireland, and when I joined him at Spurs I found no reason to change my rating of him. He was a magician with the ball at his feet, a different style of player to my Irish idol George Best but sometimes more effective in the way he could cut through a defence. We had a great laugh in 1961 when I scored with a clearance that went first bounce over the head of Alex Stepney in the Manchester United goal in the Charity Shield. He turned to Alan Gilzean and said, 'D'you realise, Gilly, this makes Pat our top scorer.' Greavsie and Gilly were a fantastic combination. They would be worth a fortune in today's transfer market.

Steve Perryman (2021)

When I broke into the Tottenham team at the age of 17, Jimmy was just beginning to wind down but he was still as potent a striker as there was in the league. He would wander around seemingly not interested in what was going on around him and then, suddenly, he would pounce on a pass and with a clever change of pace and direction he would send defenders into a blind panic on his way to scoring a goal from out of nowhere. Jim was not only one of the greatest ever footballers but was also a lovely bloke. His stand-up comedy act was as good as you'd see from a professional comedian, and there's not a programme on TV today to compare with the *Saint and Greavsie* shows for a mix of comedy and serious football stuff. Jimmy was a very, very funny man and a footballer from the gods.

Alan Mullery (2021)

Jimmy Greaves was the greatest goalscorer I ever played with, no argument. I wanted to play like him but didn't have a tenth of his skill. He was devastating over 20 yards and could outpace, outthink and outmanoeuvre any defender. Jim could be an aggravating sod, disappearing from games. Then just as you were about to give him a mouthful, it was flick, twist, shoulder dip, accelerate and the ball is in the back of the net. Then he trundles back to the halfway line with a cheeky grin on his face. I loved Jimmy like a brother. He would be twice as lethal in today's game with defenders not allowed to whack from behind. His price in today's transfer market would be astronomical.

Peter Shilton (2000)

The best goal I ever saw was by Jimmy, and I got a close-up of it because it was against me. It was a league match at White Hart Lane and the game had only been going a couple of minutes when he picked up the ball just inside the Leicester half, waltzed around four of our defenders and then tricked me into diving for a shot he never made before passing the ball into our net. I would have applauded if I had not been so busy picking the ball out of the back of the net. Nobody scored goals like Jimmy. He was the king.

Cliff Jones (2021)

Jimmy was a Cockney cheeky chappie, who was always good for a laugh on and off the pitch. I remember him taking a ride on a milk float during a pre-season training run. He was probably the worst trainer ever, but give him a ball on the pitch and he was suddenly the greatest thing on two feet. Some of his goals were out of this world and I often found myself applauding like a spectator. But for Jim all goals were the same, whether following an amazing dribbling run or just tapped in from six inches. The only thing that mattered to him was getting the ball into the net. He was a born goalscorer. I couldn't believe it when Alf Ramsey left him out of the World Cup team. England's best player was reduced to a spectator.

On a personal level, I owe him my life because he helped me get treatment for my drink problem with good, sound advice that made me follow his example and stop drinking.

Martin Chivers (2021)

I was privileged to play with Jimmy at the back end of his career with Tottenham. We were never really given the time to perfect our act, but there were moments when I discovered just what a genius he was. He had a deceptive change of pace and could send defenders tumbling by a sudden spurt and then a change of direction. I have seen few players able to match his close ball control. Just as I thought we were starting to click, he was off to West Ham. I would liked to have played much longer with him because there is no doubt that he was one of the all-time greats. It was incredible what he achieved after retiring, beating the bottle then having a great TV career and [becoming] a very funny stand-up comedian. He lived three lives in one.

Peter Bonetti (1996)

Jimmy and I were kids together at Chelsea and I always maintain that was when he was at his best. His early performances for Chelsea were mind-blowing. It's part of his legend how he convinced Billy Wright he should hang up his boots after he had scored five goals against a Wolves team that dominated football at the time. He was like greased lightning and used to unbalance defenders with his speed and dribbling skill. After many of his goals, you would find at least three defenders on their bums wondering what had happened. He was a nightmare for goalkeepers to face because he was never predictable with his finishing. He had the knack of passing rather than shooting the ball into the net. A pure genius.

Terry Venables (1996)

I remember once Jimmy driving me to Stamford Bridge for a Chelsea home game. I was a bundle of nerves because it was one of my early games. We stopped at a restaurant for what I thought would be a light snack. While I was nibbling on lettuce, Jim went through the card and had a full roast followed by bread and butter pudding. We got to the ground with about 15 minutes to spare. I was awash with sweat and Jim sauntered in as if he was walking in the park. As I recall, he only scored four goals that day! He was the king of the castle back then. Nobody in his class.

Kenneth Wolstenholme (1968)

It was a very bold of Alf Ramsey to leave Jimmy Greaves out of the England team for the 1966 World Cup Final. I would rate him the finest English striker I've ever seen and I consider it a privilege to have commentated on some of his greatest goals. One of them against Manchester United at White Hart Lane deserved to be captured in oils. It was a thing of beauty and and is definitely up there with the best I have ever witnessed.

Bill Nicholson (1982)

Jimmy was his own man and played the game his way. He could be infuriating in not following instructions and then, just as you were getting ready to explode, he would come up with a brilliant goal that only he could score. I have read a lot of poppycock about me letting him go in part exchange for Martin Peters, as if I did it in a heartless way. Jimmy had completely lost his appetite for the game. I did not know he was drinking to the extent that he has admitted to, but I can remember giving him a few lectures about his lifestyle. He was a strong-headed young man and would not listen. He has since admitted to me that he had fallen out of love with the game before he went to West Ham. Don't forget he had been playing non-stop since he was a young lad and was just burnt out. But let's remember him at his peak. I have not seen a better finisher and he made it all look so easy. I paid £99,999 to bring him back from Italy. It was a bargain. I liked Jim a lot and I hope the feeling was mutual.

Gordon Banks (1988)

Talking as a goalkeeper, I'd put Jimmy No. 1 of all the British marksmen I'd faced in my career. He was impossible to read and could make you look a fool by forcing you into diving at a shot he hadn't made. A magician. As a mate, he was second to none. A laugh a minute. He used to score goals that were so good goalkeepers wanted to applaud him, even though they were having to pick the ball out of their net.

Billy Wright (1990)

I was there at the start of Jimmy's playing career for club and country. He was like greased lightning the day Chelsea walloped Wolves, helping himself to five goals and convincing me it was time to hang up my boots. He played in my last match for England a few months later. I had never seen a greater young English footballer, apart from the superb Duncan Edwards. We got together again when he went into television and I was head of sport at Central TV. Just as when he was a footballer, he was a one-off and always doing the brilliant and the unexpected. He was there with good advice when I started having a few problems with drink. Jim had the character to overcome his booze problems and become as popular on the TV as he had been on the pitch. He was an amazing bloke.

Gary Newbon (2021)

I went to Jimmy's funeral and paid my respects to one of the most remarkable men I ever knew. He was one of England's all-time greatest goalscorers, then had the character to overcome a major drink problem and reinvent himself as an outstanding television performer. We shared the screen many times from the Central base in the Midlands and he really conquered the medium after a nervous start. Jim and I had several well-publicised arguments but looking back they were over minor matters and I thought the world of him. What a life he had!

Gareth Southgate (2021)
Jimmy Greaves was someone who was admired by all who love football, regardless of club allegiances. I was privileged to be able to meet Jimmy's family last year at Tottenham Hotspur as the club marked his 80th birthday. My thoughts are with them and I know the entire game will mourn his passing.

Bob Wilson (2019)
My memories of Jimmy are mainly nightmares. Whenever I'm asked who I feared facing most in my career, it was Greavsie. That was even ahead of George Best or Johan Cruyff – Jimmy Greaves was that ultimate, laser-like man. Then when he joined me as a television man, he was quite superb at that, too.

Gary Lineker (2021)
Jimmy was quite possibly the greatest striker this country has ever produced. A truly magnificent footballer who was at home both in the box and on the box. A charismatic, knowledgeable, witty and warm man. A giant of the sport.

George Best (1986)
I played against Jimmy, I drank with him, appeared with him on stage and screen – he was great with his feet and his elbow. He was an artist at both football and boozing. He showed enormous

character in managing to give up the bottle and then carving a new career for himself on television. Jim never tried to lecture me to stop drinking. We have each decided how we want to live, and I think we both deserve respect. One thing's for sure, there has never been a better British goalscorer than Jim. A pity he didn't do it for the Irish, his ancestors!

Ian Wright (2021)

The first footballer's name I ever heard from my teacher. 'No, Ian! Finish like Jimmy Greaves!' May he rest in peace.

Rio Ferdinand (2021)

His passing is a big loss to the footballing world. I send my condolences to the Greaves family. His was the first autobiography I ever read! Inspiration. For me, *Saint and Greavsie* was must-watch television. Nobody to touch them for entertainment while informing as well. Brilliant. I used to run home to catch their show.

Bob Hall (2021)

I was an ITV sports reporter when Jimmy arrived at ATV as a pundit for Saturday-night highlights. 'Hello Bobby (no-one had ever called me that before) – I'm Jim. Good to meet you.' Firm handshake, twinkle in the eye. We bonded over endless black coffee. My dad was a Spurs fan. Jim especially. Now I was working with him. Never got any better than that. What a footballer. What a man.

Richard Keys (2021)

So sad to hear the passing of Greavsie. He was funny, irreverent – a genius. He was a Messi before Messi was born. Sleep well, Jim. You deserve the rest. I was honoured to know you.

Ron Atkinson (2021)

I am devastated at the passing of Jimmy. We used to work together with Gary Newbon at Central TV and he was a fantastic pundit, full of fun and mixing in some seriously sensible opinions. When I was a young pro just coming into the game, he was established as one of the master footballers. George Best and Denis Law ranked him as the best striker of their generation. You can't get higher praise than that.

Sir Geoff Hurst (2021)

If there has been a greater British-born goalscorer, then I've not seen him. I followed his career closer than most because he first made a name for himself in the Essex district where I played my schoolboy football. He was phenomenal then and maintained the sky-high standards throughout his career. It was a twist of fate that he was not in the 1966 World Cup-winning team, and my luck that I was there to get the goals and the glory. But I have no hesitation in saying that he was the No. 1, and a great entertainer and broadcaster off the pitch. Jimmy was an amazing bloke and I was always in awe of him.

John Bromley (1988)

I was quick to spot the chemistry between Jimmy and Ian St John, and the *Saint and Greavsie* show was born. Credit the two of them for running with the ball and turning the show into a phenomenal success. Jimmy and I had known each other since he was a teenager with Chelsea, and he was comfortably the best goalscorer around in my football reporting days before I went into television. He can be a stubborn so-and-so and we had a couple of rows about how we used him on ITV, but I was very fond of him and rated him a gifted performer on TV, just as he was on the football field.

Jimmy Tarbuck (2016)

As a Scouser, I loved it when Jimmy used to come to Anfield and I watched the duels between him and Tommy Smith with an appreciation of combative football at its very best. He never got to score at Anfield but he always used to have us dreading him getting the ball. He was a rascal of a footballer and could thread a ball through the eye of a needle. Later, when he teamed up with my chum Ian St John on the Saint and Greavsie show, the pair of them proved they were the Morecambe and Wise of football. Facts and figures delivered with a laugh. It didn't get better than that. Jimmy scored in everything that he did.

George Cohen (2002)

I first played with Jim when we were 14-year-old boys. It was for London schools and he told me he was going to join Chelsea. I said I was going to Fulham and we wished each other luck in our careers. He developed into a fabulous player and I was choked for him when he failed to make the '66 World Cup Final team. The injury against France did for him, otherwise he would have been a certainty to play. I was lucky to pick up a winners' medal, and I was choked for Jim. All of us in the game were shocked when he admitted he had become an alcoholic, and then we watched open-mouthed as he re-emerged as this magical performer on the box. Everybody loved *Saint and Greavsie*. He was one of my favourite of all characters on and off the field. I can never remember being in his company without him putting a smile on my face.

Chapter 24

The Great Entertainer
By Norman Giller

WELL, IRENE did instruct me, 'Warts 'n' all.' I just hope that now you've finished reading this book, you feel you know the one and only Jimmy Greaves a lot better than when you started at the first page. As for me, I am an emotional wreck after revisiting so many memories. Being friends with the great man was like being caught in a tornado, but one that warmed rather than harmed you.

Remember, I am the same vintage as Jim and this is my 119th and probably last book. What a way to go out, painting a word portrait of my most unforgettable character.

If I have captured Jimmy properly, you will have a picture in your head of a complicated yet remarkable man who did everything he turned his ambidextrous hands to perfectly, including when it came to being an alcoholic. He even did drunkard better than most.

Those five lost drinking years were no fun for us onlookers, particularly Irene. He became something of a monster when fully and forlornly in the grip of alcoholism. For those of us who were horrified witnesses, it was nothing short of a miracle that he beat the bottle. What a triumph. Metaphorically speaking, we should have been carrying him on our shoulders when he stuck to his pledge of never having another drop. Yes, he kept his promise and got sober out of his mind.

That was his greatest victory, and he could not have done it without the support of the only woman he loved, Irene (along with his daughters Lynn and Mitzi, of course). She was his rock of sanity and security when he was losing his grip on everything. Yes, a very special lady.

I have endeavoured to keep a low profile in the previous chapters, handing the reins to Jimmy thanks to my files quoting him in 20 books and scores (how appropriate) of magazine and newspaper articles. I have been pleased and proud to be the Boswell to his Johnson (I can hear Jim on my shoulder, 'what the fuck are you waffling on about?'). He had a gift for cutting through gibberish and coming straight to the point in similar style to how he could cut through the tightest of defences.

In his 81 years on this mortal coil, he managed to be several different people, every one of them interesting and, dare I say, intoxicating. There was the boy wonder who could make a football talk a language that was music to the ears of those of us who watched him waltzing to goals galore. Then the seasoned professional, still canny and cunning on the pitch but with an eye to the future as a businessman. Next, the out-of-control drunk who was the puppet of alcohol to the point where he was warned that booze was killing him. Nobody who knew him well in those desperate days gave him a chance of beating his demons.

But this was no ordinary person. This was Jimmy Greaves, the one and only. He sobered up and reinvented himself, first as a media pundit and then as a television celebrity who became a national treasure with his wit and wisdom, particularly alongside Ian St John on the irreverent and innovative *Saint and Greavsie* show. When they pulled the television mat from under his feet, he responded by becoming – with the help of entrepreneur Terry Baker – a travelling theatre celebrity and stand-up comedian.

Finally, we had the wheelchair Greavsie. This was the saddest sight of all, and it was a release and a relief when he finally let go after six years locked in a world where he was unable to express himself. It's a cruel old game.

Before his disabling stroke we had agreed on one more book venture together, and we were going to call it *The Truth*. I just hope I have managed to get some of his thoughts down the way he would have wished.

What a character! I have worked with the likes of Eric Morecambe, Ricky Tomlinson, Cloughie and Muhammad Ali, and so feel qualified when calling Jimmy the Great Entertainer. First with a ball at his feet, then a glass to his lips, next a camera in his face and finally a microphone in his hands. He was always ahead of the field.

You need to be well over 50 to have seen Jimmy at his peak as a player. And what a player. He was the Artful Dodger of the penalty area, nicking goals rather than picking pockets. A lot of his 495 goals were tap-ins, purely because he had the instincts to invariably be in the right place at the right time. He might have been dyslexic, but he could read a game better than anybody.

I could have written a book three times thicker than this and still not have covered all his achievements and ups and bruising downs. I am still chuckling at some of the stories I have not managed to shoehorn in. There was the great *Dallas* barbecue showdown when Jimmy, wearing chef's hat and cooking apron, innocently got involved in a brawl at a charity pig roast that Irene had organised in the grounds of their Essex home to raise money for disabled children. Jimmy finished up with a black eye at the end of a mass fight and later sold an exclusive photo of his shiner to *The Sun* to raise £3,000 for the charity. Hilarious (though not at the time).

Jimmy was so often a volcano waiting to erupt and there were always prying newspapermen and photographers watching out for the rumbles of the first tremors. They had a field day when it was reported that he had gone after daughter Lynn's now ex-husband with a five-iron after an altercation at their home. It found its way into the newspapers after police had been called, but Jimmy's version was completely different. 'It was *not* a five-iron, it was a seven-iron – and I only took it to force entry and get our grand-daughter Victoria out of a nasty situation. The old bill had a word but there were no charges.'

Tempus fugit. That same granddaughter Victoria is now an accomplished artist living in France with her husband, Oliver, and they are perpetuating her Granddad's memory with a series of exclusive art productions.

Hazily, I recall getting legless in my drinking days with Jimmy in a nightclub after a Tottenham match in Split (then in Yugoslavia, now capital of Croatia). Spurs' Scottish winger Jimmy Robertson pulled my polo-neck sweater over my head and threatened me with a 'Glasgie kiss' over something I had written about him months earlier. A drunken Greavsie came to my rescue and the next day we both got a long lecture about our behaviour from a very sober Tottenham manager Bill Nicholson. Carry On, Fleet Street.

When we were working on our first book together *This One's On Me*, Jimmy used to join in a garden kick-about with my then 12-year-old son Michael and me at our Thorpe Bay home. On this particular day, Jimmy miscued the ball into the garden next door, where there was a grumpy neighbour who had been refusing to return our balls. I climbed up and asked if we could have our ball back, and he gave me his usual line of, 'You should learn to kick straight.'

I said, 'It wasn't me, it was Jimmy Greaves.'

'You needn't be sarcastic,' said my neighbour just as Jimmy's head appeared above the fence.

Without pausing, he added, 'Great to meet you, Jimmy. I used to watch you in the good old Chelsea days.'

We got all our balls back.

It was Michael's 13th birthday just after we finished the book and Jimmy arrived with a parcel that he quietly left in our porch. When Michael opened it, he found the England cap that Jimmy was awarded for his appearance against Argentina in Chile in 1962, the match in which he scored his only World Cup finals goal. Try to tell Michael, now 55, that Jimmy is anything but a giant.

I was moved to poetry and song by Jimmy's footballing deeds and penned this ditty that you will find on YouTube under 'Jimmy Greaves Song', with slightly amended lyrics.

Jimmy Greaves Jimmy Greaves Jimmy Greaves
Always pleased with goals scored with ease
Defenders teased and brought to their knees
Left like scattered leaves by his expertise
Jimmy Greaves

Jimmy Greaves Jimmy Greaves Jimmy Greaves
It was as easy for Greavsie as shelling peas
Goals often in threes, goalies rooted like trees
And drowning in seas as he skimmed by as if on skis
Jimmy Greaves

Jimmy Greaves Jimmy Greaves Jimmy Greaves
For him it was just a breeze, natural as honey for bees
Unlocking without keys, an acrobat on the trapeze
Confounding referees, giving us lasting memories
Jimmy Greaves

My favourite grand-daughter Kate likens me as a poet to Kipling
– Mr, not Rudyard.

Tottenham fans (I am out of the closet as one of them) hate it
when I say that Jimmy was at his best at Chelsea, but it's true. He
played with the innocence and cockiness of youth, nipping past
defenders with blinding speed and close ball control – a gift that
could never have been taught. A summary of the rest:

> Milan, what-a big-a mistake-a to-a make-a.
> Tottenham, the glory years with goals galore.
> England, still many who would have picked Jim for
>   the 1966 final.
> West Ham, should have stayed at Spurs.
> World Cup rally, drove Bill Nicholson mad.
> The lost years, looking at life through the bottom of a glass.
> *The Sun* columnist, start of the fightback.
> Abbey Life insurance salesman, sound policy.
> Central TV, the happiest years with occasional blips.
> TV-am, breakfast with Anne and Nick.
> Chat show host, car crash television.
> *Saint and Greavsie*, brought much-needed fun to the
>   football world.
> Stand-up comedian and after-dinner speaker, king of
>   the punchlines.
> The Stroke, a sad finale.

Now all the shooting, the shouting and the spouting is over, we are
left to consider the Jimmy Greaves legacy. He will be remembered
long after you and I have left this mortal coil but not – as he would
have wished – for his television broadcasting and stage presence. It
will be for his goals, yes, scored with ease, often in threes, defenders
teased and brought to their knees.

Jimmy Greaves. The one and only.

Extra Time

The Jimmy Greaves Facts and Stats File

Compiled by Michael Giller

PERSONAL

Born: East Ham Maternity Hospital, London, 20 February 1940
Died: Little Baddow, Essex, 19 September 2021
Father: Jimmy senior, a London tube train driver (died August 1989, aged 80). Mother: Mary.
Younger sister Marion and younger brother Paul, both of whom gained teaching diplomas.

Married Irene Barden in 1958. Children: Lynn, 'Baby Jim' (dec.), Danny, Mitzi, Andy. Grandchildren: Gemma, Victoria, James, Louise, Thomas, Shane, Hannah, Sam, Harry, Madeline. Great grandchildren: Jack, Rebecca, Cecilia, Rafa, Stanley, Isabelle.

Divorced 1977, reconciled 1978, remarried 2017.

Education: Southwood Lane School, Dagenham; Kingswood Secondary School, Hainault. Left school in April 1955, aged 15.

'Discovered' by Chelsea football scout Jimmy Thompson, aka 'Mr Pope'.

PROFESSIONAL FOOTBALL CAREER

CHELSEA (1957–1961)
The most prolific goalscoring season of his career was in 1956/57 while still an apprentice professional. He scored 114 goals in youth team matches and Chelsea presented him with an illuminated address to mark the feat.

On 24 August 1957, the first day of the following season, he made his league debut against Tottenham Hotspur at White Hart Lane and scored what Spurs skipper Danny Blanchflower called 'one of the greatest goals I ever witnessed'.

Between 1957 and 1961, Jimmy scored 124 goals in 157 league games for Chelsea. He was the First Division's top goalscorer in 1958/59 with 33 goals and in 1960/61 with 41 goals (the season that Spurs clinched the Double of league championship and FA Cup).

He scored three or more goals in 13 First Division matches for Chelsea:

4 v. Portsmouth (57/58)
3 v. Sheffield Wednesday (57/58)
5 v. Wolves (58/59)
3 v. Nottingham Forest (58/59)
3 v. Preston (59/60)
3 v. Birmingham City (59/60)
5 v. Preston (59/60)
3 v. Wolves (60/61)
3 v. Blackburn (60/61)
3 v. Manchester City (60/61)
5 v. West Bromwich Albion (60/61)
4 v. Newcastle United (60/61)
4 v. Nottingham Forest (60/61)

Jimmy scored three FA Cup goals for Chelsea: v. Newcastle United (58/59); v. Aston Villa (58/59); and v. Bradford (59/60). He scored two goals in the League Cup for Chelsea: v. Millwall (60/61).

He was sold to AC Milan for £80,000 in June 1961.

AC MILAN (1961)

Jimmy made his debut for AC Milan on 7 June 1961, scoring in a 2-2 draw with Botafogo at the San Siro Stadium. He made 14 appearances for AC Milan and scored nine goals.

In November 1961, he was bought by Tottenham for £99,999. Manager Bill Nicholson did not want to burden him with the extra pressure of being British football's first £100,000 player (a distinction that went to Denis Law when Manchester United bought him from Torino for £116,000 in 1962).

TOTTENHAM (1961–1970)

Jimmy played his first match in a Tottenham shirt in a reserve match at Plymouth Argyle on 9 December 1961, scoring two goals in a 4-1 win. The 13,000 attendance was a record for a Football Combination match.

On 16 December 1961, Jimmy made his debut for Spurs against Blackpool at White Hart Lane and scored a hat-trick. Between 1961 and 1970, he scored a club-record 220 league goals in 321 matches for Tottenham.

He was the First Division's top scorer a record six times, twice with Chelsea and four times with Tottenham:

1958/59: 32 goals
1960/61: 41 goals
1962/63: 37 goals
1963/64: 35 goals
1964/65: 29 goals
1968/69: 27 goals

Jimmy won two FA Cup winners' medals with Tottenham, against Burnley in 1961/62 (scoring a classic third-minute goal in the final on 5 May 1962) and against Chelsea in 1966/67.

He netted two goals to help Spurs win the European Cup Winners' Cup Final with a 5-2 victory over Atletico Madrid in Rotterdam in 1963. Spurs became the first British club to win a major European trophy.

Jimmy scored three or more goals in 12 First Division matches for Tottenham:

3 v. Blackpool (61/62)
4 v. Nottingham Forest (62/63)
3 v. Manchester United (62/63)
3 v. Ipswich Town (62/63)
4 v. Liverpool (62/63)
3 v. Nottingham Forest (63/64)
3 v. Blackpool (63/64)
3 v. Birmingham City (63/64)
3 v. Blackburn Rovers (63/64)
3 v. Ipswich Town (64/65)
3 v. Burnley (67/68)
4 v. Sunderland (68/69)

Jimmy scored 32 FA Cup goals for Spurs:

3 v. Birmingham City (61/62)
2 v. Plymouth (61/62)
2 v. West Bromwich Albion (61/62)
1 v. Man United (semi-final, 61/62)
1 v. Burnley (Final, 61/62)
3 v. Torquay United (64/65)
3 v. Ipswich Town (64/65)
1 v. Preston (65/66)
1 v. Portsmouth (66/67)
2 v. Bristol City (66/67)
2 v. Birmingham City (66/67)
1 v. Nottingham Forest (semi-final, 66/67)
2 v. Preston (67/68)
1 v. Liverpool (67/68)
1 v. Walsall (68/69)
1 v. Wolves (68/69)
2 v. Aston Villa (68/69)
3 v. Bradford City (69/70)

He scored five League Cup goals for Spurs: 3 v. Exeter City
(68/69); 1 v. Peterborough (68/69); 1 v. Arsenal (68/69)
West Ham United bought Jimmy on 14 March 1970 for £54,000
as a makeweight in the deal that saw Spurs sign Martin Peters in
British football's first £200,000 transfer.

WEST HAM UNITED (1970/71)

Jimmy scored two goals on his debut for West Ham against Manchester City at Maine Road on 21 March 1970. He notched two more goals in the 1969/70 season and netted nine for West Ham in his final season. In May 1971, Jimmy Greaves retired at the age of 31.

While battling with alcoholism, he made a comeback of sorts with non-league clubs Brentwood, Chelmsford, Woodford Town and Barnet (1974–79).

ENGLAND

Jimmy scored two goals on his England Under-23 debut against Bulgaria at Stamford Bridge on 25 September 1957 (and also missed a penalty).

His 13 goals in 12 England Under-23 international matches is a record.

On his full international debut, Jimmy scored England's only goal in a 4-1 defeat by Peru in Lima on 17 May 1959.

Between 1959 and 1967, he scored 44 goals in 57 full England internationals. Only Bobby Charlton (49 in 106 matches) had scored more at the time. Greaves's total has since been overtaken by Wayne Rooney (53), Gary Lineker (48) and Harry Kane (48).

Jimmy's goals for England:

1959: Peru (1), Wales (1)
1960: Yugoslavia (1), Northern Ireland (2), Luxembourg (3),
    Spain (1), Wales (2)
1961: Scotland (3), Italy (1) and Austria (1)
1962: Peru (3), Argentina (1, World Cup finals), Northern
    Ireland (1), Wales (1)
1963: Czechoslovakia (2), Wales (1), Rest of World (1),
    Northern Ireland (4)
1964: Eire (1), Brazil (1), Northern Ireland (3), Holland (1)
1965: Scotland (1), Hungary (1)
1966: Yugoslavia (1), Norway (4)
1967: Spain (1).

Appeared in seven World Cup matches for England:

1962 in Chile v. Hungary (lost 2-1), Argentina (won 3-1, scored one goal), Bulgaria (0-0), Brazil (lost 3-1 in the quarter-finals).
1966 in England v. Uruguay (0-0), Mexico (won 2-0), France (won 2-0). Injured and missed the rest of the tournament.
England beat West Germany 4-2 after extra-time in the final, with Jimmy as a spectator and Geoff Hurst scoring a hat-trick.
Played his last international match against Austria in Vienna on 27 May 1967. In his 57 international appearances, England won 30 games, lost 14 and drew 13.
Jimmy played in 516 Football League matches and scored 357 goals, all of them in the First Division (a record that cannot be beaten because the division has been superseded by the Premier League):

Chelsea 124 (1957/61)
Tottenham 220 (1961/70)
West Ham 13 (1970/71)

These are the teams against which he scored his league goals:

Nottingham Forest (24)
Burnley (19)
Blackpool (18)
Birmingham City (17)
Manchester City (17)
Wolverhampton Wanderers (16)
West Bromwich Albion (16)
West Ham United (16)
Leicester City (15)
Blackburn Rovers (14)
Manchester United (13)
Newcastle United (13)
Fulham (12)
Arsenal (11)
Aston Villa (11)
Everton (11)
Liverpool (11)
Leeds United (10)

Preston North End (10)
Sunderland (10)
Ipswich Town (10)
Sheffield United (9)
Sheffield Wednesday (8)
Stoke City (7)
Southampton (6)
Bolton Wanderers (5)
Coventry City (5)
Portsmouth (5)
Tottenham Hotspur (5)
Chelsea (4)
Cardiff City (2)
Derby County (2)
Luton Town (2)
Northampton Town (1)
Leyton Orient (1)
Queen's Park Rangers (1)

His average score per First Division game was .691 and he was leading First Division goalscorer a record six times. He was top scorer for his club in 12 of the 14 seasons in which he played in the First Division.

Jimmy missed five months of the 1965/66 season following an attack of hepatitis that robbed him of half a yard of pace.

At 21, Jimmy became the youngest player to score 100 league goals. At 23 years and 290 days, he scored his 200th league goal, which was exactly the same age at which Dixie Dean had reached the milestone with Everton.

He also scored ten European Cup Winners' Cup goals, three in the Fairs Cup, six in Inter-League matches, two in the Charity Shield, 12 in England Under-23 internationals, two for England v. Young England, two for the Rest of Europe team and one for England v. the Football League.

His total goals in all matches at the time of his retirement in 1971 was 491.

He played non-League football with Brentwood, Chelmsford, Barnet and Woodford Town from 1974 until 1979.

FOOTBALL VIEWS

Most memorable goal: A left-footed scissors-kick in his debut for Tottenham v. Blackpool at White Hart Lane in 1961/62.

Favourite goal by another player: A Bobby Charlton left-foot shot after a 35-yard run for Manchester United against Tottenham at White Hart Lane in 1967/68.

Greatest footballing moment: Helping Spurs to become the first British club to win a European trophy – the European Cup Winners' Cup in 1963.

Greatest disappointment: Missing the 1966 World Cup Final.

Greatest managers (during his playing career, 1957–1972): 1. Bill Nicholson; 2. Sir Alf Ramsey; 3. Sir Matt Busby; 4. Bill Shankly; 5. Don Revie; 6. Joe Mercer/Malcolm Allison; 7. Stan Cullis; 8. Tommy Docherty; 9. Dave Sexton; 10. Bertie Mee/ Don Howe.

JIMMY'S FAVOURITE BRITISH PLAYERS

(Against or with whom he played)

Goalkeepers: Pat Jennings, Gordon Banks, Peter Shilton, Peter Bonetti.

Full-backs: Roger Byrne, Ray Wilson. George Cohen, Cyril Knowles.

Centre-halves: John Charles, Roy McFarland, Mike England, Billy McNeill.

Wing halves: Danny Blanchflower, Duncan Edwards, Dave Mackay, Pat Crerand.

Central defenders: Bobby Moore, Norman Hunter, Ron Flowers, Frank McLintock.

Midfield schemers: Bobby Charlton, Colin Bell, Jimmy McIlroy, Johnny Haynes, Martin Peters.

Wingers: Stanley Matthews, Tom Finney, George Best, Jimmy Johnstone.

Strikers: Denis Law, Brian Clough, Roger Hunt. Geoff Hurst.

Centre-forwards: Bobby Smith, Ron Davies, Ian St John, Alan Gilzean.

Favourite captains: Danny Blanchflower, Dave Mackay and Bobby Moore.

Favourite managers: Bill Nicholson, Bill Shankly and Brian Clough.

Favourite Premier League players: Dennis Bergkamp, Didier Drogba, Gianfranco Zola

Jimmy's 'dream England team' selected in 1990, 4-4-2: Gordon Banks; George Cohen, Maurice Norman, Bobby Moore, Ray Wilson; Bobby Robson, Bobby Charlton, Johnny Haynes, Duncan Edwards; Bobby Smith, Jimmy Greaves.

MISCELLANEOUS
Hobbies: Gardening, keeping tropical fish, driving (Jimmy and co-driver Tony Fall finished sixth out of 96 starters in the 1970 World Cup rally that started at Wembley Stadium and finished in Mexico City), golf, cricket (batsman-wicketkeeper).

FAVOURITE THINGS:
Other sports: Tennis, cricket, rugby union, golf, boxing, horse racing (watching, not betting).
Sportsmen: Ian Botham, Rod Laver, Lester Piggott.
TV programme: *Fawlty Towers*.
TV soap: *Coronation Street*.
Film: *The Godfather*.
Actor: Alec Guinness.
Actress: Katharine Hepburn.
Comedian: Eric Morecambe.
Singers: Frank Sinatra, Ella Fitzgerald
Food: Fresh lobster, salad
Drink: Tea, coffee, Perrier water.
Newspapers: *The Sun, Daily Mail, Sunday Times*.
Authors: Tom Sharpe, Robert Ludlum, Jeffrey Archer.

TELEVISION CAREER

BOOKS with Norman Giller
This One's On Me
Stop the Game Ref (I Want to Get On)

GOALS!
The World Cup History
Taking Sides
Book of Football Lists
The Final (novel)
The Ball Game (novel)
The Boss (novel)
The Second Half (novel)
Sports Quiz Challenge I
Sports Quiz Challenge II
It's A Funny Old Life
The Sixties Revisited
Don't Shoot the Manager
Greavsie's Greatest (The 50 Greatest Post-war British strikers)
Funny Old Games (with Saint and Greavsie)
World Cup '90 (with Saint and Greavsie)
Let's Be Honest (with Reg Gutteridge)
Greavsie's Heroes and Entertainers

Other major books: *Greavsie* (autobiography with Les Scott);
The Heart of the Game (with Les Scott); *The Natural* (biography
by David Tossell); *A Funny Thing Happened on My Way to Spurs*
(Nicholas Kaye); *Football is Still a Funny Game* (Bob Patience)

Newspaper columnist: *The Sun, Daily Mirror, Sunday Mirror,
Sunday People*

Index